THE CITY
OF ABRAHAM

THE CITY
OF ABRAHAM

History, Myth and Memory: A Journey through Hebron

EDWARD PLATT

With photographs by Sarah Beddington

PICADOR

First published 2012 by Picador
an imprint of Pan Macmillan, a division of Macmillan Publishers Limited
Pan Macmillan, 20 New Wharf Road, London N1 9RR
Basingstoke and Oxford
Associated companies throughout the world
www.panmacmillan.com

ISBN 978-0-330-42027-3

1 3 5 7 9 8 6 4 2

A CIP catalogue record for this book is available from the British Library.

Printed and bound by CPI Group (UK) Ltd, Croydon, CR0 4YY

For Sophie

and for Benjamin, Eliza and Ava

'A myth . . . is an event that – in some sense – happened once, but which also happens all the time.'

Karen Armstrong, *A Short History of Myth*

Contents

PART TWO

CHILDREN OF ABRAHAM

2000–2009

Names

Israelis refer to the city as Hebron or Hevron with a short 'e', as in bread, while Palestinians use the longer 'e' of eat. The name derives from the Hebrew word 'hever', which means 'friend'. Its name in Arabic has a similar derivation: it is called Al Khalil, 'the friend', in honour of Abraham, the friend of God, and its inhabitants call themselves Khalilis. I use the name most widely used in the UK, vowel length unspecified.

Hebron's holiest shrine also goes by several names. According to the Book of Genesis, Abraham buried his wife Sarah in the Cave of Machpelah. Jews call the Herodian structure above the cave Harat HaMachpelah, or the Machpelah Cave, and Muslims call it the Ibrahimi Mosque. It is also known as the Tomb of the Patriarchs. The largest and most famous room in its interior is called the Yitzhak or Isaac Hall.

Some of the other place names are also disputed. Since Tel Rumeida is the site of ancient Hebron, the settlers refer to it as Tel Hebron, but 'Tel Rumeida' – the name coined by the American archaeologist Philip Hammond, who linked the Arabic name of a nearby mountain, Jebel Rumeida, with the Hebrew word 'tel' – is much more widely used. The settlers call the main road through the centre of the city King David Street or King David's Steps. Everyone else knows it as Shoada Street.

Dates

All dates of Hebron's mythic history are taken from the conventional biblical chronology. According to the Jewish calendar, the world began 5,771 years ago, in 3760 BCE. Abraham was supposedly born in the year 1948, or 1812 BCE, in the archaeological period known as the Middle Bronze Age. 2011 CE equates to 5771 in the Jewish calendar.

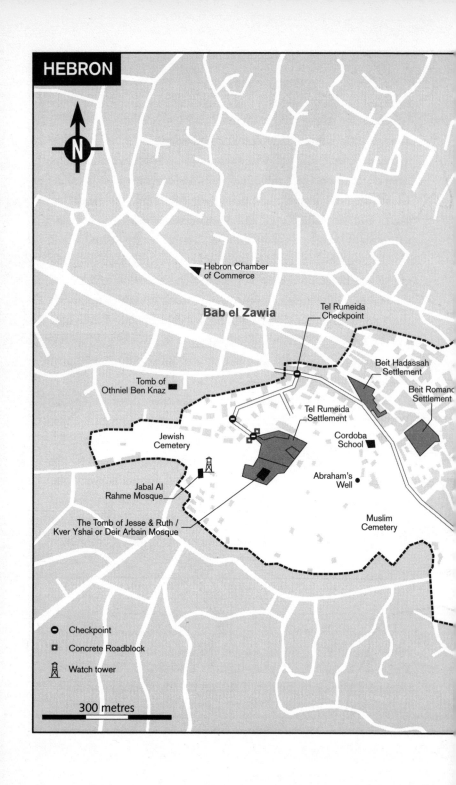

HEBRON

N

Hebron Chamber
of Commerce

Bab el Zawia

Tel Rumeida
Checkpoint

Beit Hadassah
Settlement

Beit Romano
Settlement

Tomb of
Othniel Ben Knaz

Tel Rumeida
Settlement

Cordoba
School

Jewish
Cemetery

Abraham's
Well

Jabal Al
Rahme Mosque

Muslim
Cemetery

The Tomb of Jesse & Ruth /
Kver Yshai or Deir Arbain Mosque

Checkpoint

Concrete Roadblock

Watch tower

300 metres

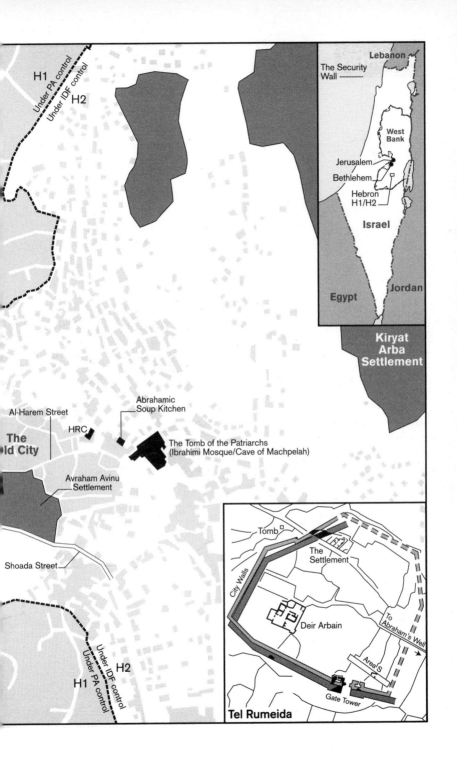

H1

Under PA control

Under IDF control

H2

The Security Wall ------

Lebanon

West Bank

Jerusalem

Bethlehem

Hebron
H1/H2

Israel

Egypt

Jordan

Kiryat
Arba
Settlement

Abrahamic
Soup Kitchen

Al-Harem Street

HRC

The
Old City

The Tomb of the Patriarchs
(Ibrahimi Mosque/Cave of Machpelah)

Avraham Avinu
Settlement

Shoada Street

Under IDF control

Under PA control

H2

H1

Tomb

The
Settlement

City Walls

Deir Arbain

To
Abraham's Well

Area S

Gate Tower

Tel Rumeida

INTRODUCTION

Say: 'God has declared the truth. Follow the faith of
Abraham. He was an upright man, no idolater.'

The Koran, 3:95

I wanted to write about Tel Rumeida since I first heard of
its existence. In June 2001, when the Second Intifada was
at its height, a friend of mine organized a conference at the
ICA with the laudable aim of 'creating a space where the
intractable futures of Israelis and Palestinians, Jews and
Arabs can briefly be re-imagined.' The invited speakers
included a woman whose daughter had been killed by a
suicide bomber and an Arab member of the Knesset, the
Israeli Parliament, who was being prosecuted for treason,
but it was the Israeli architect Eyal Weizman who presented
a way of thinking about the conflict that was entirely new
to me. He maintained that it was no longer defined by international treaties or by military force, but by how and where
one chose to build. 'The landscape and the built environ-
ment become the arena of conflict,' he wrote in an essay
called 'The Politics of Verticality'. Since Israel captured the
West Bank and East Jerusalem from Jordan in the Six Day
War of 1967, the state has been engaged in what Weizman
called a 'colossal project' of territorial and architectural
planning, building military bases, hilltop settlements and
'security roads' that bypass Palestinian towns. Occupying

land was not merely an end in itself: it was also a way of rendering the idea of a Palestinian state a logistical impossibility. 'The thing must be done first and foremost by creating facts on the ground', one planner said: 'cut apart' by Israeli roads and settlements, and enjoying only limited areas for self-rule, the 'minority population' would find it hard to 'create unification and territorial continuity'.

Weizman said that mapmaking was a national obsession in Israel, and yet if you wanted to understand the nature of the occupation, it was no longer enough to view the West Bank in plan, as a flat territory, seen from above: 'The separation between Israeli and Palestinian areas in the Occupied Territories was not articulated in the surface of the terrain alone,' he wrote. Israel had created a multidimensional road system, with the highways reserved for settler traffic raised on bridges, and the narrow Palestinian roads sunk into underpasses, and it had also sought to control the militarized airspace above the West Bank, and the mountain aquifer beneath it. The territory that had resulted was a kind of 'hollow land' – 'cut apart and enclosed by its many barriers, gutted by underground tunnels, threaded together by overpasses and bombed from its militarised skies.'

Yet it was another element of Weizman's 'hollow land' that intrigued me most. Israel has never annexed most of the West Bank, but it annexed East Jerusalem at the end of the Six Day War, and at the same time it 'declared the archaeological and historical sites in the West Bank, primarily those of Jewish or Israelite cultural relevance to be the state's "national and cultural property"'. The sub-terrain was 'the first zone to be colonised', Weizman said, and in passing he mentioned a 'notorious episode' in which a group of settlers had occupied an archaeological site called

Tel Rumeida, and built a block of flats on stilts above the exposed remains of the Bronze Age city of Hebron.

I tried to find out more about it, but the reports were confused and contradictory: one claimed that the settlers had been drawn to Tel Rumeida by the news that an archaeologist had uncovered remnants of King David's palace, but others said it was not until the settlers occupied the site that its archaeological significance became apparent. It seemed that there had been several digs during the last forty years, but when they had taken place, and what they had found, was not clear. The nature of the settlement was not clear, either: Eyal Weizman said the settlers had placed 'seven mobile homes' on 'an elevated cement roof' supported by concrete pillars placed around the site of the dig, but other sources suggested they had built – or were building – a block of flats.

The confusion was intriguing in itself – the Israeli–Palestinian conflict is reported in great detail even in relatively peaceful times, and during the upheavals of the Second Intifada there were more or less daily updates in the media. Yet the constant coverage has not proved enlightening: a study conducted by the Glasgow University Media Group in 2003 found that many people did not even know who was 'occupying' the 'occupied territories'. Perhaps it was not surprising that the history of a single building in the most bitterly contested city in the West Bank should have been so hard to establish.

Hebron lies at the heart of the struggle for control of the land because it is the city of the matriarchs and patriarchs – the family of named individuals from whom all Jews, Christians and Muslims claim lineal or spiritual descent.

According to Genesis, Abraham settled in Hebron when he obeyed God's command to leave his home and travel to the Promised Land. He had two sons: the elder, Ishmael, is believed to have become the father of the Arabs, while the younger, Isaac, had a son called Jacob, who became the father of the Jews.

When Abraham's wife, Sarah, died, he buried her in a tomb called the Cave of Machpelah, on the outskirts of the town, and he was later buried beside her. Since Isaac and Jacob, and two of their respective wives, are also believed to be interred in the family tomb, Hebron is regarded as the birthplace of the Jewish people, and the immense Herodian structure that stands above the traditional site of the Cave of Machpelah in the south-west corner of the city, half a mile east of Tel Rumeida, is Judaism's second holiest shrine.

Yet it was Ishmael's heirs who dominated Hebron when the Jews' two-thousand-year exile from Israel began. When the Muslim armies led by Mohammed's successors emerged from the Arabian peninsula and captured Palestine in 632 CE, they renamed Hebron Al Khalil, 'the friend', in honour of Abraham, whom Muslims venerate as a 'friend of God', and turned the building above the Tomb of the Patriarchs into a mosque. Jews began returning to Hebron in the medieval era, and a small group lived in peace with their Palestinian neighbours until 1929, when sixty-seven of their number were killed in a riot provoked by growing tensions over Jewish immigration to Palestine, and the British authorities decided to evacuate the rest.

For most of the next forty years there were no Jews in Hebron, but in 1968 an atavistic rabbi called Moshe Levinger led a small group back to the city. According to the Israeli writer Amos Oz, the 'settlers' who led the return to the territories that Israel had captured in the Six Day War of

1967 made up 'a stupid and cruel messianic sect, a band of armed gangsters . . . that emerged from some dark corner of Judaism'. Rabbi Levinger and his followers were some of the most extreme of all. In most places in the West Bank, the settlements were established on isolated hilltops or other defensible locations, at one remove from the local population, but the settlers of Hebron chose to live in the middle of the largest Palestinian city in the West Bank.

Levinger believed that the biblical legends on which their claims to the land were based should supersede all other considerations: 'The Jewish national renaissance is more important than democracy,' he once said. 'No government has the authority or right to say that a Jew cannot live in all of the parts of the land of Israel.' Since many of his followers belonged to the outlawed Kach Party that advocated the expulsion or 'transfer' of the 'Ishmaelites' from the territories they called 'Judea and Samaria', it is little wonder that their presence provoked resentment and resistance, yet they were not easily intimidated. In the early days of the settlement, Palestinian stallholders in the Old City would identify their new neighbours by their antisocial tendencies – one might be known for turning over market stalls; another for spitting in people's faces – but over the years, the minor antagonisms escalated into violent confrontations, and on the morning of 25 February 1994 a doctor from Brooklyn called Baruch Goldstein walked into the Tomb of the Patriarchs during dawn prayers and shot and killed twenty-nine Muslims.

The Israeli army responded to the massacre by imposing a year-long curfew on the Palestinian residents of the Old City of Hebron, increasing the number of roadblocks and checkpoints, and banning Palestinian cars, and in some cases Palestinian pedestrians, from its streets. Complaining of constant harassment, and finding themselves increasingly unable to pursue their lives, the Palestinians began abandoning the area, and the settlers expanded their presence. In 1984, they placed seven caravans on a plot of land on the eastern edge of Tel Rumeida within the line of the ancient city walls, and in 1999 they gained permission to turn the encampment into permanent homes. Building on such an important site would never have been permitted in Israel itself – one Israeli archaeologist told me that it was like building on Stonehenge, and the legal challenges that delayed the progress of the work were one of the sources of the confusion that I had encountered when I began my research.

The building was finally completed in 2005. The Israeli archaeologist who had conducted the 'rescue excavation' that prepared the ground for construction had left intact some of the structures he unearthed, including two sections of the city walls, and the settlement was raised on stilts placed among them. The settlers' American-born spokesman David Wilder called the first tenants 'keepers of the keys' – guardians of Hebron's Jewish shrines, and inheritors of a tradition lasting almost four thousand years: 'It is the site of the original Hebron, home of Abraham and Sarah, Isaac and Rebecca, Jacob and Lea', he wrote. Seemingly unconcerned by the fact that they had destroyed the heritage they claimed to revere, Wilder said that the 'beautiful new apartment complex' built above 'the roots of our existence' symbolized 'the buds of the rebirth of the Jewish People in the City of the Patriarchs and Matriarchs' and 'represents, perhaps more than any other place in Israel, the moral and historical justification of our existence, not only in Hebron, but in all of Israel. That is why we are here, and that is why we will stay here, forever.'

The building that stood on stilts above its own foundations also stood above the foundations of the state of Israel
itself. Here, or so it seemed to me from a distance of several
thousand miles, were the mythic roots of the struggle to
control the land – and here was the modern conflict in its
most incestuous form. In 2005, the liberal Israeli journalist
Gideon Levy said that 'an annual field trip' to Tel Rumeida
should be mandatory in Israeli schools: 'This is where every
student in Israel – every citizen, in fact – should be brought.'
The fate of its Palestinian residents would form the curriculum of a course in civics and social studies, for barely fifty
of the five hundred families who once lived in the area were
left: the rest had been driven out by 'a reign of terror'
imposed by the 'violent lords of the land' who had become
their neighbours.

To Levy, Tel Rumeida has become 'the gutter of the
settlement enterprise', a 'military barracks' that had become
'a shelter for purest evil', while to Wilder, it is not only the
birthplace of monotheism but 'the roots of all civilization'.
There was only one point on which they might agree: as
Levy put it, there was no other neighbourhood like this one.

It was not just the violence of the Second Intifada that
stopped me going out to Hebron straight away. At first, I
did not feel entitled to write about the Israeli–Palestinian
conflict: I do not speak Arabic or Hebrew, I have no Israeli
or Palestinian relatives – no Jewish or Muslim ones either as
far as I'm aware – and I had never been to the region. I have
no history of engagement in the subject and no expertise to
offer. The lack of an instinctive commitment was not neces-
sarily a disadvantage – you might argue that it was the best
qualification I could have – and yet the idea of an outsider

writing about such a tortuous and agonizing situation seemed at best inappropriate, and at worst a gross intrusion.

I told myself that Hebron was a place of significance to everyone who grew up within the cultural sphere of the three great Abrahamic faiths of the Middle East, but I did not believe it until I found my life converging on the lives of the matriarchs and patriarchs in one fundamental respect. In the summer of 2006, my wife and I had discovered that we belonged to the small group of people who cannot have children without help, and when I re-read the Book of Genesis shortly afterwards I was surprised and moved to discover that all three generations of Hebron's first family also suffered from what our doctors call 'unexplained infertility'. Naturally, the solutions that our societies proposed were very different – theirs preached obedience to the dictates of a priestly cult; ours offered all the benefits of post-Enlightenment medical science – but the dilemma was essentially the same, and the knowledge that Abraham, Isaac and Jacob and their respective wives had suffered the same frustrations as us made their stories more real to me than they had ever been before.

I was particularly fascinated by the story of Abraham's attempts to produce an heir, for it dramatizes the mythic origins of the ethnic struggle that has endured until today. From the moment that Abraham's wife, Sarah, appears in the Book of Genesis we are told that she was 'barren: she had no child', and before God intervenes to grant her a son at the age of ninety, she tells Abraham to 'go in unto' her Egyptian maid, Hagar: 'It may be that I may obtain children by her.'

Such arrangements might have been conventional in the time that Genesis was composed or redacted, but its authors were nonetheless aware of their ability to create resentment. The King James Bible conveys what happened next in a verse of concise dramatic power: Hagar conceived, and 'when she saw that she had conceived, her mistress was despised in her eyes.' To be supplanted by her servant was bad enough, but to be 'despised' by her was too much to bear. Sarah – or Sarai, as she was known before Isaac's birth – complained to Abraham, whose answer, seems, to a modern reader, perfectly pitched between affection and exasperation: 'Behold, thy maid is in thy hand. Do to her as it pleaseth thee.' Sarai was unforgiving: she 'dealt hardly with Hagar', who 'fled from her face', and yet God did not abandon her. An angel of the Lord found Hagar wandering in the wilderness, and told her to go back. Hagar and her unborn child were part of God's design – the angel told her that her descendants 'shall not be numbered for multitude', and that she could call her son Ishmael 'because the Lord hath heard thy affliction' before adding an ominous prophecy about his nature: 'And he will be a wild man; his hand will be against every man, and every man's hand against him.'

Hagar went back to her mistress, as instructed, but the feud between Abraham's wives was renewed after Isaac's miraculous birth. Ishmael's behaviour at the 'great feast' that Abraham gave on the day that Isaac was weaned is the source of the dispute, though it is not clear exactly what he did: the King James Bible says that Sarah saw Ishmael 'mocking', without explaining who or what provoked his scorn, but the Jewish writer Elie Wiesel offers a different translation – he says that Sarah saw the fourteen-year-old boy Ishmael 'playing' with his younger brother, and could not abide the growing intimacy between the boys.

Her reaction was as unforgiving as before: she told Abraham to 'cast out this bondwoman and her son', and God, who seemed to have infinite patience for the matriarchs' and patriarch's domestic affairs, advised her to obey. 'In all that Sarah hath said unto thee, hearken unto her voice; for in Isaac thy seed shall be called,' he said, though he added that he would also make Ishmael 'a nation'.

Abraham gave Hagar bread and water, and expelled her and Ishmael into 'the wilderness of Beer-sheba', where the boy would have died of thirst if the angel had not intervened again. This time, Hagar and Ishmael did not return to Canaan: Ishmael 'dwelt in the wilderness', and married a woman from Egypt. He had twelve sons, 'princes according to their nations, and when he died, aged one hundred and thirty-seven, he was gathered 'unto his people', who 'dwelt from Havilah unto Shur' – an area that is sometimes said to correspond to the Arabian peninsula. Isaac and Ishmael only met once as adults, when they buried their father in the family tomb in Hebron, but nonetheless the warring residents of the city are aware of their shared heritage: as one Palestinian man was to say to me, Arabs and Jews are 'brothers with different mothers'.

The costly and time-consuming process of IVF delayed my visit to Hebron by another year, but it also gave me a new appreciation of the drama and richness of the legends located in the city, and made me even more curious to see where they were set. My son was born in July 2007 and four months later I went to Hebron for the first time.

Since I had never been to Israel or the West Bank, and did not even know how to negotiate the short journey from Jerusalem to Hebron, I joined a tour led by one of the many groups with an interest in the city. The Hebron Rehabilitation Committee (HRC) had been set up in 1996 after the massacre in the mosque, and with the aim of addressing its

consequences: when it began operations, more than a third
of the densely packed stone buildings in the Old City were
abandoned or neglected, and it was home to no more than
five hundred people. The HRC began renovating the frayed
buildings and offering subsidized rents, and during the next
ten years its population increased ten times over. Reviving
its commercial life proved much harder: our guide, Walid,
told us that if he had not held his father's hand when he
visited the Old City as a child, he would have got lost in
the crowds, but such precautions were hardly necessary any
more – Sunday is a normal day of business in Hebron, but
most of the stalls that lined the winding course of Al-Harem
Street were shut, and the few that had remained open had no
customers, apart from us.

The settlers never enter the covered part of the souk
without an army escort, but it was not hard to detect the evidence of their presence: there were Israeli flags flying from
the rooftops, and the unroofed sections of the souk that
abutted the settlements were covered with a veil of chicken
wire to catch the stones and bottles thrown from above. The
side streets that ran south towards the settlement established
on the site of the old wholesale market on the southern edge
of the Old City were blocked with rubbish and barbed wire,
and the main street that used to run towards it had been cut
in half by a barrier built from the immense concrete blocks
that form the 'separation fence' or 'apartheid wall' that runs
between Israel and the West Bank. The street must have been
abandoned in great haste, for the doors to the shops were
standing open, and there were traces of chicken shit and
feathers stuck to the pallets stacked on the pavements. The
city had been divided into two zones in 1997, but the
process of segregation had not been completed, for the area
called H2, where the Israeli army retained control, had been

torn in half along a jagged line that ran through the middle of the Old City.

When we first emerged in the sunlit square beyond the last line of houses that had once formed the Old City's outer wall, it felt like we had stepped off a forest trail onto the edge of a treeless plain, but the sense of openness diminished as I looked around. The camouflage netting covering the facade of the building on the east side of the square indicated that it was one of many that had been requisitioned by the army, and the military presence was even more apparent on the western side, where there was another settlement in a large grey building called Beit Romano – a watchtower had been set up on the concrete roof above its yard, and the road that ran past it, and climbed the hill towards Tel Rumeida, was sealed by a heavy metal gate flanked by two more watchtowers.

Six soldiers were coming to the end of their patrol as we went past: 'There's another side of the story,' one of them said in an American accent, when he recognized the affiliation of our group. They went through the gates and locked them behind them. I looked through the gap by the chain and saw them standing in a circle, heads bowed in prayer. The soldier's assertion did not have the effect that he intended: I have been a journalist for most of my working life and I have always believed that it is my job to listen to what people have to say, regardless of their reputation, and to tell their stories as accurately and honestly as I can. Until that afternoon, I had not doubted that there was 'another side to the story', and yet now that I had been confronted with the worst effects of an occupation that smothers the lives of four million people, the idea of engaging with the settlers seemed a shameful compromise, a paring away of the anger that was the only reasonable response to the situation.

I wondered how anyone could justify the damage that had been inflicted on the city, let alone the cost in human life that the settlers' presence had entailed; and yet my indignation did not blind me to my nature. I am not an activist or a polemical writer. I admired the people who resisted the depredations of the settlers of Hebron, but I could not join them, and I could not write about the city if I was arguing a case. I could not evade the political dimension of the conflict, but it wasn't what had caught my attention – I wanted to understand the city's mythic history, and the ways in which it continued to inform its inhabitants' lives. Above all, I wanted to understand the history of Tel Rumeida.

I only saw it from a distance. At the end of the tour we climbed onto the roof of the HRC's office in a restored palazzo near the Tomb of the Patriarchs and looked out across the Old City. The buildings were so closely packed together that they seemed to form an unbroken surface, an undulating, dun-brown landscape, like a dried-up riverbed or wadi, riven by the cracks of the streets. Tel Rumeida was 500 metres to the west: its lower slopes were populated by the gravestones of a Muslim cemetery, and its upper slopes were a blur of dark green foliage. As I gazed at the spot where I thought the settlement ought to be, the rattle of gunfire drifted across the rooftops.

Four months later, I went back to Hebron on my own.

PART ONE

ISAAC AND ISHMAEL

c.3000 BCE TO 1999 CE

CHAPTER ONE

THE GATE OF THE CITY

And Ephron the Hittite answered Abraham in the
audience of the children of Heth, even of all that
went in at the gate of his city, saying, Nay, my lord,
hear me: the field give I thee, and the cave that is
therein, I give it thee; in the presence of the sons of
my people, give I it thee: bury thy dead.

Genesis 23: 10–11

I spent the night in a hotel in East Jerusalem, and in the
morning I discovered that the Israeli military's latest assault
on the Gaza Strip was entering a new phase. 'Operation
Warm Winter' was designed to stop Hamas militants firing
rockets at towns in southern Israel. Whether they were
responding to the blockade of the Gaza Strip or the other
way round was a matter of debate, but it was indicative of
the corrosive circularity of the Israeli–Palestinian conflict
that Israel's assault had begun on the day the rockets reached
Ashkelon, where many of the inhabitants of Gaza had lived
until 1948, when they were driven from their homes in the
fighting that followed Israel's Declaration of Independence.
For the first two days Israel had attacked suspected bomb-
making factories from the air, but on the night of Saturday,
28 February 2008, two thousand soldiers invaded northern
Gaza. In protest, Mahmoud Abbas, the President of the
Palestinian Authority, had suspended relations with Israel,

and in the West Bank a day of strikes and demonstrations had been called. There were no buses and few taxis on the roads, and the man at reception told me it might not be possible to get to Hebron.

Even on a good day the journey is not as straightforward as it should be. Hebron is only twenty miles south of Jerusalem, on an ancient trade route that runs down the spine of the Judean Hills, but the road is often closed or the flow of traffic impeded by checkpoints and roadblocks. The Ministry of Tourism has tried to re-brand Route 60 as a heritage trail called the 'Way of the Patriarchs', and its resemblance to a Bronze Age cattle trail is more than cosmetic: it often takes as long to drive the road in the first decade of the twenty-first century as it would have taken Abraham to herd his flocks along it.

For those who do not drive, or cannot afford a taxi, things are even more problematic. A settler bus runs between Jerusalem and H2, the part of the city controlled by the Israeli army, but there are no direct buses to the Palestinian districts of H1: you have to change at Bethlehem, and pass through a checkpoint in the wall. I had travelled that way earlier in the week, and I had been reminded that it was not a rhetorical flourish to call the West Bank a prison. The taxi driver who picked me up in the centre of Bethlehem did not have a Jerusalem permit, and he was forced to leave me at the entrance to the street that led to the checkpoint in the wall. There were roadside stalls selling snacks and drinks and double-parked taxis waiting to pick up fares. A trade in images of the wall is another of the micro-industries that have flourished in the unpromising spaces created by its brutal rearrangement of Jerusalem's topography, and as I entered the grilled passageway that ran beside it, I had to step over a man lying on the floor with a camera pressed to his face.

The passageway was so narrow that as I walked along it the fingers of my left hand brushed against the concrete. Had there been a queue, it would have been unbearably claustrophobic. A turnstile admitted me into a dark hall with scuffed lino floors and unpainted walls. Soldiers behind frosted windows watched my bag pass through an X-ray machine, while another soldier moved back and forth on the gantry above my head, the clatter of his boots resounding through the hall. 'Further Inspection Rooms 1 and 2' said the labels on the doors on the other side of the airport-style metal detector. The Palestinian man at the head of the queue waiting to come the other way asked me how I was, and politely repeated my answer: 'Is it fine, waiting like this?' The line stretched out of the door and along the Jerusalem side of the wall. 'Peace Be With You' said the sign, in English, Arabic and Hebrew, which the Israeli Ministry of Tourism had fitted between the coils of barbed wire above the gate that controlled the flow of traffic in and out of the West Bank. As a foreigner, I was given preferential treatment, and I was going against the flow of people on their way home from work, but even so it had been a disorientating experience, and I was relieved when Reception told me they had found me a driver who was willing to take me to Hebron.

There may have been a connection between Ashraf's willingness to defy the strike and his desire for self-improvement, for as soon as he found out that I was English he produced his course folder and asked me for help with his homework. He was a football fan: I taught him the English words for the positions on a football pitch, and as we emerged on the edge of Jerusalem, he taught me the Arabic terms for the elements that enclosed our horizons – rain, sky and wall.

Israel began building 'the separation barrier' during the
Second Intifada, when hundreds of its citizens were killed in
suicide attacks, but no Palestinian believes it is a 'security'
measure: since its looping course drives far inside the West
Bank, dividing villages from their fields, they see it as a
means of appropriating yet more land in anticipation of the
ever-receding peace agreement that is supposed to lead to the
creation of a Palestinian state.

Yet it is not just the Palestinians who resent the Wall: the
settlers hate it too. Many of them live east of its projected
course, and fear being excluded from the 'Greater Israel'
that it appears to define, though there is little indication that
Israel ever intends to relinquish any part of the occupied
territory. Within weeks of capturing East Jerusalem from
Jordan in June 1967, the state had annexed the city and
claimed it as the 'eternal and indivisible capital' of the Jewish
people, but the demographic equation forbids it from annexing the West Bank as well. It wants the land, but not the
people – or as the Prime Minister, Levi Eshkol, said to the
Foreign Minister, Golda Meir, in the aftermath of the Six
Day War: 'the dowry pleases you but the bride does not'. It
cannot swallow the West Bank, an Israeli once said to me,
for absorbing the Palestinian population of the West Bank
would mean the end of the Zionist dream of a state with a
Jewish majority, and yet it cannot spit it out, either. The Wall
is the most visible symptom of the confusion. I have yet to
hear a more coherent explanation of the logic of binding
together the West Bank and Israel only to then divide them
again than the challenge to the Palestinians that the politician
Moshe Dayan issued in 1985: 'We have no solution,' he said.
'You shall continue to live like dogs, and whoever wants to
can leave – and we will see where this process leads.'

Sometimes, the Wall retreated to distant hillsides, but

sometimes it ran close beside us. As we approached Bethlehem we ran between two long tunnels linked by bridges,
and passed between the settlement of Har Gilo and the
village of Beit Jala. During the Second Intifada, Palestinian
militants and Israeli soldiers had traded fire across the 'tunnels highway', and barriers built from the same protective
material as the battle tanks that had entered Gaza earlier in
the morning enclosed the road.

There were many Israeli cars on the road, and at every
junction and roadside hitching spot we passed off-duty
soldiers, girls in long skirts and headscarves and Orthodox
Jews in black hats and coats waiting for lifts. The Palestinian villages gathered in the folds of the land, while the
houses and apartments of the settlements stretched across
the hilltops in neatly serrated rows of uniform off-white
stone. This was Eyal Weizman's 'hollow land' – part housing estate, part prison archipelago, an endlessly subdivided
and ceaselessly monitored zone, in which two national
identities compete for space.

Raised concrete blocks and empty huts marked the site
of a disused checkpoint, and we passed an army jeep parked
beneath a watchtower. A high net sealed the curve of the
road that led past the refugee camp of Arroub. There was a
field filled with the rusting hulls of abandoned buses, and
another planted with vineyards and fruit trees. The contrasting idioms merged on the slope beyond the village of
Beit Ummar, where a scrapyard had been set up in an olive
grove. Rocks the colour of dried chickpeas tumbled down
the hills.

At an unused checkpoint on the edge of Halhoul, a town
that lies to the north of Hebron, we turned onto a smaller
road lined with tin-roofed shacks and stalls. The luxurious
vines that produce Hebron's famous grapes adorned the

frames of the stone houses beside the road. We passed unfinished buildings with blank, empty windows and shops
selling stacks of second-hand tyres, prams and office furniture. The traffic slowed, and I saw people in the road ahead.
An elderly man in a red keffiyeh and a young boy were
holding the ends of a rope stretched across the road. They
lowered it as we approached and we weaved through a
chicane of rocks. There were so many people in the road
that Ashraf had slowed to walking pace, and from my
elevated seat I watched a boy with a sling pick up a stone.
The soldiers were standing at the bottom of the hill.

The boy with his sling raised his left arm and pointed it
in the direction of the soldiers. He was not alone: there were
half a dozen other kids in the road, with scarves tied around
their faces, advancing and retreating, like a breaking wave,
re-forming behind the invisible line that defined the limit
of their daring. Ashraf was tapping the steering wheel, and
murmuring in fear or disapproval. If I had been able to speak
to him, I would have told him to stop or go back, but we
had established that all we could talk about was football.
Besides, there was another car coming up the hill towards us.
It seemed easier to keep going.

I did not see where the stone landed, but it did not seem
to trouble the soldiers. They were standing beside two jeeps
parked beside a set of yellow gates that sealed the entrance
to Halhoul. The one nearest us was leaning against the jeep,
with his rifle pointing at the sky. His hand was on the grip,
not the trigger, and he looked more relaxed than I was.
Beyond the gates, the road climbed again, past a mosque
and a car showroom. We turned right at a roundabout, and
began to descend into the city, past burning skips and piles
of rubber tyres that sent plumes of oily smoke uncoiling
across our windscreen. It was strangely quiet: there was no

traffic on the road, and few people to be seen, but the fires
that lit our path showed that the unrest had gone before us.

My hotel was the only one in the centre of Hebron: it
was on Ain Sarah, the main street in the centre of the town,
and occupied the upper floors of the large concrete building
that also housed the city's only supermarket. My room was
sparsely furnished, but it was clean and quiet and had a
phone and an Internet connection. I was not planning on
leaving again, but at half-past three I heard the sounds of a
demonstration going past on Ain Sarah and I went out to see
what was happening.

A set of steps led down the side of the building. As I
joined the back of the crowd, a young boy threw a bucket
at my back, and ran away, but no one else paid me any
attention. Three hundred metres beyond my hotel two
asymmetrical green towers serve as a gateway to the commercial heart of Hebron, funnelling traffic downhill towards
Bab al-Zawia, and the crowd stopped at a roundabout
beneath them. I was standing at the back, when a man called
Najaf Abu Sneineh introduced himself. Despite his broad
Texan accent, he was a Khalili, a native of Hebron. He had
left home when he was nineteen, and spent thirty years in
Houston. He had made a lot of money, but money wasn't
everything, and he had moved back to Hebron two years
ago, aged forty-nine, and built his 'dream house' on a hill
above the centre of town.

'The Israelis say we have to do this or that, but if they
want to stop the violence they have to end the occupation.'
The Americans were to blame, though the Arab leaders
hadn't helped: 'They ain't nothing but a bunch of fools.'
His Texan accent made the phrase seem vivid and authentic.
'Give me freedom or give me death, the Americans say.
These people aren't violent: they just want a better life.'

Most of the demonstrators were women, and many of them were carrying the green banners of Hamas, for the conservative city of Hebron is the party's stronghold in the West Bank. The men were standing on the pavement in small groups, smoking and watching. There were no policeman and more importantly no soldiers to be seen. That was why there was no trouble, Najaf said.

His brother, who was also in the crowd, shared his same imposing build, but in other respects they could not have looked less alike: Najaf's hammer-loop jeans, denim shirt and scuffed leather boots made him look like an American workman, but his brother had the shaved head, thick beard and long robes of a stereotypical mullah. He did not speak English, but he kept clasping my hands enthusiastically, and Najaf said that he wanted to welcome me to Hebron.

Najaf invited me to dinner at his house, which he pointed out as we walked back up Ain Sarah: it looked like a big place, though the building behind it was even bigger. Najaf said it was the concrete shell of a half-built basketball stadium, which had only been put there because a foreign government had offered to pay for it, and the puppets in Fatah had taken the cash. It would not be finished until another government offered more money, most of which would go in bribes. Fatah was run by people who had come back from Tunisia and Lebanon in 1993 and enriched themselves: was it any wonder that people voted for Hamas?

Najaf went up and down the hill several times a day to pray at the mosque, but he was out of breath by the time we were halfway up. As we approached the house he pressed a button on a keyring, and the metal grille that served as the gates began cranking upwards. The house was five storeys high, and faced south-east across the city. Its windows were modelled on a design in a French chateau, and it had a lift in a semicircular turret on the side. The marble in the stairwell alone had cost $150,000. Najaf had done a lot of the work himself, though some people thought that it was for 'the idiot president Arafat'. There were four cars parked on the tiled forecourt, and piles of sand and building rubble by the gates.

Inside, the ground-floor sitting room reserved for guests was low and dark, designed for the summer heat. Two stiff-backed sofas upholstered in dark fabric and a set of matching chairs were drawn up around a vast television screen. Najaf turned on the news: seventy people had been killed in the fighting in Gaza, and a boy had been killed at a demonstration in a village outside Hebron.

Najaf took me on a tour of the house, though his youngest son, Ahmad, did most of the talking: he kept up a non-stop monologue about his toys and games as we went from floor to floor, but when we got to his room, it was his father who lifted up the base of the bed, and showed me the storage space beneath it.

On the fourth floor, we went out onto one of the balconies overlooking the town, and I took a photograph of the two of them standing by the railing above the city. It was getting dark, and you could not see far through the mist hanging over the city, but Najaf pointed out the lights on a hill that he said was Tel Rumeida.

The tiles on the balcony were spattered with white droppings, deposited by the pigeons roosting beneath the flat roof on the floor above. Najaf wanted to chase them out. We went up the last flight of the stairs to the glass-walled penthouse. It was half-finished: the floors were bare concrete and the air smelt of damp and plaster. A door opened onto a narrow landing beneath the eaves where the pigeons had settled. Najaf chased two of them away, but he could not reach the last one. He fetched a ladder and climbed level with its perch. He swiped at it with a plank. It was hard to generate much momentum and the bird evaded the blow with ease, rising into the air and letting it pass harmlessly beneath it. It settled back on its perch. Ahmad was delighted: 'It's a fast bird!' he said.

His father corrected him: 'It's a stupid bird.'

He changed his grip, and tried to bring the plank crashing down on the bird's head, but it flew across the open space above us and landed on the other side of the ledge. Finally, Najaf caught it as it flew past him. He tucked it under his arm, and carried it down the ladder. In the cold empty penthouse, he stuffed it in a cage, and handed it to Ahmad, who swung it back and forth as we went downstairs. He was concerned that the cage was too small, for its wings were pressed against the mesh, but Najaf assured him that it would not be for long: he was going to the mosque to pray, but when he got back they would drive the bird into the hills outside Hebron, and release it.

Najaf's wife and two youngest daughters had been in the kitchen, preparing dinner, but they sat with us as we ate. Rabihah and Muna, who were sixteen and fourteen, were dressed in college sweatshirts and headscarves. They were courteous and enthusiastic: they wanted to know why I had come to Hebron, and they wanted to see photos of my wife and son. 'Where did y'all meet?' Muna asked me in a Texan accent even stronger than her father's.

At seven o'clock, Najaf said he was going to the mosque to pray, and we walked down the hill together. When we said goodbye, at the turning to my hotel, he hugged me and told me to call him if I needed anything. Travellers often report such kindnesses, especially in Arab countries where the culture of hospitality is well established, but that does not lessen their impact – as I walked back along the litter-

strewn screes above the empty plot of land next to my hotel
Hebron seemed a much less intimidating place than it had
earlier in the afternoon.

The next morning's protest was in the same place as the
demonstration the day before, but it was not organized, and
it was not peaceful. When I got up, the mist hanging above
the city was so thick that I could not see the compound of
the United Nations Relief and Works Agency for Palestine
refugees at the bottom of the hill, but by half-past nine it
had been displaced by plumes of smoke, and a low rumble
pierced by the blare of car horns was emanating from the
city centre. Skips had been set alight on Ain Sarah and there
were groups of kids gathering in the road: some had stepped
into a side street to tie scarves around their faces, but others
were engaged in the ritual dance I had watched the day
before, advancing and retreating across the invisible line that
marked the limit of their daring.

I knew there must have been soldiers ahead, and I asked
a taxi driver to take me round the protests. He said the road
was closed, but he pointed out a dark-eyed teenager with a
limp and an abscess on his chin who would show me the
way. We passed the Hebron Chamber of Commerce, which
was housed in a prow-shaped building on the far side of the
road, and went through a gap between two stone buildings,
where the road narrowed to a single lane. My guide was
wearing ripped tracksuit trousers, and he walked with a
limp. He stayed several metres ahead of me looking back
from time to time to make sure that I was with him. There
were fewer people around, and as we passed the junction
above the roundabout where the soldiers were gathered
some of the kids came sprinting up the hill towards us.

The trouble was very local: New Al Shalallah Street was only 200 metres beyond the centre of the disturbances, but most of its shops were open for business. I stopped and bought a banana, partly to reassure myself that such mundane transactions were still possible. A stall selling coffee had been set up on the edge of an empty forecourt with smoke-blackened walls, and the rattle and pulse of trance music spilled through the speakers of a ghetto blaster on the handcart. A stretch of green-shuttered shops led to the square called the Baladiya where I had met the soldier on my first trip.

According to my map, the most direct route to Tel Rumeida was through the locked gates flanked by the squat concrete watchtowers on the western side of the square, but I should have known that they would only open to admit settlers and soldiers. I had to go the long way round, via the Tomb of the Patriarchs, and halfway through the souk I stopped for a cup of tea at a shop run by a woman called Nawal, who told me that the demonstrations had a simple aim: 'They are to say stop killing the people in Gaza. Stop killing the children. They didn't kill people from Hamas. Maybe two or three – but most of them are women, and children, not people from Hamas or Fatah. And all we can do is make demonstrations to tell them to stop – we can't fight them. All we have is stones, and we can't kill soldiers with stones.'

Like most Khalili women Nawal was dressed in an oppressively modest style: a black coat, black trousers and a neatly tied headscarf that framed her dark-skinned face as neatly as a nun's wimple. She was friendly and persuasive, and her shop, which lay at the entrance to the covered alleyways, where the wide, cobbled road became too narrow to admit a car, sold cushions and dresses embroidered by members of a women's cooperative.

It was a meeting place for Hebron's international activists, and we were joined by a young Englishman called Philip who worked for the Palestinian Solidarity Project in Beit Ummar, a 'village' of some twelve thousand people on the road to Jerusalem. Beit Ummar had lost much of its land to the surrounding settlements and was the scene of many confrontations between the villagers and the settlers and soldiers. That morning, the army had been firing blindly into the fog with live ammunition. A man had been shot in the head and been taken to hospital in Hebron, and a boy had been hit in the leg.

Philip was dressed in jeans, boots and Gore-Tex jacket, which made him look like any other young Western traveller, and yet he had a pale, introspective face and a disassociated manner that seemed to imply he had contemplated the prospect of his martyrdom and found it not displeasing. He was regarded as an anomalous figure amongst Hebron's activist community: one day, he had simply turned up in Beit Ummar and adopted it as his personal territory. He had checked what was happening in the centre of Hebron: apparently the army had occupied empty buildings in Bab al-Zawia and were using them as sniper positions, though they were only firing rubber bullets. He seemed to think that such trivial confrontations were beneath his notice.

When I reached the Tomb of the Patriarchs at half-past eleven, I asked one of the blue-uniformed Border Police on duty in the square if I could go to Tel Rumeida, and he said, 'You sure can, sir,' in an accent that made it sound like he was directing traffic in Times Square: 'You just go to the end of the road and turn right.' I could not see his eyes behind his dark glasses and I was surprised he was so amenable: given that the morning's protests had turned violent, he might have felt that he had more important things to deal with than an English tourist looking for the site of ancient Hebron. Besides, I knew the Border Police's reputation. An Israeli once told me that of all the many branches of the country's security forces, it was the paramilitary Border Police who 'ate the most shit', though the inhabitants of Hebron would not have spared them much sympathy. Even the soldiers stationed in the city are intimidated by the Border Police – one who served in Hebron at the end of the Second Intifada told the Israeli veterans' organization Breaking the Silence that they often saw them 'beating up Arabs', and another said he watched a Border Policeman stop a Palestinian man outside the Tomb of the Patriarchs and ask him if he had got a hard head: 'The guy went "yeah", just to be left alone,' the soldier said. '"Well, mine's even harder," the Border Police-man replied. He put on his helmet, and butted the man in the face. The guy bled something terrible.'

Yet it is not just the Border Police's brutality that causes resentment. The fact that an organization called the 'Border Police' operates inside the Occupied Territory of the West Bank is proof that the state of Israel no longer knows where its borders lie, and the confusion is particularly marked in Hebron, where Israeli security forces are a constant presence on the streets.

I had reached the edge of the old wholesale market that used to cater to Hebron and the surrounding villages. It had once been the busiest shopping district in the city but had been abandoned during the Second Intifada, and the empty shops were sealed with green metal shutters daubed with racist slogans: 'Arabs are sand niggers'; 'Hebron is ours'. I could hear my footsteps rebounding from the walls, and I began to understand why Hebron is routinely described as a 'ghost town'.

A soldier stopped me at the end of the alley and asked me where I was going. When I said that I was meeting someone at Tel Rumeida, he asked me if they were Jewish, and then if I was, too. When I said no, he radioed ahead for permission before he let me through. Another street of empty green-shuttered shops brought me to the edge of the area that used to be the wholesale market, which the settlers now call the Avraham Avinu 'neighbourhood'. Most of the buildings that faced the street had been stripped of their roofs, doors and, in some cases, their outside walls, leaving the concrete floors and sagging rafters of their dusty interiors exposed. There was an office chair sitting in the middle of one open-ended room, and a desk in another. Unlike the pristine streets I had just walked through, it looked like it had been ripped apart in bitter fighting, though beyond the outer ring of honey-combed wrecks there was a collection of renovated buildings, which included a synagogue and offices and homes neatly faced in Jerusalem stone. It was typical of the intimate nature of life in the city that the settlers' homes abutted the main alleyway running through the middle of the souk.

The road forked at the corner: one fork climbed past an army watchtower, and into a low range of sparsely occupied hills, but I went along the one that ran beside the souk, along the bottom of the Islamic cemetery on the lower slopes of Tel Rumeida. 'Take care up there,' said the soldier at the next checkpoint, 'it's a bit of a mess.' I asked him what he meant and he said, 'Oh, Arabs throwing stones,' as if the Khalilis were naughty children who could not be trusted to clear up after themselves.

By the time I had circumvented the Old City, and reached the top of the short road that led downhill to the Baladiya, it was half-past eleven. It was typical of the inconvenience of daily life in Hebron that it had taken almost an hour to cover a distance of no more than 100 metres. I was getting closer to Bab al-Zawia again, and the noise of the demonstrations was getting louder. Beit Hadassah – the settlers' first home in the centre of Hebron – lay ahead. It was a large stone building reached by a footbridge spanning a basement playground.

I passed more soldiers, and entered another row of boarded-up shops. It was narrower than the ones I had passed through before, and the green shutters made it look like a curving metalled racetrack, or the lower slopes of a bobsleigh run. The rumble of sound had begun to break down into its component parts: there were isolated shouts and coordinated chants, interspersed with the peppery crackle of gunfire and the sharp retorts of detonating tear-gas canisters. The road forked again: one fork climbed steeply uphill, and the other ran straight ahead and ended at a dun-brown bungalow with shuttered doors and windows. It looked like another of the abandoned houses that proliferate in H2, but in fact it was the most important crossing-point between the two halves of the city.

Normally, its doors would have been standing open and the soldiers would have been monitoring the people passing through the metal detectors in its interior, but today it had become the focus of protests: the Palestinian kids were gathering on the far side of the concrete barriers that restricted access to the street, periodically surging forward to hurl stones and bottles at the checkpoint, while the soldiers in the empty buildings that overlooked the square drove them back with tear-gas rounds and rubber bullets.

The noise of the protests became even louder as I climbed the hill, though the concrete barriers on the side of the road blocked the view to the city below. I passed a row of empty shops and an abandoned army post. There was another army post further up the hill consisting of an Israeli flag, a metal hut and two three-sided, waist-high concrete blocks set up to provide overlapping lines of fire down the hill.

Two bored-looking soldiers looked at my passport and let me through. I turned into the short, steep road that led to the settlement of Tel Rumeida. A blast of static issued from a radio hanging in another army post in the trees, and a cat perched on a skip darted away into a yard filled with rubbish. I passed the double-stacked caravans that had been the settlers' first home in the neighbourhood and reached the fenced-off area where the excavated remnants of ancient Hebron had been preserved. The settlement was fifty metres further up the hill. It was an imposing building, several storeys high, with pale cream walls and green window frames, and it was supported on a line of pillars planted in the gap beyond one of the sections of city wall. At the front, it faced a stone house clad in the kind of metal grille that adorns the windscreens of the Border Police's armoured jeeps, and at the back a balcony propped on concrete pillars faced north across the city.

I was not looking forward to meeting Noam Arnon. I was not looking forward to meeting any of the settlers, but I had been told that I had to talk to them first. The week before I left England, I had met an elderly English activist called John Lynes, who had spent the last five years patrolling the streets of Hebron with the red-capped members of the Christian Peacemaker Teams. He had said that once the

settlers saw me with anyone that they regarded as their
enemy, including the international activists like him, they
would refuse to have anything to do with me. That would
be inconvenient, since I would need their permission to see
the site beneath the building. Trespassing on a settlement in
the West Bank would be extremely unwise, he added. He
had managed to see the site once but he said I would run the
risk of getting shot if I tried to do the same. Consequently,
I had rung David Wilder when I arrived in Hebron the day
before. He had told me that he was going to pass me on to
an 'expert' on ancient Hebron, and I was surprised to discover that he meant his fellow spokesman, Noam Arnon.
Newly apprised of his credentials, I assumed that he would
be happy to show me the site that supposedly underwrites
the settlers' presence in the city, but the manners of the
sabra, or native-born Israeli – the nickname derives from
a desert cactus or prickly pear – do not conform to English notions of politeness. 'What, you want a private tour?'
he said, abruptly. He did not disguise his reluctance to
indulge my request, and he was so eager not to waste time
on me that he started talking as soon as he got out of the
battered people-carrier he had parked on the other side of
the road.

'So here we have the identification of the ancient town,
which is doubtless of ancient Hebron.' He gestured vaguely
at our surroundings. He was a big man, tall and round-
shouldered, dressed in a blue fleece and dark blue trousers.
He had a woven kippah perched on his thick black hair, and
there were black hairs sprouting from his nose. I asked him
why Wilder had billed him as an expert on ancient Hebron,
and his answer – 'I read a lot and go to museums' – was
further evidence that he did not intend to deviate from his
standard speech.

The wind was bustling through the gaps between the caravans as we walked over to the railings. 'Welcome to the Tel Hebron Excavations' said the sign beside us. Since 'tel' is the Hebrew word for the mound formed over centuries of occupation, and Tel Rumeida is the site of Bronze Age and Biblical Hebron, the name is accurate, but only the settlers use it: everybody else, including the Israeli soldiers that protect the settlements, calls the hill 'Tel Rumeida'.

Arnon was breathing heavily through his nose as he gestured at the section of the Middle Bronze Age wall that ran across the slope. The structure was built from worn-down blocks of mottled stone clamped together by cement, moss and grit, and it looked like a massive set of molars, cast in stone, or the mould of a giant tractor wheel. It was one of the first structures that Emanuel Eisenberg had discovered during the course of his excavations in 1999, and the settlers were delighted when he dated it to the Middle Bronze Age, c.1850 BCE, for it fitted the biblical chronology that allowed Arnon to date the careers of the biblical patriarchs with the same certainty that he might date the lives of contemporary Israeli politicians.

Arnon was prepared to acknowledge that there were many theories about the 'days of creation', each of which might be said to stand for an era of unspecified duration, but he insisted that Abraham was a figure from recorded history, born the tenth generation after Noah, and the twentieth after Adam, in the year 1948 in the Jewish calendar. Since Genesis says he left Haran when he was seventy-five years old, he must have arrived in Hebron in the year 2023 in the Jewish calendar – or 1735 BCE – and Arnon said the Middle Bronze Age wall was 'very correct', as if the archaeological finds should be assessed for accuracy against the biblical record, and not the other way round.

Unfortunately, not all of Emanuel Eisenberg's discoveries fitted quite as conveniently with Arnon's views: 'Later on, there were some interesting surprises,' he conceded. 'The most surprising here.' The inner wall that ran across the slope, almost touching the pillars holding up the building, was wider and lower than the Middle Bronze Age wall. Emanuel Eisenberg had dated its slumped mass to the Early Bronze Age, c.2500 BCE, proving that Hebron had existed some seven hundred years earlier than Arnon's reading of the Bible implied. It could have been worse – the excavation had confirmed that the town had been occupied when Abraham was supposed to have lived, and Arnon had had more than ten years to absorb the idea that Hebron was older than he previously suspected. 'It proves that this town is one of the most ancient towns,' he said.

Despite the imposing girth of its fortifications, the first city had not lasted long. It had been destroyed in a fire, and rebuilt, and destroyed again, and Emanuel Eisenberg believed that both phases of occupation had lasted no more than a hundred and fifty years. What happened during the next four or five hundred years was not clear: it seems that Tel Rumeida was abandoned, though the presence of shaft tombs within the modern city limits suggest it was a 'tribal-nomadic centre', and when the Canaanites re-founded Hebron in 1800 BCE the city became the most important in the Judean Hills.

The Canaanites were skilful builders who left imposing fortifications on many sites across the region, and even I could see that the Middle Bronze Age wall was better made than the older one. In most places where their respective courses have been established, the Middle Bronze Age wall runs inside the Early Bronze Age one, meaning the second city on the hill was marginally smaller than the first, but in the area beneath the settlement, where we were standing, the relationship was reversed – the Canaanite wall ran outside the older one, enlarging the city's boundaries by several metres. The Canaanites had paid no regard to one of the defining features of the old city – the well-preserved stone staircase that climbed the inner face of the wall was broad enough at the far end to let several people walk abreast, but the Middle Bronze Age wall cut across it as it climbed the slope, and by the time it reached the point where we were standing it was no more than a metre wide. 'These steps are the most preserved steps that were ever discovered from this period,' Arnon said. 'You can imagine people walking up these steps to the gate. The question is why they didn't use the previous one. But this is a fact.'

He said there was another site on the far side of the tel that he wanted to show me, so we walked down the hill and turned onto the path that led past the front of the double-stacked row of caravans. They seemed much taller from below. Their small, grilled windows couldn't have admitted much light, but they commanded views across the city, and I had heard one of the settlers refer to them as 'inspirational windows': every morning, she said, she opened her curtains, and looked out across the city that she and a few hundred of her co-religionists hoped to possess. The jury-rigged balconies propped precariously on posts planted on the edge of the path, like tree-house platforms or improvised watch-towers, had advanced them marginally closer to their goal.

We passed an army post set up on the roof of an abandoned building and reached the house that stood on the north-east corner of the hill. It had a prow-shaped garden that faced east across the houses of the Old City to the Tomb of the Patriarchs. A rusting lorry with blue canvas sides printed with a yellow Schweppes logo was parked on the patch of wasteland facing the path that ran up to its front door. We turned south on a well-trodden path that wound through the edge of an olive grove. Some of the trees had been reinforced with stone ruffs or collars, which made them look as though they were sprouting from a crevice in the rock, instead of the dusty earth. Arnon said they had been planted in the second Temple period, between the fifth century BCE and the first century CE. He qualified his claim before I had a chance to question it: 'What is for sure is that these trees were here before the Arab occupation, which begins in 637, 638.' Some of their trunks had split and grown into strange, curling shapes, like desiccated elephants' trunks, armoured with a dusty bark as intricately textured as living skin.

After 200 metres, we reached the south-east corner of the city – the furthest point from the settlement – where a section of smooth, honey-coloured stones had been exposed to a height of four or five courses. The stones had been dated to the Middle Bronze Age, and they were part of one of the two ancient city walls that encircled the summit of the hill. This was the structure Arnon wanted me to see but since English was his third or fourth language – he had learnt French and German at Hebron University – he could not find the word to describe it: he tried gate, watchtower and checkpoint, but he realized it was absurd to compare Hebron's ancient walls to the concrete huts and steel barricades that befoul the biblical landscape he reveres. He tried again: 'A tower of the keepers of the town? A keeping tower?'

I could not supply the word he wanted, though later I learnt that it was 'gate-tower'. It was the only entrance to the town that has been discovered so far, and Arnon believed it was the location of the place described in Genesis chapter 23,

when Abraham stood at 'the gates of the city' and bought the tomb in which to bury Sarah, who had died, aged one hundred and twenty-seven. The transaction is described in great detail: Abraham approached the inhabitants of the town, describing himself as 'stranger and sojourner' in Canaan, and frequently 'bowing himself down before them', and the 'sons of Heth' responded with equal courtesy, calling him a 'great prince', and saying that he was welcome to bury her in any of their sepulchres. Yet Abraham had a specific site in mind, and he asked them to ask Ephron the Hittite to sell him 'the cave of Machpelah, which he hath: which is in the end of his field.'

Arnon turned and gestured towards the Tomb of the Patriarchs, which lay half a mile to the east: 'You see the valley of Hebron, and the building over the cave,' he said. 'The town was here, and the tombs were there, and the Bible says the tombs were at the end of the fields: here's the ancient town and the valley, and there's the cave in the end of the field.' Arnon had lived in Hebron for most of his adult life, yet he still seemed enraptured by the superficial resemblances between its landscape and the verses he knew by heart.

Ephron the Hittite told Abraham that he could have the cave for nothing, but Abraham wanted to pay him: he said he would give him 'as much money as it is worth'. Even when Ephron was persuaded to name a price, he refused payment – 'the land is worth four hundred shekels of silver: what is that betwixt me and thee?' – but Abraham insisted: he 'weighed to Ephron the silver, which he had named in the audience of the sons of Heth, four hundred shekels of silver, current *money*.' A price had been agreed, money had changed hands in the presence of witnesses, and 'the first Hebrew possession in the land of Israel' had been secured.

The account of Sarah's burial which concludes the chapter – 'After this, Abraham buried Sarah his wife in the cave of the field of Machpelah' – seems no more than an excuse to reiterate the terms of the deal: 'And the field, and the cave that is therein, were made sure unto Abraham for a possession of a burying-place by the sons of Heth.'

The Tomb of the Patriarchs is often said to be one of the three places in Israel that no one can accuse the Jews of stealing – the Temple Mount and Joseph's tomb in Nablus being the others. Yet Arnon did not believe that Abraham was merely buying a piece of real estate. Both Jews and Muslims maintain that Abraham had a uniquely intimate relationship with God, and Arnon believed he went to such lengths to secure the cave because he understood its 'sacred' place in creation. Genesis 18:1 says he was sitting in his tent in the plains of Mamre, in Hebron, when God sent an emissary to tell him that he would have a son: whether the visitors were men or angels is not clear, but Abraham, who was renowned for his unstinting hospitality, told them to sit under a tree while he prepared food and drink. According to a Midrash – or Hebrew biblical commentary – he went to fetch a calf 'tender and good', but it ran away and entered a cave in the hillside. When Abraham went after it, he found Adam and Eve sleeping on their biers: 'lights were kindled above them, and a sweet scent was upon them'. It was the fragrance of the Garden of Eden. Abraham constantly returned to the field of 'supernal scents' to pray, and he told God that he wanted to be buried there himself: 'his heart and his wish were always in the cave', while Ephron 'saw only darkness', which was why he was prepared to sell it.

Arnon was gazing towards the cave: 'It should be excavated. It should be developed. You know Hebron, in Hebrew, means "friend", and I have a dream that Hebron will be one of the most wonderful archaeological and touristic sites in the world.'

It was strange to hear an apologist for a community of people routinely characterized as violent racists adopting the trope of a black American civil-rights leader. I asked him what would have to change for his dream to be realized, and the old harshness returned: 'Well, first of all the Arabs will have to forget their dream of destroying the Jews, and throwing them out.' He seemed oblivious to the way the settlers' presence had disrupted the lives of the vast majority of Hebron's inhabitants.

An Israeli parliamentarian said recently that Genesis 23 inspired the Zionists who bought land in Palestine at the end of the nineteenth century to pay 'full price in order to cement our historical entitlement', and the story also inspired the settlers of Hebron in their attempts to re-establish a Jewish presence in the city. When Arnon and I got back to the settlement, we crossed the road and set off in the other direction, following the Middle Bronze Age wall as it curved around the north-west corner of the tel. Only a short stretch of it had been exposed: after a few metres, a much newer stone wall, surmounted by a metal fence, replaced the cyclopean stones. To our right, the ground fell away steeply and I looked down on two Palestinian kids assembling piles of stones beneath a tree. Arnon stopped when we reached the corner. The patch of sloping hillside ahead was studded with half-buried stones that marked the site of an old Jewish cemetery, and there was another cemetery on the far side of the road where the victims of the 1929 massacre had been buried in a 'common grave'.

The cemetery had been desecrated after 1929, but the

settlers had reclaimed it in 1975, thanks to a family called the Nachsons, who had been among the first settlers to arrive in Hebron in 1968. Baruch Nachson is a painter who claims to have received 'profound revelations' of the 'wisdom of the creator', and his faith was said to have helped the family find meaning in the brief life of their second son. Avraham Yedidia Nachson was the first Jewish boy to be circumcised in the Tomb of the Patriarchs in the modern era, and when he died of cot death at the age of six months, his mother, Sarah, decided that she wanted to bury him in the old Jewish cemetery in Hebron. There are many versions of what happened next, but the one on the settlers' website says the Nachsons' funeral procession was stopped at a military checkpoint outside Kiryat Arba and told it couldn't go any further: the cemetery was off-limits. Sarah Nachson was undeterred: she told the soldiers that they had their orders, and she had hers. 'Returning to her car, she cradled her dead son in her arms and began to walk past the military block-ade,' writes the American academic Jerold S. Auerbach. 'Women from Kiryat Arba, and men with shovels and flash-lights, accompanied her' as she walked past the Tomb of the Patriarchs, and climbed the hill to the site of the new cemetery.

'Moonlight illuminate[d] the field' as the grave was dug, and the body was interred, and when the ceremony was over Sarah Nachson made another speech that has entered the settlers' folklore: she said that God had given them Avraham for one reason – to re-open the ancient graveyard in Hebron, and now the task was accomplished, he had taken him back. 'We are very privileged,' she said.

The grave was a few metres from the one in which the victims of 1929 were interred, and Auerbach says that the settlers believed that the burial 'linked past and present, death and life, in Hebron': it had 'symbolically reclaimed Hebron for the new Jewish community of settlers while reconnecting them to their martyred predecessors.' It was a vivid proof of what the Israeli authors Idith Zertal and Akiva Eldar call 'the organizing principle of the Jewish settlers' existence in Hebron' – their attachment to a 'national-religious martyrology' which sees the massacre of 1929 as 'a creator of meaning, and a catalyst of the project of revival and renewal'.

It was also a means of affirming a connection to Hebron that stretched much further back in time: 'Avraham Yedidia, you closed a circle in history,' Sarah Nachson said. 'Avraham our patriarch purchased for his children the first property in the Holy Land when he bought the field of Machpelah with his money and buried his wife Sarah there, and now the circle has been closed, with Sarah burying Avraham. If we open the Jewish cemetery, we open the gate of the city.'

The building looked much taller from the back. The balcony seemed as inaccessible as the decks of a flyover from the hard shoulder of the carriageway below, and the gap beneath the building was a deep shadowy pocket. We stepped over the railings and entered the basement. It was four or five metres deep and ten or eleven metres wide with white-washed concrete walls and a dusty, unpaved floor. The pillars holding up the building divided the shadowy space into several smaller rooms. They looked like sturdy petrified tree trunks, rooted in deep pools of concrete, and they were marked with red figures that might have been part of a construction sequence or an occult code inscribed by the messianic inhabitants of the flats above.

I saw the four-room house before Arnon pointed it out

to me – it was the largest structure in sight – but he was still keen to show it off to its best advantage: 'Come – stand here,' he said, in his abrupt manner, gesturing to a spot near the entrance to the two rows of parallel pillars that marked out its floor plan. The pillars were no more than a metre high, built from piles of flat stones, of irregular shapes and sizes. They looked like crude totem poles and they mimicked the shape of the taller pillars that held up the building.

Examples of the so-called 'four-room house' have been found on many other sites in what was once Judea. Typically, they contain an entrance hall which opened into three rooms – two matching ones to either side, and another at the end. The ground floor was usually a manger, and the human inhabitants lived on the first floor, which began below the roof of the apartment, a metre above our heads. Arnon pointed to its dusty interior: 'We found five seals with the inscription *lmlk*, which means *Lamelech Hebron* – belonging to the king of Hebron.' He corrected himself: 'Well, belonging to the king, but the jars were made in Hebron.'

More than five hundred *lmlk* handles have been found across Judea. Archaeologists believe they were produced during the reign of King Hezekiah in preparation for the attack by the Assyrian king Sennacherib in 701 BCE, which is one of the earliest events in the Bible corroborated in other sources. Judea had been a vassal state of Assyria since 720 BCE, and Hezekiah had made the mistake of refusing to pay tribute. II Kings 18:13 says that Sennacherib 'attacked all the fenced cities of Judah, and took them', and a clay prism discovered in the ruins of his palace at Nineveh and kept in the British Museum offers a similar report: 'As for the king of Judah, Hezekiah, who had not submitted to my authority, I besieged and captured forty-six of his fortified cities, along with many smaller towns, taken in battle with my battering rams.'

The destruction of the town of Lachish, which was portrayed on a series of reliefs on the palace walls, was the most famous event in the campaign, but Hebron was also attacked: the four-room house burnt down and the second floor collapsed on top of the ground floor. Hebron revived in the seventh century and the house was rebuilt – Eisenberg found another layer of occupation with pottery of the seventh and sixth centuries BCE. Hebron was sacked again in the Babylonian invasion of 586 BCE: parts of the Middle Bronze Age city wall were destroyed, the gate-tower was prised apart, and the four-room house burnt down again. Eisenberg rebuilt the pillars on the spot where he had found them. 'The whole area belongs from the Early Bronze Age to the Byzantine period, and actually we wouldn't have known nothing about it if we hadn't wanted to build this house,' Arnon said. 'The Arabs built here in the Jordanian period, without any digging, without any preservation, but we think that first of all you have to excavate, you have to preserve the site, so we had first to dig, and then we built the house right on the place of the old Jewish house.' He indicated the way that the regular concrete surfaces of the modern apartment enclosed the fragile pillars of the Iron Age house: 'You have a chain of Jewish presence here of three thousand years.'

In a sense, he was right. While the figures of Abraham and Moses belong in the realm of folklore, Hezekiah's ill-advised revolt against the Assyrians is part of recorded history, and the four-room house is an authentic Jewish artefact. Yet no one had ever doubted that Jews had lived in Hebron, and Eisenberg's excavation had uncovered evidence of many other phases of occupation. I appreciated the wonder of the four-room house, and yet as I sat in the half-light beneath the building, listening to the distant noises of the protests provoked by the renewed Jewish presence in Hebron, I thought it was perverse to attempt to annex the site to a narrow nationalistic cause: the five-thousand-year history of the hill was richer and more diverse than Arnon wanted to admit.

CHAPTER TWO

WE DO REMEMBER

If the inhabitants are to be believed, Hebron is more
ancient than any town in the country.

Josephus, *The Jewish War*, IV, 519

Everyone told me I should talk to Dandis. They said he was
an expert on local history and would have a lot to say about
Tel Rumeida. They also said he was one of the richest men
in Hebron, though he had not made his money from his
shop on the edge of the covered alleys of the souk. I looked
out for him every time I went past, but the shop was always
shut, and several weeks passed before I found Dandis sitting
in a plastic armchair behind a wooden desk. He was wearing black shoes and socks and a white vest beneath a blue
pin-stripe djellabah. He was a good-looking man in his early
seventies, with short white hair, green eyes and a straight
nose. His aristocratic bearing befitted his reputed wealth,
though the cane he was holding undermined the effect – it
could have been the kind of prop a rich Khalili trader might
own, if there hadn't been a dozen like it in a box behind him.
He was one of the many stallholders in the Old City who
had been reduced to selling pieces of plastic tat to the few
tourists who wander past, but the piece of folded paper
propped on the front of his desk attested to a more serious
aim: 'We do remember', it said.

It was Friday morning – the Muslim day of prayer: the

rest of Hebron was much quieter than normal, but life in the Old City continued at the pace to which its inhabitants have become accustomed. As I made my way across the Baladiya, the square beneath Beit Romano, a patrol of soldiers entered the alleys of the souk, followed by a group of foreign visitors escorted by a pair of uniformed observers of the Temporary International Presence in Hebron (TIPH), the six-nation mission set up after the massacre in the Tomb of the Patriarchs to monitor 'the efforts to maintain normal life' and 'promote . . . a feeling of security' amongst the Palestinian population. Fifteen years later, its representatives were still shadowing Israeli soldiers through the streets of the Old City.

Dandis said the occupation had cost him everything he owned. His family had originally come from a village called Dan, in the north of Palestine; they had moved north to Tripoli, where they became known as Dandis, and then to Spain. When Queen Isabella expelled the Arabs, five hundred years ago, his 'grandfather' had returned to the home of 'his father' Abraham. At one point, the family had owned a lot of property in the Old City, but over the years their holdings had been reduced to twenty shops and five houses. Fifty years ago, each building had been worth more than $100,000, but the Israeli military had requisitioned one of his houses and closed several shops, and Dandis was not getting 'even one pound income'.

When I told him that I was interested in the history of Hebron, and the history of Tel Rumeida in particular, he seemed amused by my presumption – it would require all the students at the university to tell the whole story from the beginning, but he was prepared to offer me a summary. He believed that the American archaeologist Philip Hammond, who had led the first excavations on Tel Rumeida in the

1960s, had written the best report: 'I think this is the correct report. Other reports have other aims – political aims.' Dandis mistrusted the Israeli archaeologists who had dug on the hill, for their version of history had been used to dispossess the Palestinians. It was also incomplete: the version in the Torah was correct insofar as it went, but it omitted the pre-history of Hebron and the Judean Hills, which was his particular interest.

Pre-Abrahamic Hebron was the birthplace of civilization, the place where Adam and Eve were created. Adam wasn't the first human, Dandis maintained, but those who lived before him were like animals, and God had taught Adam to talk and to walk upright in the Judean Hills. 'Everybody knows that Adam is the first civilized man in history, and we have many evidences that he stayed in the mountains of Judea. Then, after Adam, Noah – very clear that Noah stayed here.' Local legend places Noah's tomb in the village of Dura, seven miles south-west of Hebron. 'We have the mountain of Noah and the city of Noah – and then his son, Canaan.' The first 'a' was short and hard, the second two long. 'You know Canaan, the son of Noah, and Canaan stayed in this land – so the old history called all this area Canaan land. It is very old history.'

I was sitting on a low plastic stool that placed my head on a level with his knees, and yet he spoke so quietly that I had to lean forward to hear what he was saying. His English was good, but it was far from fluent, and he spoke slowly, with many pauses. His two young grandchildren were playing in the street in front of the shop where joss sticks and coloured beads were on display, and he raised his voice and spoke to them in Arabic. 'I want them to go because I want to collect my . . .' He was interrupted by the younger boy who came inside and picked up one of his plastic canes, then stood behind me, swishing it to test its flexibility. It passed so close to my ear that I heard the whistle. He moved past me, snatched a lighter from Dandis's desk and dashed into the street where he stood out of reach while he lit a joss stick. 'I love that boy, but I can't control him,' Dandis said. Bribery was the only answer, and he made his offer in Arabic, before reporting his grandson's response with a certain pride: 'I request them five minutes to stay calm, and I will pay him, but he will not do it. He say, give it now.' The boys disappeared up the street waving their joss sticks, and Dandis resumed his summary of Tel Rumeida's history.

The American academic Jeffrey Chadwick, who inherited the records of Philip Hammond's excavations, says that Tel Rumeida satisfies the four classic requirements of a settlement in ancient Canaan – it was easily defensible, it had a good supply of water and arable land, and it was well positioned at the end of the ancient trade route that ran down the spine of the Judean Hills. Dandis concurred; the water was particularly important: 'In Hebron, always, in all seasons, you can find food for the animals, and you can find water.'

The caves beneath the Tomb of the Patriarchs, where Abraham and his family are interred, were holy long before he arrived in Hebron, for the sons of Adam and Noah were not heathens: 'They worshipped the One God.' Dandis held up his middle finger. The nail was long and dirty. 'They don't pray to the stones or other things: Adam and his people, Noah and his people, Canaan and his people – all the people who stay in Tel Rumeida pray to the One God.' Hammond found no evidence of idolatry, Dandis insisted: no temples to Phoenician gods or Baal or Ashtar.

The name Tel Rumeida derived from its inhabitants'

religion, though Dandis could not think of the English word he wanted: he called it 'the rust after the fire', and when I suggested 'ashes', he was pleased. 'Ashes!' he repeated. Ashes are clean, and the inhabitants of Tel Rumeida sought purification by sleeping naked in the ashes and asking God for forgiveness: 'This is from the way with the One God, not other gods, the One God we believe in, both of us.' The dirty fingernail indicated the two of us. The inhabitants also discovered material for sealing wells, he continued, and they mined gold, silver and bronze. It was the capital of a great empire that united twenty-eight king-doms, and it was ruled by a king called Melech Hebron, or King Hebron, who took his name from the city, or gave his name to it. King Hebron and his successors controlled the area for more than four thousand years before the coming of Abraham. 'I believe that this land, this mountain, Hebron, is the greatest city in the past, for a long, long time, from Adam to Abraham.'

Genesis repeatedly refers to Abraham as a stranger in the land, and Dandis confirmed that he was a 'clever guest', who adapted to his hosts' expectations: 'Abraham come here as a visitor – he didn't have any land, or any history but he believe in this God, so he can live in this city.' According to Genesis, Sarah and Abraham travelled to Canaan together, but Dandis had heard a version of the legend that flouted the codes of modesty that prevail amongst Jews and Muslims in the conservative city of Hebron: he said she was a local woman, and that Abraham had fallen in love with her when he saw her bathing in the spring that bears her name.

Ain Sarah, which stands beside the road of the same name in the centre of Hebron, was not far from my hotel, and I had walked past it several times before I realized what it was. The owner of the house next door had built a garage above the point where the spring emerged on the street but he showed me the source in his back garden: according to the British surveyors of the Palestine Exploration Fund (PEF) who visited Hebron in 1875, it lay 'under a stone arch, at the end of a little alley with drystone walls', but the walls of the cave had been reinforced with breeze blocks, and the entrance was sealed by a metal sheet. Behind it, steps led down to a small enclosure, and a pool of muddy water. Mr Zalloun did not believe that the water had magical properties, but he thought the settlers might think so. That was why he had sealed the spring on the street. He was right to be concerned – the settlers have a long-established habit of claiming territory by asserting its spiritual significance, though the spring does not appear in the biblical narrative until long after Sarah's death.

Dandis's version of the conquest of Canaan also deviated from the biblical story. He said that when Moses led the Israelites out of Egypt, he collected an army of Bedouins in the east, and returned to the 'dream land' or 'green land' of Hebron. I could not tell which word he used, though either seemed to suit his perception of the fertile kingdom in the Judean Hills. Tel Rumeida was a place of beginnings and endings: mankind was born in 'the Hebron mountain', and the souls of the dead return there. It was such a significant place that Moses' successor, Joshua Ben-nun, did not fight its inhabitants when he invaded Canaan: he only fought the people who prayed to the stones. 'He never say that we go to Hebron to kill, because Hebron is holy, like our Mecca.'

His interpretation of religious duty was as personal as his version of Hebron's history: he accepted the teachings of all the prophets, including Abraham, Jesus and Mohammed, because they contain much that is good, but he saw no need to follow the procedures of religion 'like a soldier'. 'I am not against believing in God, but I don't accept the way of praying used by Muslims and Christians. You can't say that because you pray to God you are a good man.' He has five daughters and four sons, but he does not insist that the girls wear the veil: he does not believe he has the right to decide.

Religion is useful to some people, but Dandis has evolved a more personal creed. 'I believe in Adam and his family, and Canaan. I believe in my mountains, and my land and my rules.' As I left him sitting behind the desk where the folded piece of paper professed the other element of his creed, he raised his long yellow finger again in a gesture of exhortation or admonition: 'You need to study more,' he said. 'We need more information to write correct book about Tel Rumeida: study more!'

I liked Dandis, though I was not persuaded by his version of Hebron's history. Archaeologists agree that the first city was established on the hill in the Chalcolithic era, towards the end of the fourth millennium BCE, though they do not know exactly where it was. Philip Hammond, the American archaeologist Dandis had commended, who had dug on the hill in the middle of the 1960s, found evidence of a 'distinct proto-urban settlement' that may have endured for one or two centuries: 'Some of its inhabitants lived in cave dwellings, but others in houses, and the community boasted the ability to produce both architecture and ceramic vessels,' say the notes of his expedition. The Israeli archaeologist who excavated the site of the settlement, on the north-west side of the summit, found pottery dating to the same era on the bedrock, but no traces of buildings, and he believed that it had spread across the mound from a 'proto-settlement'

elsewhere, possibly beside the perennial spring on the lower eastern slopes that had been the city's source of water. It used to be called Ain Habra – a name that preserves an echo of Hebron – but since the medieval era, when retaining walls were built around it, it has been called Ain Jedida, or the 'new spring'. Today, most people know it as Abraham's Well.

I walked past it many times, once with Hisham Sharabati, the Palestinian journalist that I hired as a guide to show me some of the city's Abrahamic sites. Hisham had worked with many of the foreign news teams that came to Hebron, though when I met him he was reporting human-rights abuses for an organization in Ramallah, and trying, without much success, to develop a tourist business in the Old City: he had a cafe in the Baladiya, run by a man called Ishmael, and a guest house nearby. His parents were both Khalilis, but his grandparents had fled to Jordan at the outbreak of the Six Day War, taking his mother who was heavily pregnant, and he was born on the last day of fighting, as Israeli forces prosecuted their military advantage by capturing the Golan Heights from Syria. His family were concerned that if he only had a Jordanian birth certificate, he would not be allowed to return to the West Bank, and they decided to re-register him with the new military authority that Israel likes to call the Civil Administration. Consequently, he has two names: to the Jordanians, he is Hashem, born 12 June 1967, and to the Israelis, he is Hisham, born six weeks later. For the first two years of his life, he lived in Bethlehem, but when his father died he came back to Hebron with his mother, and for the sake of convenience he has always called himself Hisham: 'I cannot be two people,' he had told me one morning, as we walked down Al-Harem Street.

His family used to have a house on the edge of the

wholesale market, which became the Avraham Avinu settlement, but it has been empty since July 2002, when the settlers went on a 'mass rampage' at the funeral of a man called Elazar Leibovitz who was killed by Palestinian gunmen. The house's last tenant, Nur Adin Sharabati, who was Hisham's uncle, told an Israeli journalist that the settlers had attacked the house, and destroyed everything they could get their hands on. Mr Sharabati had shown the journalist photographs of the house furnished with 'ancient carpets, beautiful oil lamps, a large library of rare and antique books'; only 'ashes and dust' remained. The police told him he would be risking his life if he remained at home, and when he left the army sealed the nearest entrance to the Old City with a padlocked metal gate.

Hisham said he would show me where it was, and as we left the uncovered section of Al-Harem Street and entered a stretch lit by dim bulbs high in the vaulted roof, we turned into an alleyway that ran south towards Avraham Avinu. It was pitch-dark, dank-smelling and strewn with rubbish. I could not see where I was putting my feet, and I stepped on a bag that squirmed unpleasantly beneath my weight. I was relieved when we turned a corner and emerged by the gate in the arch that used to open into the wholesale market.

In 2004, the Israeli High Court ordered the army to unseal the gate and allow the Sharabatis to return home, but it did not help: the army built a wall around the house but they could not protect the family or the builders, and they used to tell them to shelter in the alley, as if the hail of stones that greeted their arrival was a natural phenomenon, 'like rain'. Sometimes, they could not get security clearance to pass into the other half of the souk, and when they did they had to wait for the soldiers to unlock the gate. On the rare occasions that they managed to get things done, the settlers always tore it down, and eventually the family had given up and moved elsewhere: 'This is what the Israelis do,' Hisham said. 'They keep postponing, and in the end the family gives up.' The workers' tools were still stacked in a pile against the gate. Even if the army unlocked it, and allowed the family to rebuild the house, most of them would choose to live elsewhere, but Hisham still hoped to return to the house in the Old City where his father was born.

His sister had also abandoned a home in H2. Ten years ago, she had lived on the lower slopes of Tel Rumeida, but by 2002 she had grown tired of the constraints of the curfew and moved elsewhere. Hisham offered to take me there, and we went through the Tel Rumeida checkpoint then down the row of shuttered shops that leads to Beit Hadassah. A set of steps opposite the buildings leads on to the lower slopes of Tel Rumeida, and we passed the front gate of Cordoba Girls' School and along a concrete alley, where 'Gas the Arabs' had been spray-painted on a gate. An unpaved road lined with houses led to the lower edge of the Muslim cemetery that overlooks Shoada Street. It was a hot morning; we paused in the shade of the renovated houses as we climbed the path through the cemetery. The sloping patch of dusty earth was enclosed by pine trees and studded with low, flat tombs and headstones inscribed in black.

Abraham's Well was on the next terrace. Since the settlers like to immerse themselves in the water as a form of ritual cleansing, I had often seen clothes hung over the breeze-block walls that enclose the entrance, but this time a man with a long beard was standing beside them. He was dressed in a white shirt, sandals and grey combat trousers, and he had a guitar slung around his neck. He gestured that we should wait, and the reason became clear when a woman in a white shirt came up the steps that lead down to the water, drying her hair with a towel.

Hisham and I had almost passed the man before I guessed who he was. A Khalili called Ra-eed, who used to work as a labourer on Tel Rumeida, had given me the phone number of a man called David, whom he said was nothing like the other settlers. I had never met David, but I had spoken to him once while I was in Jerusalem: he had offered to pick me up and take me to Hebron, but he had sounded so chaotic that I had decided I would be better off on my own. Clearly, my instincts had been right.

'Hey, you should get in the water, man,' he said, when I introduced myself. 'Take all your clothes off and get in. The main thing is to be naked. All your body without clothes.' David laughed. He was very tanned with dark brown eyes and a long greying beard.

'It's water – it's not a drug – but you're like another person.' He touched my arm, and strummed a chord on his guitar. 'It's the best – always just the best.' He was half-singing and half-speaking in a lilting melodic voice. 'Everything's just the best.' His voice rose in pitch and volume as he leant in towards me. 'You will see one day that everything was the best. You will feel – everything just the best.' A fly landed on his nose, and he brushed it away. His voice was hoarse because he had been singing at a wedding.

The woman who was with him looked ten years younger than him – no more than forty – and when he told us she was his wife, I remembered what Ra-eed had said about him. David confirmed the rumour before I had a chance to ask: he had another wife in Kfar Etzion, a settlement by the road to Jerusalem, and he spent his time moving between them. 'I'm like a boy that wants just one more toy.' He laughed. 'No, it's good. King David had eight wives and forty children.'

Until then, Hisham had been standing several metres away, pretending not to listen, but he was so intrigued by David's boast that he asked him if it was legal to have two wives. 'According to the law of the government, it's not allowed, but we don't care about the government. We love each other, we're happy, and if you're happy, you want everyone to be happy. I wish all the people happiness.' He touched me on the arm and began to sing again: 'The more you think the best, the more it will be, all over the world – the best, always just the best . . .' The fly landed on his nose again.

Many legends have accumulated around the spring. Claude Regnier Conder, one of the British surveyors of the Palestine Exploration Fund, said it was believed to be the cave in which Adam and Eve lived for a century: 'Here Adam mourned for Abel, and hence the spot is called by some chroniclers the Vale of Tears; here also Adam was made of the red earth of the place,' he wrote. Yet when David came to Tel Rumeida and sat under the trees, 'talking and singing to God', he was emulating another biblical character, King David, who had come to prominence in the household of his predecessor, Saul, partly because of his skills as a harpist. The Zohar – the defining text of the mystical Jewish sect, the Kabbalah – recorded that in the seven years David reigned in Hebron, the souls of Abraham, Isaac and Jacob entered his body: 'They got inside his belly, like he's pregnant,' David said. 'That's why he was a king.'

I asked him if that was why he came here, but he dismissed the question with a laugh: he was no king – just a man who wished everyone the best. He had to go and sit under the trees for a couple of hours – he mentioned it as if it was scheduled in his diary – but before he walked away he tried again to persuade me to take a dip. 'You'll be a different person, man.' I walked to the top of the steps. The spring had once been much closer to the surface, but now the steps curved down between retaining walls until they reached the entrance of a cave. The roof was no more than a metre high, and the surface of the water was glossed with a layer of oil or soap. It did not look very appealing. The distant thrum of David's guitar and the fading sound of his voice wishing me the best drifted down the steps.

A local dentist called Dr Yusuf Abu Meizer, who had been billed as another expert on local history, told me about another site with Davidic associations on the lower slopes of Tel Rumeida.

Dr Yusuf was a member of the family that owned my hotel, and he lived in a house on Ain Sarah. Reem Al Sharif, the headmistress of Cordoba School, which lies on the lower slopes of Tel Rumeida opposite Beit Hadassah, had taken me to meet him. She led me down an alleyway to a dusty backyard, and through a glass door to a brightly lit room with a tiled floor. Dr Yusuf's daughter's bike was resting on its saddle and handlebars in the middle of the room, and the dentist squatted down beside it, fiddling with the chain as he explained his version of Hebron's history. He was wearing a striped shirt and green trousers, and he had a neat beard and henna-tinted hair, in the fashion supposedly pioneered by Mohammed. He could not disguise his delight at my obtuseness: 'Now do you understand?' he kept repeating, as we attempted to resolve some of the absurdities in his account, of which his reckoning of the difference between the real age of the earth and the age revealed in scripture was the most egregious.

'OK, when you say something is a hundred million or fifty millions or six millions, we must divide the number by fifty thousand years to have the real age.' He held up his hand: 'Please, this is very important. Very important. All over the world, the age of our earth – this football, which we know now – is only a matter of five or six thousand years old. When you discover the skeleton of dinosaur, sixty millions or six millions years old, you must divide the number by fifty thousand years old to get the correct age of this dinosaur. When you speak about the human, you must divide by one thousand years old. Do you understand?'

He laughed when I said I didn't, and his air of benign condescension was so comical that it made me laugh as well. He did not mind: 'They will discover later that my theory is correct. You laugh now, but in ten years or twenty years, please call me and say, "Dr Yusuf, your theory is correct."' I was curious to find out how he had arrived at the calculation. His first answer did not help – it was something to do with the speed of light – but the second was easier to understand: 'In our Koran, it maintains that when we speak about the creation of animals or mountains or anything, we must divide by fifty thousand. When we speak about humans, we must divide by one thousand.'

Presumably, he was referring to sura 22:47, which says 'a day in the sight of thy Lord is like a thousand years of your reckoning', and sura 70:4, which says 'the angels and the Spirit ascend unto him in a day the measure whereof is fifty thousand years', and it hardly seemed to matter that he had replaced 'day' with 'year', and hence underestimated the ratios by three hundred and sixty-five to one. I decided to stop worrying about the details, and enjoy the mesmeric drift of his folkloric version of Hebron. He dismissed the idea that Adam was buried in the Cave of the Patriarchs as 'a legend', but he shared Dandis's belief that human history had started in Hebron: 'It's the beginning here – Palestine, this area, this country: it's the beginning of the world.'

No one knows what happened during the thousand years after creation, he asserted: there were only stories and legends. Noah was born in approximately 3000 BCE, and history began with the great flood, which extended across the Levant from Syria in the north, to Iraq in the east, and Saudi Arabia in the south. 'It was not all over the world!' Dr Yusuf insisted. 'There is a big mistake here: not all over the world!' He spun the wheel of the bike, and gazed at me through the blurring spokes: 'Some say that the flood was all over the world. It's a big mistake!'

Paradoxically, it is the presence of deserts in southern Syria, western Iraq and Saudi Arabia that indicate the extent of the flood: those areas had once been fertile paradises, like the Yemen and Palestine, but the water had dried them out. It was not entirely clear how floods induced desertification, but Dr Yusuf seemed to be suggesting that the waters had brought up sand and stones from beneath the surface. The American invasion of Iraq had confirmed the theory, he told me, for the soldiers had found the bodies of drowned people four or five metres beneath the earth.

Noah and his wife and their three sons were the only survivors, and they had lived an agrarian existence in the vicinity of Hebron. Noah's grandson Canaan had established the first city in a hill south of Hebron called Jebel Al Sharif, which was also known as the 'Canaanite mountain', and Dr Yusuf believed that the people who established the first civilizations in Africa and Europe had originated there.

The Egyptian pharaohs, for instance, were the grandchildren of Canaan: 'They left from here.' As Dr Yusuf leant forward, his voice echoed off the cold tiles and became faint and indistinct. 'All the Africans were black. The pharaohs are like us – white, semi-white. You understand now? The origins are Hebron. They left from here, for Africa, for another land.'

He went through the locations of the various cities that had existed after Canaan's – one was on the lower slopes of Tel Rumeida, on the road that led uphill from the check-point, and another was in the place known in the Bible as Mamre, or the plains of Mamre, where Abraham was sitting in his tent door in the heat of the day when God sent three messengers to tell him that Sarah would have a son, despite her age. The account of the supernatural visitation is so vivid that people have always sought to identify the tree under which Abraham's guests were supposed to have sat while he served them 'butter, and milk, and the calf which he had dressed.' For most of the last two thousand years the favoured location was 'an immense terebinth, said to be as old as creation' that stood in a field north of Hebron, beside the road to Jerusalem. The area is now called Al Rami – the name is said to be a corruption of Mamre – and it has now been drawn within the city: a furniture showroom, and a boy's school overlook the dry, dusty field where the tree is supposed to have stood. Not surprisingly, no trace of it remains – some sources say it was picked apart by early pilgrims seeking souvenirs – but the field contains other Abrahamic shrines: the remains of the unfinished church, or basilica, in one corner is known as Beit el Khulil, or Abraham's house, and the well which was tapped by a hose feeding the window boxes in the nearest block of flats is called Abraham's Well.

Many other legends had accumulated around the site –
one said that Abraham had begun to build the tomb in
Mamre, when a flash of light in the sky to the south alerted
him to God's preferred location – but it was the first
time that I had heard anyone claim that it was the site of
a city.

By my reckoning, Dr Yusuf believed that the city on Tel
Rumeida was Hebron's fourth incarnation, and it had been
destroyed and abandoned by the time Alexander the Great
conquered the region in the fourth century BCE. There was
much more which I did not follow, much to Dr Yusuf's
amusement – I felt that he wanted to help me understand,
and yet he also relished the occult nature of his knowledge,
for he told me with great pride that his source was an
untranslated book of eighteen volumes stored in the Vati-
can library. The author was a writer called Josephius, or
Yusufius: 'He was a Jewish, but his loyalty was for the
Romanians. Understand?'

For once, I thought I did. Josephus was a Jewish priest
who became Governor of Galilee in the first Jewish revolt
against Roman rule in the first century CE. When the
Romans invaded his province in 67 CE, he retreated to the
fortified town of Jopata, and survived the siege 'in circumstances which redounded little to his credit', as the academic
Mary E. Smallwood puts it. According to the only surviving
account of the incident, which is, of course, the one he wrote
himself, he persuaded the defenders of the town to 'draw
lots and kill each other in turn', rather than committing
suicide en masse.

Thanks to what he calls 'divine providence or just to
luck', Josephus and one other man were left alive, and they
made a pact and agreed to surrender. He won the favour of
the Roman commander, Vespasian, by prophesying that he

would become Emperor, and when he was proved right, he moved to Rome, where he lived under imperial patronage, and wrote his two famous works – a history of the Jewish people from the creation of the world to the outbreak of the war, and an account of the war itself.

Dr Yusuf was surprised that I had heard of him and adamant that his books had not been translated into English: 'No, no, no, no, no, no, no!' he said, rising from the floor, and wagging his finger in my face. I assured him that you could get copies of *Jewish Antiquities* and *The Jewish War* in most libraries and bookshops in Britain, and he seemed so disappointed that I wished I had left his illusions intact: 'Here, we haven't,' he said mournfully. I couldn't tell if it was the inadequacy of the Palestinians' resources or the loss of his exclusive ownership of Yusufius that he regretted most.

It was strange to think that an Arab-Palestinian dentist should have come to rely on the partially apprehended accounts of a Jewish priest turned Roman citizen in order to explain the history of his city, but perhaps it was appropriate. By the time I left Dr Yusuf's surgery, I had begun to think that the countless layers of legend and rumour that made up his mythic city were more real than the sun-baked tarmac and the biscuit-brittle houses of Ain Sarah. Dr Yusuf was quite right to say that I did not understand: I was beginning to wonder why I had ever thought I might.

Beersheva Street climbs steeply from the Tel Rumeida checkpoint. High-rises and shopping malls fill the city centre below, and the tightly packed roofs of the old stone houses resume on the slopes on the far side of the valley. The street was lined with taxis that had been displaced from their

old rank on Shoada Street when it was closed to Palestinian traffic. Halfway down, a set of steps led up to a terrace beneath a tall stone house. On one side, a line of oil drums barred the entrance to a dusty field, and on the other a set of steps led up to the front door. The army sometimes closed the road to allow the settlers access to Beersheva Street, and Dr Yusuf had told me they were visiting the tomb that lies beneath the house. He had said it was always locked, but on the day that I visited the metal door in the front wall of the house was standing ajar. I had to stoop to get through it. Inside, it was damp and dark. The walls were smudged with candle smoke, and there was rubbish strewn across the floor. A square archway led into another, smaller room at the back. There was a deep pit in the floor and low window-like openings in the back wall.

Dr Yusuf had told me that it was the tomb of a prince called Hebron or Habron, and the last relic of the city that had been established on the lower slopes of Tel Rumeida, but the settlers believed that it was the tomb of Othniel Ben Knaz, one of the 'judges' who led the Israelites in the years between the conquest of Canaan and the establishment of the monarchy under Saul and David. The Israelites repeatedly 'did evil in the sight of the Lord' by worshipping other deities, and He punished them by allowing them to be enslaved by foreign kings. Whenever they repented, the Lord would 'raise up' a 'deliverer' or 'judge', who would defeat their enemies, but they soon fell back into bad old ways: 'In those days there was no king in Israel: every man did that which was right in their eyes,' says the last verse of the final chapter of the Book of Judges.

The appointment of the first king did not solve the problem: the Lord repented that he made Saul 'king over Israel' because he disobeyed an order to 'smite' a tribe called the

Amalek – he 'utterly destroyed all the people with the edge of the sword' but he spared the king and a few sheep and cows – and He chose David to succeed him. David became an important part of Saul's household – his armour-bearer, his favoured musician and his son-in-law – but Saul was so jealous of his growing fame that he tried to kill him several times; eventually David allied himself with the Philistines, who defeated Saul at the battle of Gilboa, and nailed the king's body to the walls of Beth-Shean.

In the aftermath of the battle, David was crowned King of Judah in Hebron: he had gained control of the territory that Joshua had allotted to the house of Judah, but Abner, Saul's former commander-in-chief, set up Saul's only surviving son, Ish-bosheth, as ruler of the ten northern tribes, who were known collectively as Israel. For the next seven years, while David ruled in Hebron, and Judah and Israel remained at war, 'David waxed stronger and stronger, and the house of Saul waxed weaker and weaker.'

Eventually, Abner had lost patience with Ish-bosheth when his ward made the mistake of reproaching him for marrying one of Saul's concubines – an act that implied pretensions to the throne. 'Am I a dog's head . . . that thou chargest me today with a fault concerning this woman?' was Abner's wonderfully terse rebuke. Abandoning the attempts to assert Ish-bosheth's right to the throne of Israel, he offered David his support instead: 'Make thy league with me, and behold, my hand shall be with thee, to bring about all Israel unto thee.'

He visited David in Hebron, and assured him that he would 'gather all Israel unto my lord the king', but not everyone was prepared to welcome him. During the 'long war' between the rival houses that had followed the battle of Gilboa, Abner had killed a man called Asahel, whose brother, Joab, wanted revenge. Joab was a captain in David's army, and when Abner set off on his journey back to Jerusalem he sent messengers after him. They caught up with him by the 'well of Sirah' – Ain Sarah, where Sarah was believed to have bathed – and brought him back to the city, where 'Joab took him aside in the gate to speak with him quietly, and smote him there under the fifth rib.'

When Ish-bosheth learnt that Abner was dead, 'his hands were feeble', and two of his soldiers, Rechab and Baanah, assassinated him, and brought his head to David in Hebron. They had removed the last obstacle in David's path to power, but they did not get the thanks they expected. David's response was brutal and unforgiving: 'When one told me, saying, Behold, Saul is dead, thinking to have brought good tidings, I took hold of him, and slew him in Ziklag, who thought that I would have given him a reward for his tidings: How much more, when wicked men have slain a righteous person in his own house upon his bed?

Shall I not therefore now require his blood of your hand, and take you away from the earth?'

David's 'young men' slew Rechab and Banaah, 'cut off their hands and their feet, and hanged them up over the pool in Hebron'. They also took 'the head of Ish-bosheth, and buried it in the sepulchre of Abner in Hebron'. Both sites – the 'pool' and the sepulchre – were nearby, and when I left Beersheva Street, I went to find them.

It was Sunday – the beginning of the working week for Israelis – and the Tomb of the Patriarchs was busier than usual: there were tourist buses drawn up in the square and men with machine guns sunning themselves on the grass. I assumed they were settlers, but when I asked a woman with an Uzi where I could find Birket es-Sultan, she told me to ask her guide. He did not want to help: he told me to look inside the building, though I knew he knew it was not there.

Instead, I crossed the road to the row of shops opposite the Gutnick Center, where three men were sitting at a table painting trays of pottery. The owner, Khaled, did not stop working as he talked: every few seconds, he picked up another pot, and spun it in his fingers beneath the paint-brush, leaving it encircled with a perfectly drawn red line. He offered me tea, and I sat down to drink it, reminded once again of the contrast between the unfailing hostility of the settlers and their friends, and the hospitality of the Khalilis.

A car arrived, and a group of five settlers in their early twenties got out, dressed in checked shirts or T-shirts, heavy boots and combat trousers. They had sunburnt arms and long straggling hair. They looked more like squatters or New Age travellers than religious zealots, and their assorted

weaponry and air of defiant self-sufficiency confirmed their
place on the fringes of Israeli society.

Khaled said his son would show me Birket es-Sultan; he
led me out of the square and along the street of deserted
shops. We turned left into another abandoned street and past
an army watchtower. Birket es-Sultan was on the right-hand
side of the street that forms the border between H1 and H2.
The surveyors of the Palestine Exploration Fund described
it as a 'large tank' '133 feet square and 21 feet deep, of good
masonry, well cut with a stone wall around it, and steps in
the corners', and the structure had remained unchanged. I
could only just see over the enclosing wall, but I peered
through the barred window in the back wall of a roadside
shelter or recess that overlooked the dried-up floor of the
tank while my escorts played in the street. Khaled had told
me that the tank had been drained and sealed in the twentieth century because two young brothers had drowned in it,
and I wondered if their deaths were an echo of the fate of
the murderers of Ish-bosheth. That I was even prepared to
contemplate such a superstitious thought was testament to
the tank's desolate air and the unnatural quiet of the surrounding streets. It seemed a suitably funereal place to hang
the mutilated bodies of two assassins.

Khaled told me that Abner was buried beside the entrance
to the souk. I must have walked past his tomb many times.
It was a low stone building to the left of the sentry posts
beside the entrance to the covered section. You could not go
inside: the gate to the courtyard was locked, but you could
look through a grilled window into a cool dark room with a
vaulted ceiling. Two of the pale stone biers that filled the
recesses at the back were adorned with stones shaped like

mushrooms, and the third – which I took to be the tomb of Abner itself – was surmounted by a taller stone shaped like a keyhole.

Rechab and Baanah are examples of those unfortunate types who are condemned for actions that are essential for the completion of a divinely ordained plan, but Abner – Saul's former commander-in-chief – played the most important role in David's ascent to power by engineering the alliance between the northern tribes and the tribes of Judah.

David's reaction to his murder was ambivalent: he declared that he and his kingdom were 'guiltless before the Lord for ever from the blood of Abner the son of Ner', and that the crime would 'rest on the head of Joab', but he did not treat Joab as severely as he had treated the murderers of Ish-bosheth. Joab's only penance was symbolic: David ordered him to mourn Abner when he was buried in the tomb where I was standing. At the funeral, David followed Abner's bier and 'wept' at the grave. He wanted it to be understood that 'it was not of the king to slay Abner', who was a 'prince and a great man', and as a final mark of respect to Saul and his heirs he placed Ish-bosheth's head in Abner's tomb.

After Abner's funeral, 'the elders of Israel' arrived in Hebron to anoint David as their king. According to the traditional biblical chronology, the year was 1007 BCE, and the greatest period in Jewish history had begun. Avi Ofer, the Israeli archaeologist who dug on Tel Rumeida in the 1980s, says that Hebron was at its peak at the beginning of the first millennium BCE, though the city's fortunes reveals nothing about the individuals who might have lived there. Ofer had told me that most archaeologists accept that David and Solomon probably existed, though no one knows the extent of their kingdom, or for how long they reigned. Even the

Bible does not maintain it was for very long. It says that David ruled in Hebron for seven years, and once he moved his capital to Jerusalem in 1000 BCE, the city fades from the account. Hebron had been consigned to a peripheral role in the nation's affairs, and Ofer said it soon acquired the reputation it never subsequently lost, as a remote and impoverished place, home to fanatics who were inclined to go their own way.

The city of Jerusalem dominates the rest of the biblical story. After David died in c.960 BCE, he bequeathed his kingdom to his son, Solomon, who built the first temple on the Temple Mount. When Solomon died in c.920 BCE, civil war split the kingdom into its northern and southern parts, and the fabled period of the 'united monarchy' came to an end. The southern kingdom of Judea was much poorer than its northern counterpart, but it was also much more stable and less prone to dynastic intrigue. After the Assyrians destroyed the kingdom of Israel in 720 BCE, and deported many of its inhabitants, giving rise to the legend of the 'lost tribes' of Israel, Judea became 'the sole inheritor of the pan-Israelite identity', and it survived for another hundred and twenty years, until the Babylonian invasion of 586 BCE, which is usually said to mark the beginning of recorded history: the Babylonians tore down the Temple in Jerusalem and sacked many towns and cities, including Hebron, destroying the four-room house beneath the settlement in the process.

Judea became a vassal state and its elite caste of priests and leaders were exiled to Babylon, prompting the psalmist's famous lament for the lost glories of their homeland: 'By the rivers of Babylon, there we sat down, yea we wept, when we remembered Zion'. The opening verse of Psalm 137 is far better known than the imprecation against the 'daughter of

Babylon' that concludes it – 'Happy shall he be, that taketh and dasheth thy little ones against the stones'. Yet the Psalmist's rage proved misconceived: far from destroying the Jews, the experience of exile proved to be the crucible in which their identity was forged. 'A new community was formed out of the wreckage of the old, and a new faith, purified, refined, was forged out of adversity,' write two British rabbis, David J. Goldberg and John D. Rayner, in their history of the Jewish people. Parts of the Bible were written in exile, and when the Persians conquered the Babylonian empire, in 539 BCE, and allowed the Jews to return to Judea with permission to rebuild the 'house of God at Jerusalem', the collection of texts began to assume their final form.

It was most probably at this moment, as 'the remnant of the house of Israel . . . came back to a wasted and devastated Palestine', that Hebron was identified as the city of the patriarchs. As the Jewish scribes or priests who were defining the identity of the 'tiny, reconstituted people' cast back to an invented past in order to lend their claim to the land more weight, they chose to locate the patriarchal legends in the ancient city on Tel Rumeida. In other words, the patriarchal legends were not the products of an oral tradition that preserved a folk memory of an ancient tribal chieftain, but contemporary inventions that reflect contemporary concerns, and the story maintaining Abraham had bought property in Hebron might have served a simple political purpose: it was a means of asserting Jewish control of the city, and attempting to re-establish the boundaries of the shattered state.

Contemporary political realities also shaped the portrayal of Ishmael. The Canadian scholar John Van Seters says the Jews were conscious of the 'threat of hostile Arab nomads (Ishmaelites) with all their various subgroups, on the borders of the settled regions of the Levant.' The Ish-maelites were feared outsiders, rivals to the contested territory that the Jews had controlled once and hoped to control again. Yet the patriarchal legends assert the kinship of Arab and Jew, and state that the heirs of Ishmael were also distinguished by God's favour. Perhaps it is not sur-prising that the stories were to attract the attention of the religious visionary who re-affirmed the Arabs' membership of the Abrahamic family and established the third great Abrahamic faith.

CHAPTER THREE

THE TOMB OF THE
PATRIARCHS

We made the House a resort and a sanctuary for
mankind, saying: 'Make the place where Abraham
stood a house of worship.' We enjoined Abraham
and Ishmael to cleanse Our House for those who
walk round it, who meditate in it, and who kneel
and prostrate themselves.

The Koran, 2:122

Hebron is one of the oldest continuously inhabited cities in
the world, and the Tomb of the Patriarchs one of the oldest
sacred buildings never to have fallen out of use: this is one
of the few aspects of the city's history on which all its inhabitants agree. The enclosure above the tombs is not included
in the list of buildings Josephus attributed to the Roman
client king, Herod, who governed Palestine from 37 to 4
BCE, but the Palestinian academic and archaeologist Nazmi
Al Jubeh, who wrote the chapters on the Tomb of the Patriarchs in the Hebron Rehabilitation Committee's history of
the city, and acted as my guide on my first visit to the city,
is expressing a commonly held view when he says it is
'undoubtedly Herodian'. When it became a shrine is less
clear: Noam Arnon maintains there was a synagogue in the
Byzantine era, and there are various unsubstantiated references to a basilica or church in travellers' reports, but Dr Al

Jubeh discounts them all: 'the sacred nature of this site is very old indeed but its transformation into a prayer site occurred only under Islam,' he writes, though he cannot specify when the enclosure became a mosque, or 'describe how the first Islamic structure looked'.

The uncertainty is not surprising: every aspect of the city's history before the arrival of the Crusaders in 1099 CE is 'plagued with mystery', in Dr Al Jubeh's phrase. The biblical narrative maintains that a tribe called the Edomites, who inhabited modern-day Jordan and are portrayed in the Bible as the descendants of Esau, Jacob's disinherited twin, occupied Judea in the aftermath of the Babylonian invasion and the deportation of the Jews. The Old Testament prophet Nehemiah said that some of the returning exiles 'dwelt at Kiryath-Arba', but there is no archaeological evidence to support the claim, and it was still considered an Idumean or Edomite town when the First Jewish Revolt against Roman rule broke out in 66 CE.

According to Josephus, a rebel called Simon Bar Giora who was at war with both the Romans and the Jewish authorities in Jerusalem captured 'the little town of Hebron' in a 'surprise attack', though he did not keep it long before one of Vespasian's officers recaptured it: 'Forcing an entry he slaughtered all he found there, old and young alike, and burnt the city to the ground.'

When Vespasian's son Titus captured Jerusalem in 70 CE, he destroyed the Temple in Jerusalem and sold many of the rebels into slavery. Yet another revolt against Roman rule broke out in 132 CE and Hebron was one of its last strongholds: Nazmi Al Jubeh says the remaining rebels took refuge in its fortifications, while the Roman legions encircled it, 'systematically bombarding its walls and forts and setting fire to its houses', turning the prosperous city into a

ruin. The Emperor Hadrian finally suppressed the revolt in 135 CE and attempted to pacify the troublesome corner of the empire by prohibiting the Torah and the Hebrew calendar, renaming Judea 'Palestine', and turning Jerusalem into a military colony called Aelia Capitolina. Many more Jews were sent into exile, some supposedly sold into slavery at Mamre, which had been the site of a market in the Roman era.

Once again, Edomites are believed to have occupied and repaired the ruins. A Gaulish monk called Arculf who visited Hebron at the beginning of the seventh century CE said that 'its inhabitants lived in scattered clusters of houses', and Nazmi Al Jubeh says it 'consisted of a number of farmhouses sparsely spread among the ruins of the Bronze Age city'. He believes that the enclosure above the Tomb of the Patriarchs was the only building beyond Tel Rumeida, and Hebron only began to occupy 'its present location on the edge of the Hebron valley' after the Muslim conquests, when a man called Tamim al-Dari, or his tribesmen, built the first houses around the Tomb.

Tamim al-Dari, who was a *sahaba* or companion of the prophet, remains a significant presence in the city: thirty thousand Khalilis – or approximately a quarter of Hebron's Palestinian population – count themselves as his descendants, and one evening two of the leading members of the Tamimi clan came to my hotel to discuss the workings of the religious foundation, or *waqf*, set up in his name.

Ziad Jalala Tamimi was dressed in black trousers and a grey-green jacket and his thinning hair was streaked with grey. Had he been a Westerner, his bulbous nose, reddened skin and gap-toothed smile might have been construed as evidence of heavy drinking, but daily life in Hebron has effects that are as abrasive as alcohol abuse and the teetotal

Khalilis often seem prematurely aged. His son Tarek, who had come to translate, was a solid, broad-shouldered man, with cropped hair and a goatee. Ziad was a retired teacher, and his opening remark struck a suitably pedagogic tone: 'First of all, I will tell you the story from the beginning,' he said.

The full name of their ancestor is too long to write down, but they suggested that we call him 'Tamim Ben Aus al-Dari'. Most sources agree that he was a Christian merchant who used to travel through Palestine and the Arabian Desert, and the Tamimis said he exported Hebron's famous grapes and associated products, such as wine and raisins, and brought back dates and spices. The Israeli historian Moshe Gil calls him 'the prototype of a Bedouin fighter, who knew how to take good care of his horse', and the Tamimis called him 'one of the most religious people of his time'. His life changed when he met Mohammed in Medina, and declared 'his *islam*' or surrender to God. He continued to trade in wine until Mohammed issued a direct prohibition against alcohol. The next time he met the Prophet, Tamim al-Dari slit open the leather containers he had brought from Hebron, and spilled the wine on the floor.

He was said to have offered Mohammed advice on various questions related to public worship, including construction of the *minbar*, or pulpit, in the mosque in Medina, and what Gil calls 'the great innovation' of using oil instead of wood for light. He is also considered to be one of the first narrators of Islamic religious stories, including several about the end of the world. Sunni Islam bases its religious practice around six books of 'hadith', or sayings of the Prophet, which were passed on by his closest companions and collected several hundred years after his death. The collection called Sahih Muslim is believed to be the second most authentic tradition, and hadith 7028 is about a woman called Fatima, who is asked to narrate a story she 'heard directly from Allah's Messenger'. She said she went to the mosque to hear Mohammed speak, and when prayers were over he said that everyone should remain in their place. He wanted to pass on a story about the Dajjal, or Antichrist, that he was told by Tamim al-Dari, 'a Christian, who came and accepted Islam'.

His descendants re-told the story in relay, Tarek passing on his father's words. Once, he said, Tamim al-Dari was shipwrecked on an island, where he met a mythic animal called 'al Jassassa'. It was so hairy that you couldn't tell its face from its back. The animal guided Tamim and his companions to a cave, where they met the Dajjal. Tarek said he was dressed in 'metal robes', though most translations offer a more prosaic version: his hands and feet were chained together. The shackled man was called 'the lying Jesus', because he would pretend to be Jesus on the day of judgement, and lead non-believers to damnation. He had one eye, which was like a swollen grape, and he asked Tamim al-Dari three questions. Do the date palm trees of Jordan bear fruit? Is there water in the lake of Tiberius? Does the spring of Zuagghar water the land? Tamim al-Dari answered yes to all three questions, and the Dajjal told him that there would come a time when the trees would cease to bear fruit, and the lake and the spring run dry: 'These are the indicators of the end of life.' The Dajjal asked about the 'unlettered prophet Mohammed', and Tamim al-Dari told him that he had conquered Mecca and Medina. The Dajjal said he would escape from his cave on the island, and 'travel the land', but he would not be able to visit Mecca or Medina, because angels with flaming swords would bar his way.

As he told Tamim al-Dari's story, Mohammed struck the

pulpit with his staff to emphasize the message. He commended it to his followers, because it confirmed what he had told them about the Dajjal. Tarek said it was a rare sign of approval: several people in the Prophet's inner circle passed on hadiths, but the master rarely commended one of his follower's lessons.

Mohammed's esteem for Tamim al-Dari was confirmed in 631 CE, when the Prophet granted him Hebron and the surrounding villages and land as far north as Bethlehem. Palestine was not under Muslim control, but Mohammed's belief that it would be one day was vindicated shortly after his death in 632 CE. The leadership of the *ummah*, or Muslim community, passed to a succession of caliphs, and Tamim al-Dari accompanied the fourth, Omar ibn al-Khattab, when he 'liberated Jerusalem' in 638. Hebron is not mentioned in the Muslim traditions of the conquest: Gil says it may have held out longer than other cities, but once it was incorporated into the Islamic empire Omar fulfilled the Prophet's promise to Tamim al-Dari.

For the rest of his life, Tamim al-Dari lived in a village called Beit Fibrin, north-west of Hebron, and since he only had one daughter and no sons, the descendants of his brother Nu'aim inherited Hebron. They established themselves in the area around the Tomb of the Patriarchs that became known as Al Tamimiya, or Bani Al Dar, and they may have created the hostel or soup kitchen that preserved the tradition of Abrahamic hospitality.

The soup kitchen still operates today, on revenues provided by the *waqf*: it used to be in front of the Tomb of the Patriarchs, but it was moved to a side street near the offices of the Hebron Rehabilitation Committee when the area was reorganized in 1994. I visited it one morning with Hisham Sharabati, and we watched a stream of people moving past the hatch and filling containers with a thinnish-looking wheat soup cooked in one of five cauldrons. No one was turned away – even the settlers would be served, the manager said. The food was supposed to be for the benefit of the poor – the wealthy ate it because it was believed to be blessed, but negative associations persisted in Hisham's mind: he had never liked it as a child, but he'd tried it recently, and it was fine. It was the taste of poverty that had put him off.

It isn't clear when the soup kitchen was established, but it was in operation in the latter half of the tenth century, for the 'Muslim geographer' Muquddasi, who was born in 945 CE, described an inn 'open to strangers, which boasts a cook, a baker and servants, who serve a meal of lentils with olive oil to the poor and to pilgrims, and even to the rich, should they want it'.

What Dr Al Jubeh calls the first 'reasonable description' of the mosque was written at more or less the same time: 'There (in Heber) lay an impregnable fort, said to have been built by Djinns using great chiselled stones,' wrote Al Makdisi Al Bishari, in 985 CE. 'It is covered by an Islamic stone dome. The tombs of Abraham and Isaac are in the front section while that of Jacob is in the back. Next to each of the prophets, lay his wife. The enclosure was transformed into a mosque around which houses were built to host visitors.'

Nazmi Al Jubeh says that the description shows that 'the Ibrahimi Mosque was more or less in the centre of the town, surrounded by public buildings to welcome the city's visitors and those seeking to be close to God's prophet, Abraham'. By the time the Crusaders conquered Hebron in 1099 CE, 'its religious and administrative importance' had earned it the 'status of a major city'.

———

I had tried to go inside the building that stood above the gates of paradise when I came down from the hill after meeting Noam Arnon on my first day in the city, but it was closed. Triumphalist Jewish music was issuing from the loudspeakers on the roof of the Gutnick Center and drifting across the empty square. I walked home through the souk, though later I was warned against entering it after dark: Becky and Andy, two English students who had volunteered for an activist group called the International Solidarity Movement (ISM) before going to university, told me it was full of rats, and not just the animal kind. Drug abuse is an increasing problem amongst the disaffected Palestinian youth, and dealers and clients congregate in the alleys of the Old City after dark. Hebron's international activists warn against most things, but I cannot deny that I speeded up as I went past the entrances to the side-tunnels, and I was relieved to reach the relatively wide and open streets that led to the Baladiya.

On that first day, the army jeeps were still parked by the concrete blocks in the roundabout, and the taxi that picked me up near Bab al-Zawia had to weave through the rocks and stones lying in the road. It was hard to imagine that the city would return to normal overnight, but when I got up in the morning, a busy weekday market had occupied the scene of the protests: the roads were filled with taxis and vans, and the pavements were lined with stalls selling kebabs and plastic bags stuffed with pitta. Men in suits and keffiyehs leant on parked cars, drinking tea, and traders pushed carts piled with broad beans and strawberries.

The streets and pavements bore the only visible imprint of the disturbances: the pale grey flowers stencilled on the tarmac were the remnants of burnt-out tyres, their misshapen ashen hearts bound together with disintegrating rings of

charred and fibrous thread. A troop of six soldiers was going up the stairs of a house opposite the gates in the Baladiya and another troop was crossing the square behind them. Kids had been throwing stones again, someone said, and the soldiers were searching houses and shutting down shops.

At the exit from the souk, I turned left and went through the checkpoint at the foot of the long staircase that ran up the northern facade of the Tomb of the Patriarchs to the entrance reserved for Muslims. The soldiers sitting beside the metal detector at the entrance were eating sunflower seeds, and adding the shells to a gleaming black puddle at their feet. The entrance led into the Al-Jawali Mosque, which was added to the building's exterior in the fourteenth century. It was a beautiful room, with stone floors, white-washed walls and vaulted arches supported on pillars adorned with astringently elegant designs, in yellow, red and green. Stacks of carpets covered the raised area to the left and a paved passageway ran down the right-hand wall to an anteroom lined with shoe racks. The room's right-hand wall was made from one of the metal doors that seal so many empty shops and workshops in the Old City, and when I looked through a gap in the frame and saw a soldier lounging on a chair with his gun on his knee I realized that it was the barrier that runs through the middle of the building.

The interior of the tomb has been divided in such a way that the six cenotaphs marking the tombs of the matriarchs and patriarchs are equally distributed between the two faiths: there are two in the Jewish half, two in the Muslim half and two in the centre of the building, visible from both sides and accessible to neither. The soldier I had glimpsed through the barrier was sitting in the Jewish side, and the grilled window in front of me overlooked one of the shared cenotaphs. It belonged to Sarah – the first woman to be interred in the tombs. There wasn't much to see: the cenotaph was a triangular structure with a rounded top, tucked snugly in the low, dark room like a jewellery box in the drawer of a wooden chest. It was draped with rugs and tapestries and partially obscured by a mesh of unlit lamps or vases suspended on wires from the ceiling.

I took off my shoes and left them in the rack. The door in the left-hand side of the wall led into the grandest and most beautifully decorated room in the building. The Isaac Hall or Yitzhak Hall, which is only open to Jews ten days a year, has pale turquoise walls and high vaulted ceilings. The stone cenotaphs of Isaac and Rebecca sit in the middle of the carpeted floor. They were built by the Mamluk Sultan Baibars, who conquered Palestine in 1250 CE, and they were inset with grilled doors and windows and surmounted with black pyramidal roofs. They looked like small, windowless houses and I walked round them on my shoeless feet and touched the alternating bands of sandy-red and creamy-white stone inlaid in their surface.

Abraham's cenotaph was visible from another room at the far end of the hall. There was a shapeless impression in a dark-brown mould preserved behind a sheet of glass at chest-height inside the door. It was supposed to be Adam's footprint. The grilled window beside it overlooked Abraham's cenotaph. A sheet of bulletproof glass was positioned to block the line of fire past the carpet-draped form to the window that opened into the Jewish half of the building.

No one believes that the matriarchs and patriarchs are interred in the cenotaphs: they are markers standing directly above the site of their graves in the 'double chambered cave' below. No one is allowed to enter the cave, and the only connection to it is the narrow opening in the floor outside the anteroom overlooking Abraham's cenotaph. The 'lamp aperture' is framed by a tall, thin cupola and covered by a frilled stone that looked like a bleached water lily. A lit candle is lowered through the grille every morning, and when I knelt down and looked through the holes I could see a flame flickering in the darkness below.

Noam Arnon describes the 'lamp aperture' as the 'threshold to the Garden of Eden', and he is one of the last people to have entered the room below. In an article published on the settlers' website, he said that the Jews who returned to Hebron in 1968 'had strong yearnings' to enter the Cave of Machpelah, so that they might 'give supplication before the Lord of our Forefathers'. Unfortunately, Moshe Dayan, Minister of Defence during the Six Day War, had returned the site to the *waqf*, the Muslim religious authority that had controlled it for the previous seven hundred years. Dayan, who was an amateur archaeologist, had attempted to explore the caves himself by lowering a young girl called Michal on a rope through the opening in the floor of the Yitzhak Hall. Michal found herself in a round room, 'whose floor was covered with coins, candles, and written notes' and 'looking around, she saw a narrow, dark corridor, to the south', Arnon wrote. 'The brave girl entered this hallway and after 17 meters discovered a stairwell. In total darkness she climbed the steps. After 15 steps she found a wall blocking her way. A large stone prevented her from continuing.' She returned to the round room, where she was lifted back into the Yitzhak Hall.

Arnon and some of his colleagues at 'Midreshet Hebron', the girls' theological college at Kiryat Arba where he used to work, were intrigued by Michal's story: since they were too large to fit through the narrow opening, they traced the probable course of the subterranean corridor and staircase Michal had discovered, and concluded that the stone that sealed it shut lay 'on the other side of the Yitzhak Hall, covered by Arab prayer-rugs'. The opportunity to explore further came during Elul, 'the month of mercy and repentance' preceding Rosh Hashanah, the Jewish New Year, when they said special 'prayers of repentance' at midnight every night. The guards were usually inattentive, or asleep, and one night Arnon and his friends took 'a big chisel' to the midnight service: some sang and danced, creating a distraction, and others lifted up the prayer rugs and revealed the stone. 'It was held in place by metal bars, attached to surrounding stones. We began hammering on the rock with the chisel, and after a while it began to move. Finally, the stone opened. It is difficult to describe the emotions we felt when we saw the stone move off the small opening under it.' They went down the staircase, 'hearts pounding with excitement', and walked along the corridor until they reached the circular room beneath the grille. Arnon's description of it was perfunctory: 'It was round and dark. On the wall were three stones, but no cave was visible. Where was the cave? Were all our efforts in vain?'

It seems surprising that they were so baffled by the subterranean topography of the cave, for it is documented in medieval sources. When the Crusaders captured Hebron in 1099, they destroyed the mosque and built a Romanesque church in its place, though their lack of respect for its Muslim heritage did not blind them to its potential value to other faiths: Benjamin of Tudela, who visited Hebron in 1163, said that the 'Gentiles have erected six sepulchres . . . which they pretend to be those of Abraham and Sarah, of Isaac and Rebecca, and of Jacob and Leah', and that they extorted money from pilgrims who wished to see them. 'But if any Jew comes, who gives an additional fee to the keepers of the cave, an iron door is opened . . . and with a burning candle in his hands the visitor descends into a first cave, which is empty, traverses a second in the same state, and at last reaches a third which contains six sepulchres . . . A lamp burns in the cave and upon the sepulchres continually, both night and day, and you there see tubs filled with the bones of Israelites.'

The caves had been forgotten for many years before the Crusader conquest of the city, but they had been rediscovered in 1119 by a monk called Arnoul, who noticed a draught near the south-eastern wall, removed some flagstones, and found a room lined with Herodian masonry. He hammered on the walls until he heard a hollow sound, and uncovered the narrow passage – or *serdab* in Arabic – that Michal had also discovered. When he reached the round room where his near namesake, Arnon, and his blundering companions had paused, Arnoul noticed a stone in the floor that looked different from the others. He lifted it up, and entered the caves below, where he found bones that he believed were those of the matriarchs and patriarchs. He washed them in wine, stacked them neatly, and carved inscriptions into the wall. After the Kurdish leader Saladin had recaptured Hebron from the Crusaders in 1187, the Muslim rulers of the city sealed the *serdab* and pierced the hole in the roof of the circular room.

If Arnoul's account had not told Arnon where to go next, then David Wilder's interpretation of the symbolic significance of the cave ought to have supplied a clue. He believed that the darkness that Arnon and his friends encountered in the round room beneath the grille was intrinsic to their meaning: 'Beit HaMikdash, the Temple in Jerusalem, is open to all, high upon a hill. Ma'arat HaMachpela is a cave, hidden from all eyes, inner. Beit HaMikdash extends outward. Ma'arat HaMachpela extends inward,' he writes. 'One, to the heavens, and one to the depths of the earth. One bursts out and the other directed towards our roots.'

It was the breeze moving through the round room that told Arnon where to look – at first, he and his companions wondered if it had originated above ground, until one of them looked down and noticed that several stones in the floor appeared to be stuck together. 'The wind seemed to be originating from between them. Within moments, emotions flying, the stones were uplifted and . . . the cave – a cave of rock, leading into the earth.' They went through a 'very narrow opening' into a circular cave, carved in the rock, 'deep in the earth'. It was filled with dust, and the roof was so low that they couldn't stand. They crawled through the first cave, and entered a second cave, smaller than the first: 'Wind blew in the caves, but the sounds of our hearts pounding was audible.'

They said that 'no living being had been this close to the Patriarchs in thousands of years', and they were moved to find themselves 'by the entrance to the Garden of Eden, where souls and prayers ascend'. One of them noticed that the floor was littered with bones and pottery shards, some of which were in 'good condition', and they must have

rooted through them for Arnon claimed to have dated some of the pottery to the first Temple period, at the beginning of the first millennium BCE.

Arnon said it was an 'unforgettable spiritually uplifting experience' to find themselves 'united, as Sons with their Fathers', though he must have known that it was a crass and ill-conceived expedition: even if the amateur archaeologist and historian in Arnon saw no harm in breaking into an ancient tomb with a 'big chisel' and disturbing the pottery, it seemed remarkable that his religious sensibilities did not deter him from disturbing the bones that he believed to be the remains of the 'slumberers of Hebron', who 'even in death, are called living'. The former director of the Israeli Antiquities Authority, who went in to check how much damage they had done, was the last man to enter the caves, though it hardly matters that there has been no further exploration: most archaeologists accept there probably are ancient tombs beneath the building, but they are unlikely to be more significant than any of the other countless cave-tombs that pock the Judean Hills.

Besides, the symbolic significance of the rooms above ground seems more interesting than the contents of the caves below. Saladin had treated the site with more respect than the Crusaders: he removed all Christian ornaments but he did not destroy the structure of the church, and the marble pillars, vaulted ceilings and high windows that enclose the cenotaphs of Isaac and Rebecca are relics of the 'Kingdom of Jerusalem'. Saladin also installed a *minbar* in the south-eastern wall, near the entrance to the *serdab*, and built the *mihrab*, the decorated prayer niche that indicates the direction of Mecca. The accretions of Islamic worship surrounding the tomb of the father of the Jews were a reminder of how much Islam has borrowed from Judaism, but they were also a reminder of the central role that the father of the Arabs occupies in the older faith.

According to Karen Armstrong, Mohammed did not intend to establish a new religion: 'he was merely bringing the old faith in the One God to the Arabs, who had never had a prophet before,' she writes in *A Short History of Islam*. 'The Quran insisted that its message was simply a "reminder" of truths that everybody knew. This was the primordial faith that had been preached to the whole of humanity by the prophets of the past.' Mohammed felt that old tribal values had been lost in the stampede for wealth that had turned Mecca into a thriving mercantile city, and the sense of 'spiritual restlessness' besetting Arab society was aggravated by the knowledge that Judaism and Christianity were more sophisticated than the Arabs' pagan traditions. The cycle of vendetta and counter-vendetta that drove the murderous tribal warfare of the Arabian peninsula added to his growing fear that the Arabs were 'a lost race, exiled for ever from the civilised world and ignored by God himself'.

Mohammed's revolutionary teachings did not make him popular in Mecca, and his position became even more precarious in 619 CE, when his uncle and protector died: 'according to the harsh vendetta lore of Arabia', he could now be killed with impunity, and three years later he and his followers left Mecca and travelled to an agricultural settlement called Yathrib, which became known as Medina, or the City. The two-hundred-and-fifty-mile journey – known as the *hijrah*, or migration – marks the beginning of the Muslim era, for it allowed Mohammed to establish a community based on the Quranic ideal. It also enhanced his knowledge of Jewish scriptures, and introduced him to the

Abrahamic stories of Hebron. He had been invited to Medina by envoys from the nomadic tribes who had settled in the city. They included families of Jewish descent, and converts to Judaism, who told him that Abraham had had two sons, one of whom was believed to have been the father of the Arabs. He was delighted to discover that the Arabs 'had not been left out of the divine plan after all'.

Far from it: they had been accorded a central role. Since Hagar is the first woman that God addresses, there is a Jewish tradition that maintains that she was not a mere handmaid, but a princess in the Pharaoh's court, and Genesis awards Ishmael even higher status. He is prominent in Abraham's affections – when God tells him that his ninety-year-old wife is going to bear him a son, Abraham points out that he already has one ('O that Ishmael might live before thee!') – and in God's plans. The ritual act that symbolizes the sealing of God's covenant with Abraham, 'the first Jew', is not performed with Isaac, as yet unborn, but his older brother: 'In the self-same day was Abraham circumcised, and Ishmael his son,' says Genesis 17:26.

The Jews of Medina also told Mohammed the legends that connected Ishmael and Abraham to the city of Mecca, and its holiest shrine – the black stone called the Kaaba or 'cube', which the Koran describes 'as the first temple ever to be built for mankind . . . a blessed site, a beacon for the nations'. Genesis says that Abraham expelled Hagar and Ishmael into the 'wilderness of Beer-sheva' where they would have died of thirst if God had not intervened to save them, but Mohammed heard a different version in Medina: local legends maintained that Abraham had brought them to the Arabian Peninsula and left them in the desert near the Kabaa.

When the water ran out, this version of the story went,

Hagar ran back and forth seven times between two hills called Safa and Marwa, desperately scanning the terrain for signs of water, before flinging herself to the ground and praying for deliverance. An angel struck the ground with his foot and a spring called the well of Zam-Zam gushed forth. One tradition says that when Abraham returned to visit them, he was amazed to find them running a successful business, selling water to travellers, and that the city of Mecca evolved around the oasis. Another tradition states that he and Ishmael rebuilt the Kaaba, which had originally been built by Adam and subsequently fallen into disrepair.

In Mohammed's time it was still revered by the Arabs, who came from all over the Arabian peninsula on a yearly pilgrimage or *hajj*, and circled the shrine seven times, following the direction of the sun around the earth, but it was dedicated to a Nabatean god, Hubal, and contained three hundred and sixty idols – 'emblems of the days of the year, or effigies of the Arabian pantheon'. Mohammed reconsecrated it in two stages: to begin with, the Muslims had faced Jerusalem while they prayed, in acknowledgement of the city's significance to the Jewish and Christian faiths, but one day, in 624, he reversed the *quibla*, and told them to face Mecca instead. Karen Armstrong calls it 'one of his most creative gestures': it marked a return to 'the original pure monotheism of Abraham, who had lived before the revelation of either the Torah or the Gospel and, therefore, before the religion of the one God had been split into warring sects.' It also demonstrated the Muslims' growing strength and confidence, and when Mohammed returned to Mecca in 630 with an army of ten thousand men, capturing the city without resistance, he purged the Kaaba of its pagan associations and rededicated it to the One God, Allah.

He also gave the rituals of the *hajj* an Islamic significance by associating them with the story of Ishmael and Hagar, and over the years the topography of the Masjid al-Haram, the mosque that surrounds the Kaaba, has come to reflect their ordeal in the desert. The *hajj* is one of the five duties that every Muslim must observe and the millions of pilgrims who visit Mecca every year are observing a subtle conflation of rituals: they 'circle the Ancient House' seven times, as the Koran commands, honouring the practice of their pagan predecessors, and they re-enact Hagar and Ishmael's despairing hunt for water by walking back and forth seven times along a covered promenade that connects the hills of Safa and Marwa, and by sipping water from the well of Zam-Zam, which lies twenty metres from the Kaaba's eastern face. The consequences of the domestic feud that led to Ishmael's expulsion from his father's house continue to animate the greatest religious spectacle in the world.

According to Genesis, the brothers only met once after Ishmael's expulsion, when they buried Abraham in Hebron, but tradition maintains that Isaac never forgot Ishmael. Abraham never overcame his perception of himself as an outsider in Canaan and sent a servant to Mesopotamia to find Isaac a wife from amongst his 'kindred'. Rebecca welcomed the servant in a way that suggested she was the woman God had chosen and she agreed to return to Canaan with him. Isaac was living in the Negev, in the south, beside 'the well Lahai Roi', which is said to be the 'fountain in the wilderness' where the angel found Hagar when Sarah had thrown her out the first time. Isaac was aware of the coincidence – according to Genesis 24:63 he had gone 'out to meditate in the field at the eventide' when he saw the approach of the camel train bearing Rebecca. Tradition

maintains that it was Ishmael who was on his mind: thinking of his brother, he was rewarded with his wife.

These days, the descendants of Isaac and Ishmael cannot even agree who has the larger share of the family tomb: the settlers say they have the smaller parts of the building's interior, but since the Palestinians include the courtyard beneath its north-west facade in their reckoning of its size, they say the Israelis control two-thirds of the total. Since I felt no attachment to the building's shrines and cenotaphs, I thought the settlers had got the better of the arrangement, for the courtyard was the largest and most elegant civic space I had come across in Hebron. It even had a sloping patch of grass at the end of the building, where I often saw bearded men with machine guns lolling in the shade. The settlers staged music festivals in the courtyard, and welcomed hundreds of visitors on religious holidays.

Yet the courtyard was also a reminder of past humiliations: in 1267, the Mamluk Sultan Baibars, who installed the cenotaphs in the Yitzhak Hall, barred non-Muslims from entering the Tomb of the Patriarchs, and for the next seven hundred years Jews were forced to pray on the 'seventh step' in the broad staircase that ran up the building's south-east end. The Jordanians pulled down the staircase when they demolished the houses around the Tomb between 1948 and 1967, but some Jews still chose to pray on the site to which their forebears had been restricted – the creamy yellow stones were marked with candle burns, and there were often plastic chairs for worshippers placed against the wall.

I left the Yitzhak Hall, and was sitting on the bench in the middle of the courtyard, beneath a tree that offered some shade from the steadily strengthening sun, when a young settler came and sat beside me. He had long hair and was dressed in a T-shirt and combat trousers. There was a handgun in the holster attached to his belt. He lit a cigarette and smoked with quick, impatient movements, dragging it from his lips with a gasp, as if it was burning him. He got halfway down it, stubbed it out, and got to his feet, striding towards the foot of the stairs so impetuously that it looked as if he meant to attack the building. He went through the metal detector that was certified not to violate the Sabbath and handed in his gun at the armoury. The soldiers looked like college kids, bespectacled and earnest beneath the obscuring veil of helmet, uniform and gun: 'Not even a pocket knife?' said the one who searched my bag when I went through the metal detector a minute later: 'Handgun, rocket launcher, AK-47?'

Another metal detector framed the entrance to the Jewish half of the building. The book-lined synagogue to the right of the door was empty, though there were soldiers praying in the fenced-off area beside the corridor that ran parallel to the building's facade. The open courtyard at the end had been turned into another synagogue, where two people were praying, standing up, swaying back and forth in the motion known as *shockelling*. Since I was raised in the Protestant tradition that sees prayer as inward contemplation, I was impressed by the physicality of the Jewish version.

The synagogue is not as beautifully decorated as the Yitzhak Hall, but I liked its plainness: my time in Jerusalem had reminded me that my response to religious shrines is more aesthetic than spiritual, and I preferred the unadorned facade of the Western Wall, Judaism's holiest shrine, where 'the divine spirit always rests', or the sparse interior of the Tomb of the Patriarchs, to the gaudily daubed and incense-drenched interior of the Church of the Holy Sepulchre, where Christ is supposed to have been crucified and interred.

It was midday, and the voice of the imam calling the faithful to prayer reverberated around the courtyard. I crossed the synagogue and sat down in the anteroom between the rooms that housed the cenotaph of Jacob and Leah. A woman in army uniform was sitting at one of the lecterns. There must have been more people there earlier in the day – prayer shawls and copies of the Torah lay on the chairs against the walls, and despite the fans that were doing their best to alleviate the heat in the windowless room it smelt of sweat.

Isaac's marriage had been a success from the start – 'Isaac brought her into his mother Sarah's tent, and took Rebecca, and she became his wife; and he loved her' – but Rebecca, like Sarah, found herself unable to conceive. Since Isaac was a righteous man, like his father, he 'entreated the Lord' on her behalf, and twenty years later she gave birth to twins. Rebecca favoured the younger, Jacob, and she helped him displace Esau as his father's heir. Esau fell further from favour when he married two Hittite women, and Jacob secured his position by returning to Mesopotamia to choose a wife from 'amongst his own kind'.

He fell in love with a 'beautiful and well-favoured' woman called Rachel, and served her father, Laban, for seven years to earn the right to marry her, but on their wedding night he succumbed to one of those surreptitious substitutions that feature prominently in the patriarchs' marital affairs and found himself sleeping with her sister, Leah. Laban explains that he could not let the younger sister marry 'before the first-born', and Jacob had to work another seven years to earn the right to marry Rachel. Since he loved her 'more than Leah', God found an insidious way of balancing the relationship between the sisters: 'And when the Lord saw that Leah was hated, he opened her womb: but Rachel was barren.'

Clearly, the idea of male infertility had never occurred to the authors of Genesis, and yet I could not bring myself to dismiss the stories as attempts to reinforce patriarchal values or assert the primacy of the priestly codes – however insidious their ideological goals might be, the stories have a core of human warmth, and I was moved by the way that the women who cannot conceive are the first chosen and best loved of their husbands' wives.

Jacob had eleven children with his less favoured wives – six sons and a daughter with Leah, two sons with Rachel's handmaid, Bilhah, and another two sons with Leah's handmaid, Zilpah – before God 'hearkened to' Rachel, and 'opened her womb'. She gave birth to a boy called Joseph, and she died giving birth to another son, Benjamin, Jacob's youngest son. Sibling rivalry is another recurring theme in the matriarchs' and patriarchs' domestic affairs, and it proved particularly corrosive in the case of Jacob's twelve sons: since Joseph was Rachel's child, and 'the son of his old age', Jacob 'loved him more than all his children' and 'made him a coat of many colours'.

His brothers were so jealous that they plotted against him. To begin with, they planned to murder him while they were tending their father's flocks in the fields, but a passing camel train of 'Ishmaelites' gave them a better idea: they sold him to a train of 'Midianite merchantmen', who in turn sold him to an officer of the Pharaoh called Potiphar. Joseph rose to prominence in Egypt, and when famine in Canaan forced the other brothers to follow him south in search of food, they found him second in command to the Pharaoh. Jacob's sons settled in Egypt, and their descendants become enslaved by a pharaoh 'who knew not Joseph', before Moses led them out of captivity.

The story is so well known that it barely requires re-telling, but Yacov Ferrara, who came and sat beside me, felt I needed to be reminded of it. A name-tag with the logo of the Tomb of the Patriarchs implied he was a guide of some sort, though he looked like the captain of a nineteenth-century whaler: he had a white beard and dark brown skin, and he was wearing a peaked hat, a thick white sweater and a jacket with fur collars. He was born in Italy but he had lived in Israel for sixty years, and he was 'a Jew, first and foremost'. He asked me whether I was a Christian and if I was did I believe that the Jews had killed Jesus? I said I couldn't see why it mattered, since his death was part of the plan. Whose plan? Well, God's, if you believe in God. But Jesus is God, isn't he? Yacov Ferrara seemed to think he was getting the better of the theological argument. We considered the notion of the Trinity: why not four in one, or two in one? I was happy to concede the absurdity of the idea, but Yacov Ferrara wasn't a man to mock religious faith: 'I don't want to tease you,' he said. 'I just want to give you the truth. More than three thousand three hundred years ago, God gave the Bible to the people of Israel, on Mount Sinai, in front of three million people.' I had not realized there were so many. 'More than three million.' God gave the people of Israel Ten Commandments, and the idea of the Trinity is blasphemous, for it contradicts the first and greatest of them – 'thou shalt have no other God but me'.

I did not mention the emerging consensus that Yahweh had a female consort called Ashera and the Israelites were polytheists as late as the sixth century BCE, and I did not attempt to discuss the absurdities of the Sinaitic revelation, for Yacov Ferrara believed in it implicitly. Given all the fanfare with which God had delivered his first message, why would he contradict it, thousands of years later? 'He'd have to make a real effort to beat the smoking mountain, wouldn't he?' Yacov Ferrara said. 'So what happened? Two thousand years ago, before the British existed, except as a tribe, and before the French existed, a Jew killed another Jew. So what? English people kill each other all the time. Henry the Eighth killed all his wives: so why did the death of Jesus result in two thousand years of persecution, two thousand years in which Christians felt entitled to kill Jews?'

I had no answer, other than the truism that faith licenses many of humanity's worst instincts, but it did not matter: it was a rhetorical question. As Yacov Ferrara began to explain the 'deep and hidden' ways of reading the Torah, which revealed an occult text that predicted Rabin's assassination and 9/11, I began to see why the settlers felt it was wise to let Wilder and Arnon speak on their behalf. I said I was going to go and look at Abraham's tomb, and Yacov Ferrara stood up and ushered me on my way with a graceful smile: after all, his manner seemed to say, there is only so much truth anyone can absorb in a single day.

CHAPTER FOUR

HAIM THE JEWISH EGYPTIAN

> From the testimony of my grandfather, Rabbi
> Haim Bajaio:
> *How long were you in Hebron?*
> Since always, myself and my father and his
> fathers, about 400 years.
> *Did you have good relations with the Arabs?*
> Yes.
> *Until when?*
> Until a day before the riots.
>
> Haim Hanegbi, 'My Hebron'

The reign of the Sultan Baibars who defeated the Crusaders
and the Mongols, securing control of the Eastern Mediter-
ranean for the Mamluk dynasty that had come to power in
Egypt, initiated 'a golden era' in Hebron's history, according to Nazmi Al Jubeh: it became 'a magnet for mystics
seeking affinity with our Father Abraham', and an important stopping-point between Egypt and the Levant. The
Mamluks, who were former slaves, built 'mosques, schools,
meditation centres, hostels and baths', and restored and augmented the Tomb of the Patriarchs.

Their reign also witnessed the revival of the city's Jewish
community. Jews settled in the Al Dar district, around the
Tomb of the Patriarchs, during the reign of Baibars' successors, and in 1487, Obadiah of Bertinoro estimated there

were twenty Jewish families in the city, 'all of them scholars'. Hebron Jews were 'few and good and not bad like the
men of Jerusalem.' They lived in a 'closed courtyard, and no
Ishmaelite or unclean man comes among them'.

As the period of Ottoman rule began in Palestine in 1540,
a small group of Jews who had been expelled from Spain in
1492 arrived in the city, and bought land near the Avraham
Avinu synagogue, though the community was still so small
that they could not always muster the *minyan*, or quorum
of ten adult males required for public prayer. There were
only nine on the eve of Yom Kippur in 1619, wrote Rabbi
Naftali Hertz Bachrach in a book called *Emek Hamelech*, or
The Valley of the King, when an old man arrived to make up
the numbers. He disappeared after prayers, and the congre-
gation could not find him, though they searched the 'entire
courtyard'. That night, he appeared in a dream to the
chazzan, or prayer leader, a holy man who had 'wondrous
visions', and told him 'that he was Avraham Avinu' himself.

He had seen how distraught they were that they could
not pray, and he had come to make up the quorum. 'To
honour their righteous visitor, they named their new synagogue Avraham Avinu ("Our Father Abraham")', writes the
American academic Jerold S. Auerbach.

The community was bolstered at the end of the sixteenth
century by 'handfuls of Jews' from Kurdistan and Jerusalem,
Auerbach says. But its existence was far from secure. Rabbi
Abraham Gershon of Kutow, who visited in 1746, described
it to his brother-in-law the Ba'al Shem Tov, 'founder of
the dynamic movement of Jewish spiritual revival known as
Hasidim', which derives its name from the quality of *chesed*,
or loving kindness, associated with Abraham: 'In this holy
city there is a courtyard of the Jews. On Sabbaths and
holidays they close it, nobody goes out and nobody comes

in, and all night they close it and people are almost not afraid.'

Auerbach praises the 'attentive precision' of those last three words. To be 'almost not afraid' was the most that Hebron's Jews could aspire to, for they were 'fated to be without security within the walls and gates of their tiny enclosure':

> The tiny cramped ghetto at the edge of the vegetable market displayed the precarious vulnerability of its residents. Two dark and narrow streets, each less than six feet wide, separated the Jewish quarter from the surrounding Muslim city. Three gates opened from the ghetto to the hostile world outside . . . Each night, the gates were securely locked.
>
> Its stone buildings were so tightly squeezed together, separated only by narrow alleys, that a marauder could easily attack and escape by jumping from roof to roof.

The threat was made explicit by 'Muslim officials' who entreated Istanbul authorities to 'replace the Jews by another nation so that the name of Israel will no longer be remembered in the hills of Hebron.' Yet the community was slowly expanding its possessions. At the beginning of the nineteenth century, a Sephardic rabbi called Haim Yeshua Hamitzri, or 'Haim the Jewish Egyptian', who had immigrated from Egypt and described himself as 'dwelling in the city of the master Al-Khalil', signed two contracts that still underwrite the settlers' claim to property in the city: in 1807, he completed the purchase of five dunams of land on the edge of the Old City on behalf of the city's Jews, and in 1811, he signed another contract for eight hundred dunams of land, which included four plots of land on Tel Rumeida. The original lease was for ninety years, but its terms must have been extended, for one of Haim Hamitzri's descendants, a rabbi called Haim Bajaio, who was the last Sephardic rabbi of Hebron, continued to administer it after the Jews had left the city.

In 1948, the Jewish property was appropriated by an office of the Jordanian government called the Guardian for Absentee Property, and in 1967 it was transferred to the equivalent department in Israel. The Israeli Guardian for Absentee Property had been set up to administer the land that belonged to Palestinian refugees who fled in 1948. By 1950, 1,400,000 Israeli Jews had been housed on 'absentee' Palestinian property that it had transferred into Jewish hands, and yet despite its essential role in securing Israel's existence as a Jewish state, the settlers believe it has committed a gross crime against the Zionist cause by failing to reverse what it perceives to be the theft of Jewish properties in Hebron: 'These properties have never been returned. The Government of Israel decided to let the injustice stand,' writes Orit Struck, the director of the settlers' 'legal department'. Her argument that the Jews of Hebron had 'never been anyone's enemy and had been murdered and expelled for no reason whatsoever' is true, but it does not justify the settlers' claim to their property in the city, for none of them is descended from the members of the old Jewish community of Hebron.

The heir of Haim Hamitzri and Haim Bajaio was particularly dismissive of their claims. Haim Hanegbi was one of Israel's most prominent 'leftists', and a founding member of an anti-Zionist party called Matzpen, or Compass. He was a journalist, and he still wrote occasional articles, often about Hebron, but he had retired from active politics, for he was seventy-three years old, and he had recently had a heart attack. When I rang him first, he told me that he felt he had talked too much, but he changed his mind, and we arranged to meet one Sunday afternoon at a cafe near his home in the north of Tel Aviv.

It was not just the name of the Marilyn Monroe cafe that made Ramat Aviv feel so American. It stood at the end of a line of low shops that looked like a small-town mall, and there were bursts of blood-red bougainvillea in the flower beds in front of the tall white blocks of flats further up the road. Palm trees lined the pavements and the scent of the sea drifted down the long, wide avenues that ran towards the beaches. It felt like California, and it was strange to think that this pleasant seaside town was no more than fifty miles from the stone houses of the ancient city in the Judean Hills where Hanegbi's grandparents had lived.

He was a stooped figure in a black jacket, black shirt and jeans. He had a stubbled head, oval glasses and was carrying a blue denim bag over his shoulder. As he took a seat at the table, the woman sitting next to me sat up straighter: 'Oh, you're meeting Haim,' she said, as if the revelation prompted an entirely new appraisal of my worth. We had been chatting before he arrived: had she been English or American, I would have assumed she was enjoying a peaceful late middle age in semi-retirement, walking her friendly dog through the streets, and stopping for mid-morning coffee in her favourite cafe, but Israeli politics galvanizes the most improbable people, and she had told me she ran a website that monitored barriers in the West Bank. When I asked her how she knew Hanegbi, she said, 'Oh, everyone knows Haim. We're on the same part of the spectrum politically. Not that Haim would agree.' An endorsement from the 'retired revolutionary' was more than she could hope for.

———

It was obvious from the moment Hanegbi started talking that he was used to being heard. He wasn't curious about me: he did not ask what I wanted to know, or why I was interested in Hebron. He didn't even look at me; he placed his chair at an angle to the table and sat facing sideways across the cafe. His stories were long and complicated, often travelling far from their point of origin, though they normally came to a tidy conclusion, and I realized they were structured reminiscences, with a pattern and patina that came from long reflection and repeated telling. For the next two and a half hours, he talked about his memories of Hebron and rehearsed the stories he had been told by his father and grandfather. When I went through the tapes afterwards, I made a note of the points that weren't clear, and I asked him to clarify them when we met again in the same cafe three months later. By the time our second meeting came to an end, I felt I had gained a rich insight into the life of old Hebron.

I promised I would send him a transcript, though two months passed before I finished going over the tapes. The document was twenty-five thousand words long. Two days after I sent it to him, I got an email from Mi'chael Zupraner, the Israeli who had acted as interpreter on both occasions. Its title – 'URGENT: HAIM' – was surprising, and its contents even more so: Hanegbi did not like the transcript. In fact, he did not recognize it. 'Haim says that it doesn't sound like him at all, and that he would need to re-edit the whole thing, to rewrite his "Hebron story",' Mi'chael wrote. 'He asks – demands – a copy of the recording, so that he could compare it to the text and reach a final decision.' He also made a surprising request: he no longer wanted to be quoted as saying anything libellous about the settlers, which excluded large parts of our conversation. The old revolutionary was not as pugnacious as he seemed.

Since his English was almost as limited as my Hebrew, I couldn't see how a copy of the tape would help him, but I sent him one anyway. Several months later, I got another email from Mi'chael. Haim had contacted him again, saying he did not want to be quoted at all. Mi'chael said he had become quite agitated: 'those are not my words,' he had insisted, repeatedly.

I was sure they were. I could not vouch for the literal accuracy of Mi'chael's translation, but I could vouch for the fluency of his American-inflected English and for his thoughtful nature. He was aware of the difficulties inherent in all forms of translation – 'I don't sound like myself when I speak English,' he said, as if one language licensed a version of yourself that another might suppress – and he seemed particularly suited to interpreting Hanegbi's 'Hebron story'. When I met him in the spring of 2008, he was on a sabbatical from his degree in film studies at Harvard, but shortly afterwards he moved to Hebron and set up

a pirate TV station called HEB2.tv, which operated from the house with the prow-shaped garden that looked east across the roofs of the Old City to the Tomb of the Patriarchs. As the only permanent Jewish resident of Hebron who was neither a settler nor a soldier, he seemed to me the ideal medium for a family history that had become implicated in the political debates about the city's future.

Unfortunately, Hanegbi had made up his mind to be offended. I emailed him several times in English and Hebrew, and cc-ed his two English-speaking friends who had joined us in the cafe, but he did not reply, and when Mi'chael contacted him again he abruptly terminated the conversation: 'I DON'T KNOW HOW I CAN HELP YOU, MI'CHAEL', he wrote, childishly lapsing into capitals. 'GOODBYE.'

Put four Israelis at a table and you'll have eight opinions, the saying goes, yet even by the standards of this disputatious nation, Hanegbi's behaviour seemed perverse – he was entitled to change his mind and withdraw his testimony, but he was not entitled to do it in such a peremptory way. I had gone to considerable effort and expense to guarantee the accuracy of the translation and I could not understand why he was so offended. What's more, his stance seemed self-defeating, an act of erasure that only reinforced the fate of the forgotten community whose history he venerated. Most of it was publicly available anyway, in articles and interviews that had, no doubt, been rendered into English by a less articulate and sympathetic interpreter than Mi'chael Zupraner, and having put aside the repudiated transcript of our conversation, it did not take me long to reconstruct its salient points.

———

Haim Hanegbi was born in a mixed Arab–Jewish neighbourhood of Jerusalem in 1935, but he always knew that his
grandfather wanted to go back to Hebron. That did not
make him unusual in a country 'filled with people dreaming
of returning', he said, in an interview with the *Jerusalem
Post*. It was not just the Palestinians who had been displaced
in the fight for control of the land: 'Jews who had never
taken up Zionism – in Baghdad, Damascus, or Aleppo – paid
the full price for the bitter struggle between Zionism and
the Arab nationalist movement', he wrote. The six or seven
hundred men exiled from Hebron with their families in 1929
'were humble and decent craftsmen and merchants, cheese
makers, tinsmiths and tailors, established men living their
separate lives, congregating in their synagogue, "Zchor
Avraham", at the edge of Mahane Yehuda and reminiscing of
a Hebron that once was', and his childhood sense of their
diminished existence meant that he could never 'be indifferent to the plight of refugees and their descendants'.

As a child, Haim went to Hebron at least a dozen times
with his father and grandfather, and when they walked round
the market they were welcomed with 'handshakes and hugs'
from the stallholders. Later in life, he was 'forced to carry out
military reserve duty', and found himself stationed on a hill
looking south towards Hebron. It was a dislocating experience: 'I tried to share my feelings with a brother in arms, if
I can call him such,' he wrote, in a long article called 'My
Hebron: A Different Kind of Love'. 'I told him: "How
strange it is, to protect a homeland which is not behind you
but in front of you, across from where you stand. How
strange it is to point my weapon toward the place of birth of
my grandfather Haim and grandmother Marqada and my
father Mordechai . . ."' The other soldier was 'speechless':
'What could he have said to someone like myself who is

divided between two homelands?' Hanegbi wrote. He had told me the same story himself, though he had put it more succinctly in print: 'Where is the homeland and where the exile?'

In a sense, the Jewish refugees of Zionism suffered twice over – having been forced from their homes, 'they were pushed to the edges of the historical story, marginalized even in their own societies', and yet he could never overlook the fact that other people had suffered more than him. Several years before I had met him, he had told the *Jerusalem Post* that he would not go back to Hebron and attempt to reclaim his family's property until Palestinians and Jews enjoyed equal rights in the city: 'Justice can't be one-sided. In the future, when property owners, as well as those who lack property, from here and there, on both sides of the Green Line, shall hold the right to return to their place of origin, to the playgrounds of their childhood days, or alternatively be entitled to reparations, then I too will make my demands.'

Hanegbi's family held property in two capacities: on their own behalf, and on behalf of the Jewish community of Hebron. He did not have the documents to prove his ownership, but the reception he received when he went back to Hebron after the Six Day War confirmed his family's status in the city: he went into a cafe, told the waiter his name and asked him to ask the 'elderly men' if it meant anything to them. 'Suddenly they all turned around on their stools and were looking at me. I had no doubt – my name went before me and in it they also saw their own pasts.' They took him to a chicken vendor who spoke Hebrew, and helped him piece the story together 'against a backdrop of congealed blood and feathers'. Sometimes they called his grandfather 'Hakham Bajaio' and sometimes 'Sh'hadah', and they called his father Murad.

Even the mayor Sheik Mohammed Ali Al-Ja'abri knew the name Bajaio. 'His response was very civic', Hanegbi wrote: 'A fine man, Hakham Bajaio, always paid his taxes on time, every lira, until the eve of the war.' One of the other men in the room got up and walked over to him: '"You are the son of Abu-Murad," he said in a decisive tone. "How do you know?" I responded. "By the way you sit, by your hand gestures, by the manner in which you speak," he replied.'

The man was a childhood friend of his father:

> Old Hirbawi, a character in the mould of Zorba the Greek, only smaller. He already knew that my father passed away and asked how my mother was doing. He said some words in Ladino, and counted with the joy of a child, uno, dos, tres . . . I was delighted to find his name among the names of Hebronites who protected their neighbors as if they were brothers on that awful day on August 24th, 1929, such as the sons of Khamouri, Bader, Shahin and Qawasmi and many others. Human beings . . . This city of Hebron, which is always in the news and which continues to claim so many victims, is also my Hebron, by law. This is the Hebron in which many of its Muslim daughters are called Sara, Rebecca, Leah and Rachel. This is the Hebron of my grandfather.

Jewish immigration to Palestine began at the end of the nine-teenth century, but according to the historian Eugene Rogan, it was the Balfour Declaration of 2 November 1917 that provided 'the formula for communal conflict'. As the British government prepared to inherit the League of Nations Mandate to govern Palestine, the Foreign Secretary, Arthur Balfour, assured Lord Rothschild, a leading member

of the British Jewish community, that it would 'view with favour the establishment in Palestine of a national home for the Jewish people, and will use their best endeavours to facilitate the achievement of this project.'

Robert Graves has described the Balfour Declaration as an example of the 'deliberate looseness of phrase' that may be employed when a writer does not wish to be 'completely understood', and the sleight of hand is most apparent in its change of voice halfway through: having made an active commitment to the Zionist cause, it then appends the passive hope that it should be 'clearly understood that nothing shall be done which may prejudice the civil and religious rights of existing non-Jewish communities in Palestine'.

The nationalist aspirations of the separate groups in Palestine could not be so easily wished away: 'Opposed to British rule and to the prospect of a Jewish national home in their midst, the Arab population viewed the expansion of the Jewish community as a direct threat to their political aspirations,' writes Eugene Rogan. Yet the British ignored their concerns, and 'determined Palestine's future without consultation or the consent of its people. Where peaceful means failed, desperate people soon turned to violence.'

The immediate provocation was the ongoing dispute over the rights to the Temple Mount, or the Haram al-Sharif, Jerusalem's holiest shrine. Religious Jews believe the low, flat hill in the south-west corner of the Old City is the site of creation, the place where God made Adam, and the site of Mount Moriah where Abraham was commanded to sacrifice Isaac. It is also the site of Solomon's Temple, which was destroyed by the Babylonians in 589 BCE, and rebuilt by the returning exiles in the fifth century BCE. Herod strengthened the Temple Mount with masonry blocks like those that form the walls of the Tomb of the Patriarchs, but the Romans destroyed the Temple for a second time in 70 CE, and the hill was abandoned until the Muslim conquerors of the city built two mosques on its summit. The Dome of the Rock, which is the larger of the two, covers the flat stone from which the world expanded to its present form, and the smaller, Al-Aqsa, or 'the furthest place', marks the spot from which Mohammed ascended into heaven to commune with God on a mystical adventure known as the Night Journey.

Since religious Jews believe that a third Temple will one day be built on the Haram al-Sharif or 'Noble Sanctuary', the claims to the site cannot ultimately be reconciled. Yet over the centuries, an accommodation of a sort was achieved. Orthodox Jews are forbidden from walking on the summit of the hill, for fear of straying into the inner recesses of the Temple, the Holy of Holies, and since the Middle Ages they have worshipped at the base of the Temple Mount beside the last section of the Herodian fortifications that the Romans left intact.

It was not until September 1928 that the Jews of Palestine felt sufficiently emboldened to test their claims to the site that had become known as the Western, or Wailing, Wall. The collapsible screen that they erected in the small cleared area in front of the Western Wall was ostensibly to divide male and female worshippers, but the sheikhs of the nearby Muslim religious court regarded it 'as an attempt to give the wall the status of a synagogue, as a first step in taking it over', and demanded that it be taken down. As the Israeli historian Tom Segev writes in *One Palestine, Complete*, his history of the thirty years of British rule in Palestine that preceded the creation of Israel, they had always refused to let the worshippers put out chairs for the same reason: 'first they'll put out chairs, they'd said, then wooden benches, then stone benches. The next thing would be walls and a ceiling to keep out the sun and the cold, and suddenly, the Muslims would have a building on their property. This was the Palestine conflict in a nutshell.'

During the next six months, tensions escalated in the way that has become wearingly familiar, with 'protests, proclamations, telegrams to the League of Nations' leading to outbreaks of violence. On 14 August 1929, the eve of the Ninth of Av, the fast day marking the destruction of the Temple, thousands of Jews gathered at the Wall, and the next day, there was another demonstration. The rallies provided the Mufti of Jerusalem with 'a slogan to incite religious fervour in the hearts of the masses'. Fears that 'the Jews are coming' to 'conquer and defile' the holy places spread rapidly, and two days later, the Muslims responded with a counter-demonstration that turned violent.

By 21 August, one observer said, 'the situation in the city has gotten out of hand. Every day, there are attacks and stabbings.' That day, a seventeen-year-old Jewish boy was murdered when a petty dispute escalated and on 22 August the acting high commissioner initiated discussions between representatives of both sides. In principle, the Arab and Jewish leaders were prepared to sign an announcement saying that they recognized one another's rights to the site. Had they published a call for restraint before the meeting broke up at 9.30 p.m., they 'could perhaps have prevented the bloodbath that began just a few hours later', Segev writes. But negotiations broke down, and in the early hours of Friday, 23 August 1929, 'thousands of Arab villagers', many armed with sticks and knives, began 'streaming into Jerusalem'.

Jewish merchants in the Old City began closing their shops at 9.30; at 11 a.m. gunshots were heard on the Temple

Mount, and 'several hundred worshipers swarmed through the alleys of the marketplace and began attacking Jewish pedestrians.' By the end of the day 'eight Jews and five Arabs' had been killed. The British could do little to stop the violence: they only had a small force of fifteen hundred policemen, and most of them were 'Arabs' who were reluctant to intervene for fear of 'killing rioting Arabs and then becoming the target of vendettas by the victim's families'. In Jerusalem 'several English theology students from Oxford who happened to be in the city' were drafted in to help.

Raymond Cafferata, the police superintendent in Hebron, who had arrived several weeks before the riots, had similarly inadequate resources: eighteen constables on horseback and fifteen on foot, of whom only one was Jewish. Local leaders assured Cafferata that Hebron would not succumb to the violence that had taken hold in Jerusalem, but the rumour spread that Jews were killing Arabs, and that the mufti had demanded a response. Cafferata ordered the Jews to stay indoors, and attempted to disperse the crowds, but without success: they gathered at the Hebron yeshiva, and at four o'clock on the afternoon of 23 August a twenty-four-year-old Polish student called Shmuel Halevi Rosenholz became the first victim of the riots in the city.

The trouble resumed early the next morning: 'at 8.30, Arabs began throwing rocks at Jewish homes.' Soon, Cafferata was forced to confront a mob 'running amok.' In one house, he shot 'an Arab in the act of cutting off a child's head with a sword', and a police constable from Jaffa who was standing over a Jewish woman with a dagger in his hand. A tourist from Poland called Y. L. Grodzinsky, who had arrived in Hebron the week before, was attending Sabbath prayers in the house of a man called Eliezer Dan when it was attacked. 'We went to reinforce the door and ran around the room like madmen', Grodzinsky wrote.

> The shrieks of the women and the babies' wailing filled the house. With ten other people I put boxes and tables in front of the doors, but the intruders broke it with hatchets and were about to force their way in. So we left the door and began running from room to room, but wherever we went we were hit by a torrent of stones . . . I looked out and saw a wild Arab mob laughing and throwing stones.

Afraid that his mother 'would be hit', he 'grabbed her and shoved her behind a bookcase in the corner'. Grodzinsky also hid a young woman, a yeshiva student and a twelve-year-old boy behind the bookcase, before joining them himself. They heard the noise of 'the Arabs singing as they broke into the room, and the shouting and groaning of the people being beaten'. When the room fell quiet, they could barely move the bookcase because of the bodies piled against it. 'My eyes were dark from the sight of the dead and the wounded,' Grodzinsky said. 'I could find no place to put my foot. In the sea of blood, I saw Eliezer Dan and his wife, my friend Dubnikov, a teacher from Tel Aviv, and many more . . . Almost all had knife and hatchet wounds in their heads. Some had broken ribs. A few bodies had been slashed and their entrails had come out.'

The Jews of Hebron wrote to the high commissioner to report 'other atrocities': two rabbis, aged sixty-eight and seventy, and 'five young men' had been castrated, a baker called Noah Imerman 'had been burned to death with a kerosene stove', and 'the mob had killed pharmacist Ben-Zion Gershon, a cripple who had served Jews and Arabs for forty years', and 'raped and killed his daughter as well'.

Yet other Palestinians intervened to save their neighbours. In his article 'My Hebron', Haim Hanegbi quoted the testimony of a Hebron Jew called Malka Slonim, who was saved by 'an Arab' called 'Abu-Shaker', who appeared on a white horse outside their house. He told them to close the doors and windows and assured them that he would not allow anyone to touch them.

> We sat silently in the sealed house and Abu-Shaker reported what was happening . . . The rioters had arrived. We heard them growling cries of murder . . . We also heard the voice of Abu-Shaker: 'Get out of here! You won't enter here! You won't kill here!' They pushed him. He was old, maybe 75 years old, but he had a strong body. He struggled. He lay in front of the entrance to the home, by the door, and cried out: 'Only over my dead body will you pass through here! Over my corpse!' One rioter wielded his knife over Abu-Shaker and yelled: 'I will kill you, traitor!' The knife struck him. Abu-Shaker's leg was cut. His blood was spilt. He did not emit any groans of pain. He did not shout, he only said: 'Go and cut! I am not moving!' The rioters consulted with each other; there was a moment of silence. Later we heard them leaving. We knew we had been saved. We wanted to bring our saviour inside and bandage his wound and thank him. He refused and said that others might arrive and that his task had not ended yet.

Across the country 133 Jews and 116 Arabs were killed in the riots, but the toll of 9 Arabs and 67 Jews in Hebron was testament to the one-sided nature of violence in the city. David Ben-Gurion, then General Secretary of the Histadrut, the Zionist Labor Federation in Palestine, and later the first

Prime Minister of Israel, compared what happened in Hebron to the pogroms of Eastern Europe, but Segev rejects the comparison, pointing out that the authorities did not initiate the Hebron riots, and the 'police did not simply stand aside'. The surviving members of the Jewish community in exile noted that had 'it not been for a few Arab families not a Jewish soul would have remained in Hebron'. The Abu Heikels were credited with saving the lives of the Bajaio family, and they were not alone: according to a list in the Zionist archive, Arab families saved the lives of 435 Jews. 'Some of the saviours may have expected a reward in exchange for their help,' Segev writes, but 'most saved the Jews out of human decency, putting themselves at risk . . . In any case, Jewish history records very few cases of a mass rescue of this dimension.'

It was typical of Haim Hanegbi's proprietorial attitude to the history of old Hebron that he did not approve of the only other widely available account. The editor of *Sfer Hebron*, or the Book of Hebron, had committed the greatest crime of all, Hanegbi wrote, by praising Levinger, and yet Hanegbi inadvertently led me in its direction: Mi'chael Zupraner had bought a copy of the book with some of the fee I paid him for his discredited translation, and we went through it together one afternoon. The Book of Hebron is 515 pages long and incorporates all kinds of sources, documents and contributors. The exploration of pre-twentieth-century Hebron – what Mi'chael called 'this fabulous history' – was particularly leisurely: it even included certificates of payment for city taxes. There was a section about prominent Jewish figures, such as the Ramban, or Maimonedes, the Jewish medieval mystic, who came to Hebron once, and set aside a

day a year to commemorate the trip, a section devoted to the Tomb of the Patriarchs, and an hour-by-hour account of the events of 24 August 1929.

Mi'chael said the book was partly an attempt to keep the exiled community intact by preserving a collective identity, and it included an account of the deliberations that led to the attempt to re-establish the city's Jewish community in 1931: 'The joy that accompanied the rumor of the return was accompanied by anxiety', it said. 'Who would dare return to the "lion's den", and whom [*sic*] would guarantee the safety of the families returning? Opinions in the institutions of the Yishuv were divided, but while they debated the question, the families had already determined a date for their return to their ancestral home.'

The group of one hundred and sixty Jews who left Jerusalem by bus after the Passover holiday of 5691, or 1931, was led by Hanegbi's grandfather, Haim Bajaio, 'aided by advocates A. Franco and Y. Hasson'. Approximately 60 per cent of the returnees were children, but there were also 'craftsmen' who reopened their shops and workshops: 'Carpenters, tailors, shoemakers, one silversmith and one plumber. One opened a liquor store, with the purpose of serving only the faithful in need of a "remedy prescribed by the doctor". Yaakov Ezra reopened his dairy production plant.' There was 'a severe shortage of professional craftsmen in the city', and the Arabs of Hebron 'greeted the Jewish craftsmen with open arms'. Communication between buyers and sellers was difficult at first, but rapidly improved: 'Some bought their clothes and tools from the Children of Israel, and some bought grocery goods and vegetables from the Children of Ishmael . . .' Haim Hanegbi said that his grandfather dominated the community both through his physical presence and his force of character –

'tall build, always upright and powerful', he wrote – and the account in the Book of Hebron concurred: it said he ruled 'with a powerful and mighty arm'.

Hanegbi believed the experiment had been a success: 'The Levinger types, although they hold all the necessary evidence, choose to neglect this chapter of history,' he wrote, in one of those essays that so closely resembled the stories he had told me. The idea of 'a peaceful return to Hebron' was inconvenient for contemporary historians who chose 'to portray all the Arabs of the Hebron Hill as murderers and the sons of murderers'. Yet the experiment did not last long: the riots of 1929 had not dissipated the anger and frustration of the Palestinian Arabs, and a prolonged uprising known as the 1936–1939 Arab revolt began in April 1936.

The renewed Jewish community of Hebron were aware of the rising tensions: 'the atmosphere in the City of Patriarchs became more and more bleak every passing day', said the Book of Hebron. 'Rumors of another massacre spread by word of mouth', and in 'the dark night hours of 23rd April 1936', the British authorities evacuated the Jewish community from Hebron. The only Jew left in Hebron was Yaakov Ezra, 'the owner of the dairy production plant and the producer of the renowned and delicious Hebron cheese', but even he left when the Jordanian army captured the city in 1948. David Ben-Gurion said that Hebron had become 'Judenrein', or 'Jew-free', and the settlers frequently repeat the term in the hope of evoking parallels with the purged ghettos of fascist Europe.

CHAPTER FIVE

THE SHEEP TABLET

And Joshua at that time turned back, and took
Hazor, and smote the king thereof with the sword:
for Hazor beforetime was the head of all those king-
doms . . . And he burnt Hazor with fire.

Joshua, 11:10–11

On 19 July 1949, six weeks after the end of the war in which
Israel repulsed an attack from the neighbouring countries of
Egypt, Jordan, Syria and Iraq, and enlarged the territory it
had been awarded in the UN plan to partition Palestine, the
Prime Minister of the new state summoned a group of historians, archaeologists and geographers to a meeting at his
office in Tel Aviv, and entrusted them with a task vital to the
state's survival. According to Meron Benvenisti, the former
Deputy Mayor of Jerusalem, the scholars belonged to a
group called the Israel Exploration Society, which had been
formed 'to develop and advance the study of the land, its
history, and pre-history, accentuating the settlement aspect
and the sociohistorical connection between the People of
Israel and Eretz Israel', or the land of Israel, though Nazmi
Al Jubeh, who used to know one of the men who attended
the meeting, describes its mission in simpler terms: 'Ben-
Gurion said: "Look, we have a state, but we don't have
roots."' Dr Al Jubeh recalled his friend's recollection of Ben-
Gurion's words as we sat amongst the lemon trees in the

cloistered garden of a Jerusalem hotel one evening in March 2008: 'He said: "Create me roots. Go to the field – create me roots. I need historic maps to prove my relationship to the biblical period, I need archaeological evidence, I need historical texts. Go and do it."'

Ben-Gurion asked them to draw up a map of the Negev desert in southern Israel, and assign Hebrew place names to all its 'mountains, valleys, springs and roads', in the hope of convincing the public that 'a new – Jewish – reality had indeed been created' in its 'desolate expanses', Benvenisti writes in *Sacred Landscape: the Buried History of the Holy Land Since 1948*: 'It was an act of establishing proprietorship: they had been asked to draft a deed of Jewish ownership for more than half of Israel's territory.' Yet Ben-Gurion did not just rely on mapmaking as the means 'to provide concrete documentation of the continuity of a historical thread that remained unbroken from the time of Joshua Bin Nun', Moses' heir, who led the Israelite conquest of Canaan in the Bible: the excavations of biblical cities, battlegrounds and settlements also played their part, and it was one of Ben-Gurion's closest colleagues in the 1948 Arab–Israeli War who was to prove most adept at establishing the connection in the popular imagination between ancient Israel and its modern counterpart.

Yigael Yadin, who was born Yigael Sukenik and took a Hebrew name shortly after the state of Israel was created, understood the value of archaeological research early in life, for his father, Eleazar, was the most prominent Jewish archaeologist in Palestine during the British Mandate. Eleazar Sukenik's greatest triumph came at the beginning of the 1948 Arab–Israeli War, when he secured the first sections of the manuscripts that became known as the Dead Sea Scrolls. But from the start of his career he was determined to arouse the interest of the 'Jewish people' in their ancient heritage: he believed that 'the nation that gave this land its glory, that poured out its spirit and soul on the mountains and valleys' had fallen far behind in its exploration. 'The time has come for the Jewish people to fulfil our obligations to the Jewish past, and to the exploration of the land of Israel, cradle of our faith', he wrote, in 1925.

Four years later, Sukenik took his twelve-year-old son to the site of excavations at an ancient synagogue in the Jezreel Valley, and showed him how the Zionist pioneers who lived nearby reacted to the find: 'There was suddenly a feeling that this very parcel of land – for which they had suffered so much – wasn't just any piece of land but the place where their fathers and grandfathers had lived and died fifteen hundred or two thousand years before', writes Yadin's biographer, Neil Asher Silberman. 'Their history had been uncovered, and they could see it with their own eyes.'

The archaeological relics 'instil[ed] a feeling in the heart of the individual and the public that every inch of this country is ours and it is our obligation to defend and to fight for it', Eleazar Sukenik wrote. It was both a science and 'a spiritual weapon' and it would provide 'an important buttress for the State in its path to the future'. His son had an even clearer sense of its role. Yigael Yadin did not aspire to objective assessments of evidence and data: according to Silberman, he was a brilliant storyteller, who could turn 'a mere scholarly listing of artefact types and linguistic esoterica' into 'flesh-and-blood epics' that would captivate not only the Israeli public, but an audience around the world. Yadin was also a brilliant military tactician and administrator, who became Chief of Staff during the 1948 Arab–Israeli War, and he was particularly adept at dramatizing parallels between the contemporary battles the Israelis fought and their ancestors' campaigns.

His first major excavation was at the mound of Tell el-Qedah, near the Syrian border in Upper Galilee, which had been tentatively identified as the likely site of the biblical city of Hazor, which Joshua had destroyed in his conquest of Canaan. When Yadin began planning the excavation in 1954, he hoped that its scale and ambition would challenge the dominance of foreign archaeologists, and assert Israel's right to conduct its own excavations within its newly created borders. Hazor would not only be Yadin's debut as a practising archaeologist, but 'a testing-ground on which to invent, create, and shape the distinctive national endeavour that would eventually be known as Israeli archaeology', Silberman writes. Yadin hoped that the walls, gates and citadels that he uncovered at Hazor would reveal the richness of the biblical past, and he persuaded the Rothschild family to fund the dig on the basis that they would be underwriting 'the discovery of the palaces of their own noble forefathers'.

The first season began in August 1955, and yielded some significant finds. Excavations in a part of the site dubbed Area C uncovered the remains of a 'densely packed and apparently prosperous city', which seemed to have been destroyed in c.1250 BCE, the approximate date proposed for the Israelite conquest. The revelation that the officer who had directed the Israel Defense Forces' operations during the 'War of Independence' had found evidence of an ancient Israelite conquest resonated beyond scholarly circles. Yadin warned the reporters who converged on Hazor that he did not have conclusive proof it was Joshua who had destroyed the city, but he managed to convey the impression that the Israelites had sacked the city through his evocative description of the most important discovery of the season – a small statue of a Canaanite king or god, which seemed to have been beheaded by a blow at the neck with a sharp instrument.

At the same time, he was engaged in an even more 'important transformation': 'For decades the school-children of the Yishuv had imagined that biblical villages and towns resembled rural Arab villages of low stone buildings, with outdoor clay ovens, grazing flocks of sheep and goats', writes Neil Asher Silberman. The Arabs of Palestine came to be seen as the physical embodiment of the biblical past, and yet 'Plan D', the military campaign that Yadin had overseen, had driven many of them off the land: 750,000 Palestinian Arabs became refugees, and their houses and villages were abandoned, destroyed or repopulated with Jewish immigrants.

Whether or not the 'ethnic cleansing' of Palestine was an accident of war or the consequences of a deliberate policy remains a matter of debate, but the result was not: 'much of what the Jewish community had long identified as "ancient" had vanished', Silberman writes. Since a new physical connection with the past was required, the excavation at Hazor was a continuation of Plan D by other means: tels replaced Arab villages as symbols of the past, and pottery and figurines replaced sketches of Arab shepherds and farmers. As Yadin's excavations dramatized the biblical narrative of ancient Israel, collecting antiquities became fashionable, expeditions to digs became part of the curriculum in Israeli schools and Yadin became a celebrity. The man who had engineered Israel's defining military victory was now engineering an essential component of its self-image.

Yadin achieved even greater prominence with his next major excavation: between 1963 and 1965, he dug at the hilltop fortress of Masada, in the Judean Desert, which is supposedly the site of another defining episode in Jewish history. Again, Josephus is the source – and again the story is of a mass suicide. According to *The Jewish War*, the Romans had effectively suppressed the first Jewish revolt by 70 CE when they captured Jerusalem and destroyed the second Temple, but a small group of Zealots took refuge in the fortress of Masada and held out for three more years, eventually committing suicide rather than surrender to the besieging troops.

Moshe Dayan, another prominent Israeli soldier-archaeologist who used to exploit his position as Minister of Defence by sending military personnel and helicopters to plunder sites that attracted his attention, had already recognized Masada's propaganda potential: he had made it the setting for a swearing-in ceremony for new recruits to the armoured corps, which concludes with the pledge that Masada 'shall not fall again'. Yadin attended one of the services before the dig began, and told the soldiers that the 'echo of your oath will resound throughout the encampments of our foes. Its significance is not less powerful than all our armaments!'

He had raised part of the funds for the dig by selling exclusive newspaper, magazine and television rights, assuring him a global audience for the story he hoped to reveal. Yadin's career was becoming 'a larger-than-life public spectacle, in which an intense search for heroic chapters of the Jewish past was followed with obsessive fascination by the general public all over the world', Silberman writes. The Masada excavation rivalled the discovery of the tomb of Tutankhamen in the Valley of the Kings as the most widely publicized and celebrated dig of the era, and once again Yadin used its finds to the best possible effect. Archaeological data is rarely conclusive, but Yadin was reluctant to challenge a tradition that it did not clearly disprove: Silberman

does not accuse him of knowingly concealing or manufac-
turing evidence, but he says he downplayed the ambiguous
nature of his finds and 'strung together a series of narrative
assumptions that led his audience to the inevitable and satis-
fying conclusion' that Josephus' account of the defence of
Masada was true.

The propaganda value of his widely publicized work was
immense: 'At this time when we are trying to renew the
heroic period of our nation's history, the story of Masada
should penetrate into every home in the country,' the Israeli
President, Zalman Shazar, said when he opened the second
season of excavations in 1964. Yadin himself declared that
'Masada was a symbol of our refusal to live like slaves.'
Masada was as much 'an exercise in patriotic inspiration as
in scientific research', Silberman said – or as Nazmi Al Jubeh
put it, Yadin had obliged the stone to tell beautiful, potent
stories, and in the process he had fortified one of the myths
that bind the Jewish people to the land.

Yadin's aim of establishing Israeli archaeology as an independent discipline had been substantially advanced by one
of the accidents of the 1948 Arab–Israeli War: the ceasefire
line known as the Green Line ran through the centre of
Jerusalem, and almost all the foreign institutions that had
dominated archaeological research in the Levant in the early
part of the twentieth century, when Eleazar Sukenik was
struggling to make his name, fell into the eastern half of the
city, which was controlled by Jordan. Since the American,
French and British schools were no longer a force within
Israel, the field was free for men like Yadin. Yet the Israelis
had no access to the biblical sites of Judea and Samaria, and
while Yadin was conducting his first season of excavations at

Masada in 1963 an American archaeologist was preparing a much smaller expedition to Hebron.

Philip Hammond was born in New York, in 1924, and was wounded on the beach at Normandy in the Second World War. After he left the army he studied at Yale and then excavated at Jericho with the famous British archaeologist Kathleen Kenyon. In 1962, he was teaching at Princeton, and in accordance with the fashion of the time he started looking for a biblical site to excavate. Hebron was the only significant one that had not been touched, and it was so inaccessible that many people believed it would remain that way. Even Philip Hammond, who was a fluent Arabic speaker, and went on to become an adopted Jordanian, was deterred by its reputation: 'The presence of the Mosque of Ibrahim, over the traditional site of the Cave of Machpelah . . . had brought Muslim orthodoxy to an unusually high pitch in the community', he wrote: 'Tales of violence, uprisings, fanaticism, and the like, had always circulated about Hebron. Even native Jordanians found the city inhospitable for trade or residence, unless they were of local origin. No large group of foreigners had ever lived there, hence suspicion, religious and political, was directed against visitors to the site.'

It did not take Hammond long to discover that the stories about the Khalilis were unfounded. In the summer of 1963 he lived with a family in the Old City for a week while he conducted a preliminary survey, and a year later the full party of twenty-two American teachers and students arrived to begin the first season of excavations. Throughout their stay in the city, they were treated with exemplary courtesy and hospitality: 'The reaction of the local people was grossly different from that which had been darkly predicted!' Hammond wrote. 'Local interruptions *did* occur in the workday

– but by visitors coming to proffer invitations to their homes. Altercations *did* occur – as workmen vied with each other in bringing melons and grapes from their gardens for their newfound friends . . .'

The second season was shorter and smaller than the first: ten foreigners and fifty locals worked for six weeks, principally with the aim of preparing for a larger expedition in 1966, and they would have returned in 1967 had it not been for the Six Day War.

Fighting broke out in the early hours of 5 June 1967. Israel destroyed the Egyptian air force, rapidly defeated the armies of Egypt, Syria and Jordan, and occupied East Jerusalem, the West Bank, the Gaza Strip, the Golan Heights and the Sinai peninsula. The Israeli historian Avi Shlaim said that the speed and scale of its conquests 'led some observers to suspect that Israel launched the war not in self-defense but in order to expand its territory'. Shlaim, who is a noted critic of Israeli policy, maintains that it was a defensive campaign 'launched by Israel to safeguard its security' and yet it reopened questions about the 'territorial aims of Zionism'. It was evident that the occupation of the West Bank would mean the end of the Zionist dream of a state with a Jewish majority, and yet there was 'a strong expansionist current' running through Zionist ideology and Israeli society: 'There was a general feeling . . . that the territorial gains of the 1948 war had fallen short of the envisioned promised land,' writes another revisionist Israeli historian, Benny Morris, in *The Birth of the Palestinian Refugee Problem 1947–1949*. '*Bechiya Le Dorot* – literally a cause for lamentation for future generations – was how Ben-Gurion described the failure to conquer Arab East Jerusalem; leading groups in Israeli society regarded the Jordanian-controlled West Bank with the same feeling.'

The victory delighted different elements of Israeli society: a messianic minority saw the capture of the bibical territories of Judea and Samaria as a fulfilment of God's will, while warrior-politicians such as Moshe Dayan appreciated the strategic significance of thickening a country that was no more than eight miles wide at its narrowest point. Some commentators expressed concerns about the corrosive effects on Israeli society of subjugating the Palestinian population and turning them into 'hewers of wood and drawers of water', but those with an interest in Hebron had a prominent and influential supporter. On 12 July 1967, Israel's founding father, David Ben-Gurion, said it 'should take nothing in the conquered territories, with the exception of Hebron', which 'is more Jewish even than Jerusalem'. The idea of returning to the city of the Patriarchs was no longer unthinkable, and in early 1968, a short advert appeared in an Israeli newspaper: *Wanted: Families or singles to resettle ancient city of Hebron. For details contact Rabbi M. Levinger.*

Unless you share the religious faith that inspired the settlers' actions, it is hard to understand how they must have felt as they entered Hebron on Friday, 12 April 1968, the first day of the week-long holiday that commemorates the liberation from slavery in Egypt. The sense of righteous vindication at a long-delayed homecoming must have been mixed with trepidation, though it is testament to the damage that successive defeats had inflicted on the Palestinian psyche that Khaled Qawasmi – director of the Hebron Rehabilitation Committee, which he set up in the aftermath of the massacre in the mosque – believed that the Khalilis were equally afraid of them: 'They were scared that the Israelis wanted revenge for the massacre of 1929,' he said, when I met him at the

offices of the HRC, in a converted palazzo at the end of the
street that led past the Abrahamic soup kitchen to a side
entrance to the Tomb of the Patriarchs.

I was sitting on the doorstep when he turned into the car
park in a white four-by-four that resembled the vehicles
driven by UN representatives through East Jerusalem and
the West Bank. It was Friday morning, and as usual the city
was deserted: it took several minutes to find someone to
unlock the offices. The building was one of the grandest in
the Old City, a large stone house built around a central
courtyard. Dr Qawasmi's first-floor office was a cool white-
walled room, with black sofas set either side of a low table,
and a large desk. Outside, a short corridor led to a courtyard with stairs to the roof, from which you could look
across the tightly packed houses of the Old City to Tel
Rumeida. Dr Qawasmi was wearing blue trousers and a blue
and white short-sleeved shirt. His greying hair was slightly
receding, and he had a neat moustache, small glasses and a
round face.

I had come to see Dr Qawasmi not only because he was
a significant figure in the Old City's recent history, but also
because he was a member of the family that owned the Park
Hotel, where the settlers first took rooms. I went to see it
later in the week. It stands on Ain Sarah, half a mile from the
centre of town, a large, flat-fronted building, painted white,
and half-hidden from the street by a row of recently built
shops. Hisham Sharabati, who knew a member of the family,
had rung ahead, and a student called Ala Qawasmi, who
was a nephew of Dr Qawasmi, and the son of the Dean
of Engineering at Hebron University, met us at the front
steps. History doesn't look like history when you're living
through it, said the slogan on his T-shirt. The front door was

locked, but Ala found the key: 'Welcome to Reception,' he said, as he pushed open the door.

Not surprisingly, there are different versions of the return to Hebron. According to the Qawasmi family, four men bearing Swiss passports arrived at the hotel and asked to rent rooms, but David Wilder has described it as a mass gathering, which included 'families from Israel's north, south and center'. He denies they were travelling incognito, as the Qawasmis maintain, though he accepts that few foreign visitors came to Hebron. The city's hotel owners 'had fallen on hard times', he said. 'For years they had served the Jordanian aristocracy who would visit regularly to enjoy Hebron's cool dry air. The Six Day War forced the vacationers to change their travel plans.' According to Wilder, the Qawasmis were 'delighted to accept' the cash-filled envelope which Rabbi Levinger placed on the front desk, and agreed to rent the hotel to 'an unlimited amount of people for an unspecified period of time'.

The hotel had closed in 1986, and the abandoned reception was cool, dark and dusty. There were no traces of the hall's former function, except its proportions. Ala showed us where the desks had stood along the right-hand wall. If Wilder's account is to be believed, then the lobby was a dormitory on the night of 12 April 1968: men slept on its floor, and the women and children slept three to a bed in the hotel rooms. 'At least Ya'akov Avinu had a rock to place under his head,' one of those present was supposed to have said. Yet Miriam Levinger said they 'all felt deeply moved and excited', for they believed they had made 'an historical breakthrough'. Wilder claimed that eighty-eight people celebrated Pesach Seder that night, and two days later Rabbi Levinger called a press conference, and announced that they were staying in Hebron. Wilder said that 'dignitaries, Knesset members and Israelis from far and near streamed to the Park Hotel to encourage the pioneers', though in fact their presence in the city divided opinion in Israel.

No doubt the settlers believed in God and manifest destiny to secure their place, but the historian Martin Gilbert says that luck played a much greater part, for the two men who might have evicted the settlers from Hebron could not come to the city. The Minister of Defence, Moshe Dayan, who was adamantly opposed to their presence, was in hospital after a trench on an archaeological dig had collapsed on him, and the coordinator of activities in the Occupied Territories was at home, observing the traditional eight-day mourning period for his father.

The other man who might have intervened was dead: if he had been alive, Haim Hanegbi said that Haim Bajaio 'would have left his home in the Abu Al-Bassel neighbourhood, on the outskirts of the Mahane Yehuda market in Jerusalem, to go and block Levinger with his body.' He was convinced that his grandfather would have wanted to see the revival of the Jewish community, but only on the understanding that 'Bajaio's Hebron' was also the Hebron of the Arab families of Natshe and Qawasmi and Ja'abri. 'Levinger is another story completely. He allows no fellow man to place a foot.'

Had Haim Bajaio confronted Levinger, 'the conflict between them would have been settled there and then', Hanegbi wrote, though he thought it was just as well his grandfather did not witness the national euphoria in the aftermath of the Six Day War: 'he would surely have lowered his head in disgrace, for the first time in his life, to bear witness to a Jew subjugating an Arab.' Levinger's presence in the city had had an unexpected effect on the old revolutionary himself: 'This tormented colonialist, perennially reeking of self-righteousness, awoke in me an urge of possessiveness; a truly deplorable inclination, which dictates that one must identify and cling to his property endlessly', he wrote. 'Against my wishes, Levinger made me a landlord. Where my late mother, God bless her soul, had failed time and again, he, of all people, succeeded.'

Hanegbi had seen a schematic map of the Jewish quarter of Hebron, which identified site number 43, north-west of Beit Hadassah, en route to the spring, as the 'home of the son of Haim and Bajaio', and he identified himself as its rightful owner: 'I am Haim Bajaio, the sole inheritor by law and religion.' He said that the Levingers acted 'like pimps', and 'spoke pretentiously in the name of the Hebron Jewish community, as if they were real estate agents or merchants'. Hanegbi wrote a letter to the Israeli newspaper *Haaretz*, in which he forbade anyone, and especially the Levingers, from claiming his family property in Hebron. He hoped 'to put a spoke . . . in the wheels of the settlers' carriage', though he knew he would not succeed, for the 'colonialists' were operating under military protection, and with the blessing of the government.

It isn't clear who proposed that the settlers should move to the Mandate-era compound on a hill near the northern entrance to the city, where the new Governor of Hebron had established the headquarters of the city's military administration. Khaled Qawasmi says that his uncle rang the Governor of Hebron who had stayed in the hotel at the end of the Six Day War, and asked him to remove the settlers, but David Wilder, who resents the Israeli government almost as much as he resents his Palestinian neighbours, believes it was Moshe Dayan's idea. The settlers were not sure that they wanted to be displaced to the 'Memshal', as they called the compound on the hill: 'A heated debate ensued', Wilder wrote. 'There were those who felt that moving to the compound would, in effect, strangle the project. Others saw in Dayan's suggestion official recognition, albeit de facto, of their goal.'

The pragmatists prevailed: in May 1968, the settlers moved into a wing of the Memshal, while the debate over their long-term future continued. In September, the Ministerial Committee on Hebron and Gush Etzion officially approved the establishment of a Jewish neighbourhood in the city, but three months later it changed its mind. In March 1970, the Knesset finally approved the construction of a new community on the western edge of Hebron, above the Tomb of the Patriarchs, which the settlers called Kiryat Arba, the other name by which Hebron is known in the Bible. Moshe Dayan feared the consequences: he 'begged the settlers not to seek conflict with their Arab neighbours', Martin Gilbert writes: '"Don't raise your children to hate them," he said.'

The departure of the settlers from the hotel did not mark the end of the Qawasmi family's involvement in their fate, for in 1976, Khaled Qawasmi's father, Fahed, was elected Mayor of Hebron. A year later, the Labour Party lost power in Israel for the first time, and the new Prime Minister, Menachem Begin, made his sympathies plain by his insistence that he would only refer to the West Bank as 'Judea and Samaria'. Emboldened by such support, the settlers of Hebron advanced their aim to re-establish a presence in the city: Moshe Levinger's wife, Miriam, said that they had always seen Kiryat Arba as a compromise forced on them by the government. 'Our wish was and still is settlement within Hebron,' she said, and one night in 1979 she and a group of

women and children entered Beit Hadassah through the windows in the basement, where the settlers later established a museum commemorating the Jewish presence in the city. 'Hebron will no longer be Judenrein,' she said.

According to Jerold S. Auerbach, Miriam Levinger 'was fulfilling a mission for her family members who were murdered in Auschwitz', but she was also honouring the memory of the victims of 1929: 'We thought that here we would redress the wrong, not out of reprisal and blood vengeance, but from within, rebuilding,' she said. At the end of their first Sabbath in Beit Hadassah, yeshiva students from Kiryat Arba came to dance and sing in the street outside the building, and she said that they felt that the souls of the victims of 1929 had gathered with them at the window to celebrate the sight. 'I wanted to calm them and say to them, "You can rest, you have waited many years, now we have returned. What was in the past in Hebron is what will happen in the future. Always!"'

The settlers were so 'determined to eradicate the shame of their murdered ancestors who had not defended themselves' that they had 'all but assumed the identity of the martyrs of 1929', Auerbach writes. It was not an auspicious beginning: the settlement was founded on the memory of violent Jewish death, and it secured its future through further Jewish deaths. Nine months after the Israeli cabinet voted by a majority of one to allow the women to remain in Beit Hadassah, a settler from Kiryat Arba was murdered in the market. Yet the settlers did not retreat: instead, they seized five more buildings that had once belonged to the old Jewish community of Hebron, including Beit Romano.

With settlers re-established in the centre of town, it fell to Fahed Qawasmi to lead the campaign against them, in both his capacity as mayor, and as a member of a proscribed organization called the National Guidance Committee. He was not opposed in principle to a Jewish presence in Hebron, his son told me – he believed that the descendants of the original Jewish community in Hebron had the right to return, and Haim Hanegbi said he personally received a warm welcome when he went to the city. Qawasmi told him that they would receive him 'with open arms', because he was a Hebronite and held all the rights of a Hebronite.

The settlers were a different matter: Dr Qawasmi said his father was opposed to them because they were part of the occupation. When the Israeli army attempted to suppress the unrest that followed the government's decision to allow the settlers to establish a yeshiva in Beit Romano by imposing a twelve-day curfew, Fahed Qawasmi spoke at a mass rally in the city: 'We have no choice but to put force against force,' he said. 'The Zionist empire will fall, just as the British Empire and Nazi Empire fell before her.' Sheikh Raja Bayud Tamimi, the city's chief justice, was even more provocative. He responded to the settlers' racist rhetoric with an inflammatory diatribe of his own: 'The Jews have to know that this land is Muslim and that it is entirely Muslim,' he said. 'We'll fight you, until you, the Jews, are wiped out.'

Yet the violence that ensued only led to further territorial expansion. On 2 May 1980, six yeshiva students were murdered on the footbridge outside Beit Hadassah as they returned from the Tomb of the Patriarchs after Shabbat prayers, and the settlers responded by claiming buildings in the Avraham Avinu neighbourhood: 'from each Jewish death in Hebron would come new Jewish life', writes Jerold S. Auerbach. The murder of 'the six' provoked a response from the Israeli authorities as well: the Israelis arrested Fahed Qawasmi, his colleague, the Mayor of Halhoul, and Sheikh Tamimi, and deported them to Lebanon.

The Qawasmis appealed against the decision, which was taken without due process, and Fahed was allowed to return briefly, before being deported again to Amman, the capital of Jordan. Dr Qawasmi told me that the rest of his family remained in Hebron for a year, before following his father to Jordan. His father used his connections to help him obtain a scholarship in the former Soviet Union, and he was taking a degree in civil engineering in Odessa, the capital of the Ukraine, when his father was assassinated in Jordan in 1984. Some reports blamed a splinter group of Yasser Arafat's Fatah movement, called Fatah Intifada: 'There was an internal Palestinian difference of opinions, and my father was standing on the side of Yasser Arafat,' Dr Qawasmi said. 'Syria was not satisfied with his position, and they decided to kill him.' I did not feel I could ask him any more: I didn't know whether he held the settlers responsible for his father's death, though even I could discern the links in the causal chain that led back to their arrival in the Park Hotel.

No doubt they could also be blamed for the fact that the Park Hotel had been forced to close in 1978. The building had been turned into apartments for the family. Ala Qawasmi had shown me around, and as we went up the staircase at the back of the hall he pointed out the front door of the flat where one of his grandmothers had lived. The lower stairs were strewn with grit, which turned into chunks of plaster and rubble as we went up. The ceiling was falling in and you could see the metal latticework through the rotting mortar.

The house now belonged to Dr Qawasmi's brothers and cousins. Dr Qawasmi had registered another NGO devoted to the task of cultural preservation in one of its apartments, and one of his brothers ran a jewellery workshop in a building at the back. We went through a door to the roof, and Ala showed us the new houses that had been built on the land behind the hotel. It was now unsafe, and they feared it might collapse. They were hoping to build a new one in its place.

One of the senior archaeologists on Yigael Yadin's excavation at Hazor was a man called Yohann Aharoni, who later founded the Department of Archaeology at Tel Aviv University. Before he began excavating at Hazor, he had conducted a pioneering archaeological survey of the hilly areas of Upper Galilee, where he discovered a group of unfortified hilltop settlements far from major Canaanite centres. He believed that the settlements were evidence that the entry of the Israelites into Canaan had been a social process, and not a military campaign: it was 'only after the arriving Israelite pastoralists had settled down to become farmers that they came into violent conflict with the Canaanites', Neil Asher Silberman says. For those who believed in the 'divinely directed triumphs' of the Joshua narrative, it 'was a disturbingly radical theory'.

It was also at odds with Yadin's interpretation of the finds at Hazor. The two men became involved in such a bitter dispute that they could barely speak to one another, though Silberman says they both made the same mistake: they 'endorsed the pivotal Biblical notion that the rise of early Israel was a unique, singular phenomenon in the history of the country'. Aharoni's theory of 'peaceful infiltration' has proved no more durable than Yadin's championing of the Joshua narrative, and yet Aharoni left a significant legacy in the form of the approach adopted at Tel Aviv University. Yadin was raised in the Jerusalem school of biblical archaeology, which has been described as excavating with the Bible in one hand and a trowel in the other, in the hope of validating the biblical portrait of a God who acts in history, while Aharoni adopted a more sceptical attitude to the Bible as a historical source. He also pioneered the use of archaeological surveys, like the one he conducted in Upper Galilee. One of Aharoni's students, Professor Moshe Kochavi, conducted the preliminary survey of Judea after the Six Day War, and one of Kochavi's students, in turn, surveyed the highlands of Judea and became the second man to excavate at Tel Rumeida.

Avi Ofer's parents were Ashkenazic Jews of European stock, and hence members of the pioneering caste who drove the Zionist movement in its early years. His paternal grandparents had fled Russia after the Revolution of 1917 and settled in Turkey, where his father was born. He emigrated to Palestine in 1944, when he was seventeen years old, and joined the Palmach, the guerrilla organization that Ofer described as 'the elite troop of the Jewish community, half underground, half official'. Ofer told me that he 'participated in the operations' of 1946 and 1947, though not surprisingly he did not offer any details, for the British rulers of Palestine regarded the resistance to their rule, to which he was referring, as a terrorist campaign. When the Palmach was folded into the Israeli army at the beginning of the 1948 Arab–Israeli War, Ofer's father became an officer, and he remained in the military for the rest of his career.

Ofer spent most of his childhood in Tel Aviv, though the family had moved to Paris for a posting at the time of the Six Day War, and he was mobilized in October 1973, at the end of the campaign Israelis call the Yom Kippur War, when Israel repulsed the attack by a coalition of Arab states hoping to recapture some of the territory lost in 1967. He had already begun a degree in philosophy at Tel Aviv University, and when he resumed his education in 1977, after three and a half years' service, he walked past the Department of Archaeology, and decided that it looked interesting. 'And so quite by hazard I decided to become an archaeologist,' he told me, when I met him at his home on a kibbutz near Tel Aviv.

I had not been able to find his name on the published lists of faculty members at Tel Aviv University, and I had emailed Moshe Kochavi, who told me I could reach him at Kibbutz Ma'anit. Since I did not have an email address or a phone number, I had resorted to an old-fashioned form of communication, and Ofer's reply, thanking me for my 'snail-mail letter', hinted at the direction his career had taken: he worked in Israel's burgeoning high-tech industry, and when I met him in the fenced car park overlooking an open field on the perimeter of the kibbutz one afternoon, he had an Intel ID attached to his belt.

He was fifty-three years old, a tall, slender man, with dark curly hair, casually dressed in jeans, trainers and a dark green shirt. The house was a hundred yards away. Inside, the main room felt cool and clean. It was furnished with two orange sofas and a wall of glass-fronted bookshelves. There were rugs on the tiled floor, and an upright piano in the corner. A set of French windows opened onto a small garden with a pond. He laughed when I explained my interest in Tel Rumeida: 'It is very complicated. Much more complicated than anything you find in England.' It was a source of pride as well as frustration. I was not the first to ask him about Tel Rumeida, he said, and he talked about it fluently, and with little prompting. His military service had damaged his hearing and I had to repeat everything I said. His voice wasn't harsh or incapable of conveying feeling, but it had become rather flat and unmodulated as he became less aware of other voices.

He was proud of his accelerated progress through the Israeli academic system: he had finished his degree in 1980, and Tel Aviv University had authorized him to begin his Ph.D. straight away. 'It's not very common – usually, you're supposed to write your Masters first, but they trusted me, and also the subject was the subject for a Ph.D.'

He began his survey in 1981, in the middle of what proved to be a brief window of opportunity. These days, the West Bank is so partitioned that no Israeli will leave the fortified world of settlements and security roads, and no Palestinian will enter it without permission, unless intent on harm, but in the twenty years between the end of the Six Day War and the outbreak of the First Intifada, both groups mingled relatively freely – even the settlers of Hebron used to catch the local bus to Al Khalil. Ofer normally went out on survey duty on his own, or accompanied by colleagues or students. He always carried his army rifle, but he kept it hidden in a bag, because he did not want to appear 'amongst the Palestinians' armed. Even so, his work was interrupted by yet another crisis.

It is often said that Israel's invasion of Lebanon in 1982 was the first war of choice it had ever fought. It was directed by the Defence Minister, Ariel Sharon, who had made his name as a brilliant, brutal and notoriously insubordinate soldier, and whose subsequent political career had been devoted to advancing the settlers' cause. According to Avi Shlaim, Sharon believed that he could reshape the political map of the Middle East by driving Yasser Arafat's Palestinian Liberation Organization out of Beirut, and starting 'a chain reaction that would eclipse all of Israel's enemies': crushing the PLO would put an end to Palestinian resistance to Israeli rule in the West Bank and Gaza, and the influx of Palestinians into Jordan would 'sweep away the Hashemite monarchy and transform the East Bank into a Palestinian state', bringing an end to international pressure on Israel to withdraw from the Occupied Territories, and facilitating the creation of Greater Israel.

Ofer did not approve of the war, for he was an active member of Peace Now, an organization which had been set up in 1978 by a group of reservists who wrote to Begin urging him to 'accept an exchange of territories for peace', but he dismissed the suggestion that he might have refused to serve in the campaign: 'We have to defend ourselves against our enemies, and the Palestinians are our enemies – we don't deny it, like the extreme left, who are not realistic. But we say, OK this is the enemy, and with the enemy we are making peace: with the enemy we are making war, and with the enemy we are making peace.' He used to come back from Lebanon, take off his uniform and join demonstrations. Once, when he joined a march from the Lebanese border to Tel Aviv, he got changed behind a bush.

The war ended in catastrophic circumstances: the Israelis seemed to have achieved their aim when they surrounded Beirut and forced the PLO cadres to leave for Tunis, but they found themselves drawn deeper into Lebanon's internal battles. The IDF occupied the areas of West Beirut that had been controlled by the PLO, and on 16 September 1982, Ariel Sharon ordered the soldiers guarding two refugee camps called Sabra and Shatila to permit a group of Christian Phalangist guerrillas to enter. They were supposed to be searching for PLO fighters implicated in the assassination of the Christian Prime Minister, Bashir Gemayel, but during the next two days they murdered many hundreds of men, women and children. The exact number of dead has never been established, though the Palestinian Red Crescent placed it at over two thousand. The Israelis were accused of complicity in the massacre, and the official Israeli government inquiry recommended that Ariel Sharon should never be allowed to hold office. The longer-term consequences of the war were also disastrous: Sharon's strategy had disintegrated with the death of Gemayel, whom he had promoted as Prime Minister of Lebanon, and the military campaign ended in a bloody stalemate, as Israeli troops found themselves mired in a guerrilla war in southern Lebanon. Sharon's war of aggression had cost thousands of lives, dissipated the goodwill Israel had acquired in the Arab world and inspired the birth of a guerrilla movement called Hezbollah, which has threatened its northern border ever since.

The war marked a turning point in Avi Ofer's life as well, for he met his partner, Shlomit, in the course of the campaign: she was an administrative officer in his base, and they met when he was called up at the beginning of the war, and again when he was mobilized for the siege of Beirut.

Shlomit lived on kibbutz Ma'anit, which was owned by the Marxist–Zionist youth movement to which Ofer's mother had belonged in Romania as a child, and in 1984 he moved into the kibbutz. For the next few years he worked night shifts in the fructose factory outside the gates and helped run the Tel Aviv branch of Peace Now, while he continued his survey of the Judean highlands. In total, he covered some 800 square kilometres, and surveyed 240 square kilometres in detail. It was normal practice to complement a survey with longer excavations in a key site. To begin with, he said he wouldn't have dared dig at Hebron, for he was only twenty-eight years old, and he was still writing his Ph.D., but when the opportunity arose he could not turn it down.

He did a test dig in 1983, and in 1984 he began a full season of excavations. He was working on the eastern slopes of the tel on 18 August when the settlers brought their caravans up the hill and placed them on the land. Some reports maintained that the settlers had been drawn by news that Ofer had discovered David's palace, but he said they were unaware of the site's significance: 'It's really quite absurd, but those fundamentalist fascist settlers who came in the name of the Bible, claiming that God gave us the whole land, didn't know that Tel Rumeida was ancient Hebron.' They knew that Hebron was David's city, of course, but to them Tel Rumeida was just a hill. More than twenty years later he was still frustrated by his failure to prevent them – all he would have needed was a day's notice, but by the time he found out, it was too late: 'They were there, and once they were there, it was impossible to take them out.'

I never met Philip Hammond, the first archaeologist who dug on Tel Rumeida, because he died in 2008, but two years later I met the man who inherited the record of his excavations. Professor Jeffrey Chadwick – the Jerusalem Center Professor of Archaeology and Near Eastern Studies at Brigham Young University, in Provo, Utah – was a Mormon from the Midwest state of Utah who had first been drawn to Israel by the dramatic events of the Six Day War. As a twelve-year-old boy, he had been astonished to discover that the country he had learnt about in Sunday school classes was a real place, and that it was in a fight for its life: 'That was like bringing Greek mythology into modern times for me, except it was biblical stories. I just went: *What is that?*' The enthusiasm of his younger self was effectively conveyed.

It was a sweltering August afternoon at the end of the

summer season of excavations, and we were sitting on wicker chairs on the terrace at the back of the W. F. Albright Institute of Archaeological Research in East Jerusalem. It was an appropriate place to meet, for both Jeffrey Chadwick and Philip Hammond had studied and taught at the Albright Institute. It used to be known as the American School in Jerusalem, but it had been renamed in 1970 after the great American archaeologist who defined the practice of 'biblical archaeology'. Today, biblical archaeology has fallen out of fashion: most archaeologists prefer to talk about the broader discipline of 'Syro-Palestinian archaeology', though since Jeffrey Chadwick is a 'person of faith', he does not disown the term. 'I have no problem with the idea of being a biblical archaeologist, though it would be a sub-component of my whole,' he said. 'I'm an archaeologist: I'm a biblical archaeologist when the archaeology I do intersects with biblical places, biblical times, or in some other sense, with biblical studies.'

Not surprisingly, he rejects the idea that faith is incompatible with intellectual enquiry. He concedes that religious people have to be open-minded about aspects of their traditions, but the scientific community, to which he also belongs, is constantly adjusting its views as well: 'Look at any scientific journal and you'll see they're saying that what we thought five years ago ain't so. Science doesn't have truth: it pursues truth.' To the objection that religion does the opposite by enshrining dogma in place of free enquiry, he says that Mormons maintain the 'glory of God is intelligence', which is why the Church has funded a university and tenured its faculty: 'The belief of the ecclesiastical leaders is that nothing that can be discovered that is really truth would undermine the notion of the existence of God. They're that secure. So we have perhaps some of the top DNA scientists

in the world working for us. And one crazy Israeli archaeologist.'

I was surprised to hear him describe himself in such
terms, but he only qualified his commitment to his adopted
country on a technicality: 'I'm not Israeli by citizenship, but
I feel very much a part of the land and the country. I speak
the language, I've lived years and years here. I'm probably
more comfortable in Israel than in Utah.'

He was an upright man, with a full head of hair that was
just turning grey. I had seen a photograph of him standing
on top of the gate-tower in the south-east corner of the hill,
but I did not know that it had been taken twenty years
before. He was older than I expected and yet he looked
younger than fifty-five: 'Appreciate it,' he said when I
expressed my surprise. 'It's not the years, though: it's
the mileage.' His wife jokes that he commutes between 'the
Near East and the Far West', for he lives in a small dairy
town in Utah called Farr West, but has made the network of
religious, educational and archaeological institutions established by a previous generation of Christian missionaries
and archaeologists in East Jerusalem his second home.

Such a profession of loyalty made him an unlikely candi-
date for the role of Professor Hammond's executor and heir,
for Hammond was an honorary Jordanian, who regarded
Israel as an illegitimate presence in Arab land. Yet the fact
that they had taken different sides on the most intractable
and contentious dispute of their time did not stop them
being friends: 'He was the quintessential son of the desert,
and I was the quintessential Zionist dog,' Professor Chadwick said. 'It was an odd collaboration, but it was a great
honour.'

When they met in 1986, Hammond had been digging at
Petra, in Jordan, for fifteen years. He had long since given

up hope of going back to Hebron, but was looking for
someone who understood the latest developments in archaeology in Israel to make sense of the unpublished records of
his excavations. Chadwick seemed the perfect choice. He
knew Tel Rumeida, because he had got into the habit of
wandering round it when he went to Hebron, and he had
seen Hammond's trenches and met Avi Ofer in the field.
Chadwick said that Hammond had 'winced' when he told
him he had been studying at the Hebrew University in
Jerusalem, but nonetheless he offered him the chance to
write up his notes for his Ph.D. 'It was like a gift on a golden
platter,' Chadwick said: 'No one could have turned it down.'

Chadwick's greatest contribution was to identity the
structure Hammond had excavated on the south-east corner
of the hill. He had not realized it was a gate-tower, and when
Chadwick showed him the plan he had had drawn, he had
gazed at it in chastened silence for a moment: '"By God,
you're right," he said. "How did I not see this?"' Chadwick
was so determined to defend his patron's reputation that
he dismissed his self-reproach, saying that even Albright
couldn't have seen it in 1966. He was much more critical of
Avi Ofer's interpretation of his most important find.

During his final season of excavations, in 1986, Ofer dug a
long trench on the east side of the hill that he designated 'S'
for slope: it begins on the second highest terrace and runs
towards the Tomb of the Patriarchs until it meets the path
that leads through the olive grove from the gate-tower to
the house with the prow-shaped garden where Mi'chael
Zupraner lived. Trench S has never been filled in, though
the stones that pour off the surrounding walls blur its out-
line, and the rubbish that drifts across the hill collects like

standing water in its hollows. Near the point where it crosses the city wall, Ofer discovered 'the most important structure in the area' – a room that was 'used to collect ashes, animal bones and potsherds'. It contained the 'remains of sacrifices and of the vessels used for preparing and eating the sacrificial animals', and a document that Ofer coded TH1: it was the right half of a 'well-baked clay tablet', originally 7 centimetres by 9 centimetres, and inscribed with a list of 'sheep or goats fit for sacrifice' in 'Akkadian cuneiform' and 'early Babylonian'. It was very significant, Ofer wrote, for it showed that 'a small outlying town like Hebron apparently had a king, an orderly administration and a scribal school of a high standard.'

He dated the tablet to the Late Middle Bronze Age, c.1600 BCE, which he describes as a 'flourishing period' in Canaanite Hebron. Many of the cities of the Judean highland were subsequently destroyed, and Ofer believes that they were abandoned during the Late Bronze Age, c.1250 BCE, when Joshua is supposed to have led the Israelite conquest of Canaan. 'The late Bronze Age in the Judean Highland is a void', he has written. The implications for Yadin's attempts to verify the Joshua narrative are obvious: if cities like Jericho, Ai, Hazor and Hebron were abandoned when the Israelites were supposed to have conquered them, then the Joshua narrative cannot be true.

Professor Chadwick's response to Ofer's claims was dismissive: in the first place, Ofer was wrong to say that the highlands of Judea were abandoned in the Late Bronze Age. 'There is Late Bronze at plenty of places,' he told me. 'We have Late Bronze in Jerusalem: lots of it. We have Late Bronze at Schechem. We have Late Bronze at Bethel. If Avi said that the major sites along the Judean highlands don't have Late Bronze Age evidence, he's simply not representing the current state of the science. I don't know how to be gentle about that. Avi is wrong on this issue – he's absolutely wrong.' What's more, he was wrong about Hebron. Philip Hammond's dig had confirmed that there was 'Late Bronze' at Hebron: 'Avi's conclusion that there wasn't is blatantly incorrect – and I say that with all the respect I can have for a colleague.'

Since Ofer had not seen Hammond's unpublished data, he could not have known that Hammond had found evidence of Late Bronze Age in four sites on the tel, but Chadwick maintains that Ofer had evidence of it in his sites as well, most notably in the room in 'Trench S' that formed 'part of the cult complex of Canaanite Hebron'. The law of stratigraphy, one of the fundamental disciplines of archaeology, states that a layer or stratum is dated by the latest pottery it contains, and Chadwick said that Ofer found painted pottery that he described 'as being of the tradition of the thirteenth century BCE' on the same surface as the sheep tablet. 'The late thirteenth century BCE is the Late Bronze Age, but because he maintains there is no Late Bronze Age, he wouldn't call it Late Bronze pottery.' Chadwick believed that Avi Ofer knew what he had found, and chose not to say: 'You can't call it painted pottery of the thirteenth century BCE, and be a competent archaeologist, and fail to recognize it as LB pottery. I think he was being deliberately and evasively vague.'

Ofer's conclusions influenced the archaeologist who dated the sheep tablet itself: Nadaav Namaan said that there were certain elements in the language of the tablet that would have led him to date it to the Late Bronze Age, but since the excavators reported that there was no Late Bronze in Hebron, he dated it to the Middle Bronze Age. Professor Chadwick laughed: 'So Nadaav Namaan recognized that

this tablet probably should have been dated to the Late
Bronze Age but chose to date it to the Middle Bronze
because Avi Ofer, with whom he was working, had decided
that his thirteenth-century painted pottery couldn't be
ascribed to the Late Bronze Age either. Why? Because
neither one of them wants there to be a Late Bronze Age
in Hebron. Why? Here's the reason.' With the theatrical
skill of the practised lecturer Chadwick paused before he
delivered his conclusion: 'Science can sometimes become
the victim of a political agenda.'

Professor Chadwick does not believe that Ofer deliberately set out to misrepresent the data, but he believes that he
had been influenced by an attitude fashionable in the 1980s,
when 'a certain segment of intellectual society' reacted
against the way that the Joshua narrative had been used to
justify 'what some people viewed as the excesses of the
Zionist adventure'. If he was right to suggest that the prac-
titioners of the school of Tel Aviv had subconsciously
conspired to suppress evidence that might be seen to con-
firm the conscious myth-making of men like Yigael Yadin,
then they had, no doubt, fallen short of the standards of scientific objectivity to which they aspire. And yet Ofer's
assessment of the relationship between the Jews and the
land, and the political arrangements that he supported,
seemed to me reasonable and fair.

Before I left their house, Ofer and Shlomit said they were
going to take me on a tour of their very own archaeological
site, and we drove round the outskirts of the kibbutz, and
walked up the hill that overlooked a collection of cowsheds
and offices. Local legends maintain that the rebellion of 66
CE started on the hill, and in 1948 it marked the furthest
point of the Iraqi army's advance. A line of half-filled-in
trenches ran across the eastern slope, and the eastern face of

the pillbox on the summit was pitted with bullet holes. The border with the Territories was only a mile away, but the call to prayer drifting through the trees was coming from a Palestinian village inside Israel.

Far below, we could see the red and white trails of the cars on the motorway that ran between the sea and the hills, following the ancient road to Egypt. A line of misshapen white stones ran across the hill: one of them appeared to be a gatepost, and Ofer showed me the groove in both sides that would have held the bolt. He thought it might have been a synagogue or a rich man's house, and lamps with seals adorned with menorahs had been found on the land – there was evidence of Jewish presence everywhere you looked, he said, and anyone who denied it was ignorant or prejudiced. Yet that did not give the Jews the right to possess it all: 'We left, and other people settled here. Once we came back, they began to define themselves as Palestinians – before, if you had asked them, they would say they were Syrians or just Arabs, but so what? They are people, they are living here, and they have traditions – not three-thousand-year-old traditions, but still traditions. It's their country also. So we have to divide it between us.'

Ofer believed that he had a much stronger attachment to Hebron than the settlers and yet he was prepared to give it up. He had finished the basic stage of the survey by 1987. He did not have a budget for further excavations, but even if he had he would not have been able to go back to Hebron, for the events of the First Intifada made it too dangerous. The Arab–Israeli conflict had shut down Philip Hammond's excavations in Hebron after three seasons, and twenty years later it had also shut down Avi Ofer's. He returned to kib-butz Ma'anit, where he resumed night shifts and wrote his Ph.D. He finished his thesis, 'The Highland of Judah During the Biblical Period', in 1992, the year his son was born, and submitted it in 1993. There was no position at Tel Aviv University, and he began teaching at the University of Haifa in 1994 or 1995, but soon afterwards he encountered unexpected problems in his academic career. He had brought the subject up but he would not go into any more detail, except to say that 'internal academic political issues' had prompted him to leave Haifa in 1998 and join the high-tech industry. He became an 'expert of software quality', which made good use of his academic training. He enjoyed the work, and he was relieved to have escaped academia, but his survey and his excavations in Tel Rumeida were left partially completed: he said he left and never went back, but that was not strictly true. He had already told me that he had gone back to Tel Rumeida in 1999 and attempted to resume his excavations in the most unpropitious circumstances.

CHAPTER SIX

FOUR MOTHERS

'It's no accident, you know, that we're called Jews and this place is called Judea – there may even be some relation between those two things. We are Jews, this is Judea, and the heart of Judea is Abraham's city, Hebron . . . If anything is territorialism, if anything is colonialism, it's Tel Aviv, it's Haifa. This is Judaism, this is Zionism, right here where we are eating our lunch!'

Philip Roth, *The Counterlife*

Khalil Bhitar remembers 'every single second' of the morning of 25 February 1994, when Baruch Goldstein entered the Yitzhak Hall in the Tomb of the Patriarchs and opened fire on the worshippers. Khalil, who had grown up opposite the Ibrahimi Mosque, in a house built after the Jordanian government cleared the area, was nine years old. There had been trouble the night before when he had gone to pray – some of the settlers had been banging on the doors of the mosque with their guns: such disturbances were not uncommon, but his mother 'felt something', and told him not to go to *isha'a*, the last prayer of the night. He did not go to *fajr*, the first prayer in the morning, either. They heard people shouting from across the square and they knew that something was wrong. His parents would not let him go down to see what was happening, for many of their friends and neighbours were emerging in the street, bloodied and weeping. He remembers ambulances arriving from Ramallah and Jenin, and taking people away. He knew many of the victims. One was a childhood friend: 'One day we were playing football together, and the next, Kamal is dead.' The fathers of several of his friends from school were killed and so were many of his parents' friends.

In a way, it did not come as a surprise: Khalil was used to seeing settlers with guns in the streets of Hebron. 'Every day in my area, someone holds a gun in front of your face, and says they want to shoot you, or they learn some Arabic words, and they swear at you in Arabic, and spit on you.' Appropriately, given his name, Khalil was the first Khalili I spoke to. He was studying in London and we met in a cafe near the Clerkenwell campus of City University a month before I first went to the West Bank. Someone had put on a Led Zeppelin CD, and the strains of 'Whole Lotta Love' almost drowned out his descriptions of life in his home-town.

If they left their shutters open at night, the settlers would stone the house, and smash the windows, or the settlers would go into town and start shooting. He used to see Rabbi Levinger going past his house to pray in the Tomb of the Patriarchs, and people used to say that he was the Pales-tinians' 'biggest enemy': 'They say this guy is the most aggressive. And he's the leader in this area – the most extremist Zionist you can ever imagine, and he lives in Hebron.' Khalil laughed: it was a compliment of a kind. 'Nowhere else. He could live in Jerusalem, which you'd think is more famous for them, but no, his mission is Hebron. And he won't live in Kiryat Arba, either, because that's too far away: he has to live in the centre of town.'

The Israeli authorities are notoriously lax when it comes

to policing the settlers' activities, but Rabbi Levinger has not escaped their attention. He has been charged several times with assaulting Palestinian women and children and Israeli soldiers, and he was once charged with manslaughter for shooting and killing a shopkeeper in Hebron. On 30 September 1988, Levinger was being driven through the city by one of his sons, when the windscreen of their car was shattered by a stone. 'The defendant's son continued driving until they reached an Israeli army checkpoint manned by two soldiers,' the indictment said:

> The defendant reported the incident to the soldiers, asked them to send a patrol to the site, and waited next to his parked car for the patrol to arrive at the checkpoint. As they waited, stones were thrown at the checkpoint by two groups of youths located at the upper part of the street, to the north of the checkpoint, and by a group located to the south of the checkpoint . . . The defendant pulled out his pistol, a 9mm Beretta . . . advanced a few steps to the north, toward the rise of the road, and fired two or three shots in the air. The defendant then turned toward the south and advanced downhill.

Qa'id Hasan Salah had not been throwing stones: he was standing 'by the show window' outside his shop, showing girls' shoes to a customer whose daughter was waiting inside as Levinger came towards him, firing 'toward the shops and the sidewalks on both sides of the street.' Both Qa'id Hasan Salah and his customer were hit, and the shopkeeper 'was seriously wounded by a bullet that tore through his body'. Levinger 'advanced along the sidewalk . . . overturned some crates containing fruits and vegetables, threw saplings, dumped the merchandise on the ground, damaging the items and their wrappings, and shouted at the merchants to close their shops immediately.' Qa'id Hasan Salah died of internal bleeding.

When he was brought to trial Levinger read out an extraordinary statement on the steps of the court: 'As far as the substance of the case goes, the State Attorney's Office knows that I am innocent and that I did not have the privilege of killing that Arab – not that I may not have wanted to kill him or that he did not deserve to die, but I did not have the privilege of killing that Arab.'

When his case came to trial, settlers demonstrated outside the courthouse, and Levinger appeared carrying an effigy of the Justice Minister holding scales tilted toward the left, as if only his political opponents would seek to prosecute the crime. Following a plea bargain, the original charges of manslaughter and doing serious harm were dropped, but he was convicted of causing death by negligence, wounding in aggravated circumstances and doing malicious damage. In his summing up, the judge claimed that 'despite the defendant's unfortunate statement in a press interview', Levinger did not think that 'the Jews who have settled in Judea and Samaria have an innate right to take the law into their hands'. Yet the use of the biblical terms denoted his sympathies for the settlers' cause: 'The defendant is a prominent individual and the father of eleven children,' he said. 'His primary concern and care, for some twenty years, has been the interest of the public he leads . . . However, since the incident did occur, and he chose to make his own law, the punishment that the court decrees on him must express "the value placed on human life as such . . . otherwise it could be construed as acceptance of a norm of behavior which is intolerable."'

Given such an evasive and conciliatory appraisal, the leniency of the sentence could not have come as a surprise – Judge Brenner sentenced Levinger to twelve months in prison, seven of which were suspended. Noting that he had been on trial on eight other occasions with 'previous convictions for assault, criminal trespass, and causing malicious property damage', the judge refused to let him serve his punishment doing community work. He served three months in prison.

Even Levinger's most devoted defenders did not attempt to conceal his abrasive character: 'he had proven to be a formidable, indeed irrepressible, leader – and provocateur', writes Jerold S. Auerbach. One journalist called him 'a dervish', and another commentator said 'he looks like a tormented Biblical prophet and lives like a monk'. According to Auerbach, 'he was unafraid to roam, at night and unarmed, through the forbidding Arab casbah. There, oblivious to danger, he might sit on the ground, lead prayers, and conduct a Torah lesson. "Gaunt, careless of his appearance," a visitor wrote, "he seemed unconcerned about anything but his mission to settle the Land of Israel."'

Philip Roth portrayed him as a messianic rabbi called Mordecai Lippmann, in his brilliant 1986 novel, *The Counterlife*. 'I smell fascism on people like Lippmann,' a journalist from Tel Aviv says to Roth's narrator, the novelist Nathan Zuckerman. 'There is now so much antagonism between Arab and Jew that even a child would understand that the best thing is to keep them apart – so Mr Lippmann drives into Arab Hebron wearing his pistol. Hebron! This state was not established for Jews to police Nablus and Hebron!'

Yet Levinger was not the only violent extremist amongst the settlers. One of the first residents of the caravans on Tel

Rumeida was a man called Baruch Marzel, who had been a follower of Levinger most of his life: like many of the settlers of Hebron he was born in America, but his family emigrated to Israel when he was a child, and his parents took him to see Levinger in the Park Hotel when he was four or five years old. Marzel's career as an 'activist' started early: according to a self-written biography posted online, he was arrested for the first time at the age of fourteen for blocking traffic when Henry Kissinger came to Israel to finalize the arrangements for returning the Sinai peninsula to Egypt under the Camp David peace accords, and he claimed to have been one of the activists who resisted the subsequent evacuation of the Jewish settlements.

His conviction meant that he was not called up to serve in the invasion of Lebanon in 1982, but he was 'determined to volunteer at any cost', and he hitchhiked to Lebanon and 'fought in the central district in a tank'. The idea of Israeli tanks manned by hitchhikers seems no less improbable than Marzel's subsequent account of his wartime escapades, which he describes in the heroic third person: 'He was one of the first to take over the Beirut–Damascus Highway. During the conquest he identified a number of Syrian commandos. Taking decisive action, he charged toward them and killed seven of the commandos . . . he was injured by a grenade thrown at him, but after receiving medical treatment he returned to the tank and participated in the conquest of the fortress-like Beirut National Museum.'

Hashem Al Azzeh, the Palestinian man who has the misfortune to live in the house directly beneath his caravan, described him as the 'most aggressive man in Israel', and many Israelis concur. An IDF reservist who served in Hebron in 1993 reported that he had displayed a sign outside his caravan that emulated the callous attitude Levinger had displayed to 'the Arabs' on the steps of the court-room: 'I have already killed an Arab', it said. 'What about you?'

The same reservist said he saw Marzel's children throw-ing stones at 'Arab kids', and one day, when he was driving towards Tel Rumeida, he was stopped by a Palestinian man, who said that Marzel had 'beaten his son, stepped on him, and kicked him'. The man was crying, and the boy, who was no more than three years old, was unconscious. The soldier asked the company commander to intervene. He wanted to be given permission to take the boy to hospital, but the Palestinian man was afraid to tell his company commander that Baruch Marzel had hit his son. The army informed the police but they did nothing: 'I am ready to go to Hebron, find the father, and testify against Baruch Marzel, only to clear my conscience about the incident,' the soldier told the Israeli human rights organization B'Tselem.

Marzel's casual brutality is complemented by his rebar-bative political beliefs. He claims that he has devoted his life to reviving 'the values of our forefathers, who led us into this Land and fulfilled the prophecies which promised us that we would be a great nation', though his political career has hardly been a great success. He was the parliamentary assistant to the racist rabbi Meir Kahane, and when Kahane was assassinated in New York in 1990, Marzel became the head of the 'Kach secretariat'. Yet the organization's public life was coming to an end: after the massacre in the mosque, the Israeli authorities and US State Department listed Kach as a terrorist organization and banned it from participating in elections.

The fact that Marzel later set up an organization called Hazit, or the Jewish National Front, did not surprise Khalil, who said that Palestinian extremists flourish in Hebron as

well: the city elected nine Hamas representatives in the last
elections, and it is home to the three leaders of Hizb ut-
Tahrir, a party that calls for the re-establishment of the
Islamic caliphate that ruled the Middle East in the centuries
after the death of the Prophet. 'It's a worldwide movement,
but it's led by Hebronites.' Khalil laughed again as he
contemplated the absurdities of his hometown: 'Some Palestinians talk as if they were fourteen hundred years ago. In
Hebron, you are not allowed to open a cinema: they think
of it as evil. It's quite weird for me . . . why stop people
watching movies?' The stereotypical view of the Khalilis was
contradictory – how could they be stupid and yet commer-
cially astute? – but his family used to joke about the way the
settlers appeared to live up to it: 'We used to say they were
born in Hebron, so what do you expect from them? They're
crazy. They're Khalilis. You can't do anything about them.
They both have the same ideology, the Palestinians and
Israelis in Hebron.'

He had often witnessed Palestinian violence against the
settlers, as well as the other way round – during the Second
Intifada, Palestinian gunmen used to shoot at the settlements
from Jebel Abu Sneineh, the hill behind Tel Rumeida, and
since their house was an obstacle in the line of fire, ambulance crews would provide emergency treatment to the
victims in the square in front of it. He was not just a spec-
tator, either: as a child he often fought with the settlers'
children: Israelis often say that Palestinians teach their children to hate them, but Khalil believed the reverse was true.
The settlers' children fought so ferociously because they had
been taught to imbue 'the Arabs' with mystical powers of
evil: their books said that you have to be wary of an Arab,
even if you've killed him – 'forty years after you killed him,
still be careful of him'.

Khalil had reason to fear the soldiers, too. One day a soldier asked his neighbour to give him a ball, because he wanted to play with them, and when he refused he shot him in the leg. They often set up military posts on the roof of their house, because it had a good view of the area. Khalil believed that many of them were intimidated by the settlers. 'They were very aggressive with them – they'd even try to hit them with their cars, and they'd look at them as sheep, because they are the settlers, they are the people who are protecting Israel.' No matter what they did the settlers would not be happy, and Khalil believed the soldiers felt the need to prove themselves by treating the Palestinians harshly.

'The basic problem was that the soldiers just didn't know how to handle the settlers,' said the IDF soldier who had reported Baruch Marzel's assault on the three-year-old boy. There were 'a few cases where settlers confronted officers, even the commander of the Cave of the Patriarchs, and told them how they should act.' One day, 'the Arabs' put up

flags in Uri Square and the settlers attacked them. Miriam Levinger and another woman entered 'the Kasbah', where they 'spat on Arabs and overturned carts'. The soldiers radioed for help: 'The Border Police came and separated the settlers and the Arabs, but they really gave it to the Arabs. They fired in the air above the heads of the Arabs, and they shoved and beat the Arabs. They never behave like that with settlers.'

The police were no more help: Khalil used to work in one of the gift shops opposite the Tomb of the Patriarchs, and the settlers' kids would often throw stones at the window: 'I would go to the police, but the police does nothing. They say, give me proof, did you take a picture of them? How can I take a picture of someone who breaks my glass?'

The kids also fought on the rooftops of the Old City, and when I got to Hebron I found a guide to their games in one of the nine children who lived in a house just inside the entrance to the covered alleyways of the souk. The family aren't allowed to close their front door: the army insists on having access to the house twenty-four hours a day; when I climbed the narrow, stale-smelling stairwell, past the dark, dusty rooms on the first floor, and the airier rooms above, to emerge on the roof, I could see why – it was directly above the Avraham Avinu settlement, and I found myself looking down on a bearded settler with an Uzi slung around his neck loading boxes into an ambulance parked amongst the rubble in the derelict market. My guide thought I would pay for such a sight: 'Just one shekel,' she whispered in my ear, over and over again, and every time I walked through the souk she would try to persuade me to go up on the roof again: 'Come, come, Israel!' she would say, as though intoning the opening lines of a hymn. One afternoon I went up on the roof again and saw kids running like high-wire artists along the narrow parapet, high above the rubble-strewn netting that covered the street below.

The undulating roofscape and the dark claustrophobic alleys seemed to belong to different realms. Ra-eed, the young Palestinian man who had told me about David, the settler with two wives, took me to his house on the edge of the Old City one afternoon. He was pushing a double-handed coffee cart, like an ornamental wheel-barrow, and as I followed him up the steep, cobbled streets I became aware of an acrid, bitter smell in the air. At first, I thought it was dust, but it got stronger the higher we went. Ra-eed said that some kids had lit a fire, and the smoke was billowing down-hill in great clouds, flooding the tunnel-like passages of the souk. A fireman was turning his hose into an open doorway, and reluctantly I followed Ra-eed into the choking darkness of the tunnel beside it. Halfway through, I took a breath, and could not taste any oxygen in the bitter smoke. I stumbled out of the tunnel, gasping and panicky, and by the time Ra-eed hauled me up onto his roof I was so disorientated that I could not understand how we had emerged beside the Tomb of the Patriarchs.

On another afternoon I was with John Lynes in the Christian Peacemaker Teams' offices, in the most lifeless corner of the Old City, between Shoada Street and Avraham Avinu, when someone came to the door to say that the set-tlers were stoning a shop. John Lynes said he was going to see what was happening, and set off with a delegation of potential CPT recruits in tow. We walked through the souk and turned into a house in the covered alleys. We climbed a winding staircase to a flat roof beneath an Israeli watch-tower, where at least a dozen CPT members had gathered.

John Lynes was engaged in a conversation with the soldiers above. It seemed that some of the Palestinian kids had been flying a kite that had gone close to the Israeli kids on the roof of the settlement, and they had thrown stones at it. The delegation struck a tactical retreat. We went down the stairs, through the alleys of the souk, and climbed a winding staircase to another vantage point amongst the roofs. When the soldiers spotted us they climbed down from their tower and began to make their way towards us, their equipment-laden forms moving with a jolting, robotic precision. I had never been so high before. I could see across town to the army tower and the silhouette of the ruined house on Abu Sneineh. The muezzin was issuing the call to prayer, and sprays of livid green light were leaking from beneath the hat-like turrets on top of the two minarets on the Tomb of the Patriarchs. There was still a thin line of pink cloud above Tel Rumeida, but the clouds elsewhere were losing their pearly sheen, and the air was getting colder. Tel Rumeida looked very calm in the evening sunlight, the clean, dark shapes of the graves on its lower slopes in sharp contrast to the rounded roofs and the circular satellite dishes that bloomed in the foreground. The offending kite flew above our heads, anchored by the invisible thread marking the divide between the two halves of the Old City of Hebron.

Most of the confrontations were minor affairs – what child would not enjoy chasing their enemies across the rooftops of the Old City? – yet they had the capacity to turn violent. Khalil said that most of the fights stopped when he and his contemporaries turned sixteen, not because they had become more mature, but because the stakes were higher: 'They had guns, and I didn't, so any fighter can kill me.

They don't want to kill me because they know they will go
to jail, and I don't want to fight them because I know I will
be killed.' Yet it was not just his personal confrontations that
were growing more extreme: he said that the city as a whole
had become much more tense, though no one imagined that
events would take the turn they did.

On 25 February 1994, the Israeli army was preparing to
withdraw from Gaza and Jericho, while the settlers were
attempting 'to defame the government, and concoct schemes
to thwart its moves. The call to "stop Oslo" and the commandment to salvage the land became their most urgent aim,'
write Idith Zertal and Akiva Eldar in *Lords of the Land: the
War Over Israel's Settlements in the Occupied Territories*.
'One settler, Dr Baruch Goldstein of Kiryat Arba, "delivered
his soul to his maker" before dawn on that wintry Friday in
February for the sake of the commandment. Before the
Jewish children had woken up for the Purim celebrations
. . . the religiously observant doctor, a native of Brooklyn,
donned his army reserve uniform, picked up an Uzi sub-
machine gun, and set out for the Tomb of the Patriarchs.' The
sentry recognized him, and refused to let him in. 'This was
not the first time Goldstein had entered the place when it was
closed to Jewish worship,' Zertal and Eldar write:

> '"I'm in charge here and I have to go in,' Goldstein said
> in Arabic, shoving the sentry with his rifle butt, pushing
> open the door and bursting into the mosque. While
> rising from the floor, the sentry heard a long burst of
> gunfire accompanied by cries of *Allahu Akhbar*. He
> rushed out to call for the help of the soldiers, who
> seemed to have evaporated, then ran back to the mosque,
> where Goldstein was still firing at the worshipers. At
> 5.15, as Goldstein was loading the fifth magazine into his

weapon, he was hit by a fire extinguisher thrown at him
by a worshiper. Goldstein collapsed. Other worshipers
fell upon the murderer and beat him to death.'

Naturally, conspiracy theories abounded: where were the
guards, and who reloaded his automatic rifle? Did he have
an accomplice? Three days later, Yitzhak Rabin told the
Knesset that Goldstein was 'alien to Judaism', but the residents of Hebron did not accept his verdict. Zertal and Eldar
quote an Israeli journalist who said that many of them
'reversed the order of events: they repress the fear of revenge
for the incident at the Tomb of the Patriarchs. Instead, they
speak about an event that was supposed to happen, which
Goldstein, in his insane act, succeeded in preventing.' The
'massacre of Muslim worshippers was perceived as . . . a
supreme act of sacrifice that prevented a new Holocaust'.
One account maintained that Goldstein was a descendant of
the Shnerson family that had survived the pogrom in 1929,
while his victims included descendants of the murderers
who had perpetrated the killings: 'Thus the immediate,
material connection was made between the two acts of
slaughter. The Brooklyn-born Jewish doctor's deed is perceived as the closing of a circle, as a great act of healing and
the restoration of order, if only temporarily. In requital for
the twenty-nine Yeshiva students and rabbis who were
slaughtered in 1929, Goldstein slaughtered the same number
of Muslim worshipers.' His friends portrayed him 'as a
healer of the poor and a rehabilitator of the miserable',
Zertal and Eldar write: "'His devotion to the inhabitants of
the area knew no bounds,"' they report one friend saying.
"'The man bought the poor and the depressed close to him
. . . He regularly worked with retarded children."' The
inscription on Goldstein's grave at Kiryat Arba declared he

'had sacrificed himself for the sake of Israel, his Torah and his land', and the grave became a place of pilgrimage until the Israeli government demolished it in 1999.

Rabin acknowledged that he ought to evacuate the settlers from Hebron, but he feared that doing so would incite a rebellion in the settlements of the West Bank. Some effort was made to restrain the most notorious settlers – Baruch Marzel was placed in administrative detention and kept under house arrest – but Rabin admitted he felt uncomfortable that the Palestinians had been placed under a curfew designed to ensure the safety of the 'murderer's neighbours and admirers'. On 19 March, he told his Foreign Minister, Shimon Peres, that he had decided to evacuate Tel Rumeida and Beit Romano, but the next day, he changed his mind. Peres said that coexistence in Hebron was impossible, but they could not abandon the settlers, and the official report into the massacre, which was published in June 1994, reinforced Israeli control of H2. The Tomb of the Patriarchs was divided into two, and the police presence in the area was expanded. B'Tselem reported that the army had established regular checkpoints with concrete blocks and barriers, and sealed many roads to Palestinian traffic. Khalil always had to go through three or four checkpoints to get home and, sometimes, he could not leave the house at all.

Khalil understood why so many people had left, and yet his family decided to stay, despite the fact that they owned another house in a more pleasant part of Hebron. Two of his six brothers and sisters have married, but they still live nearby, and his mother lives in the house where he grew up: 'Everyone does their resistance in their own way, and our own resistance is to stay in the house, and not let them take it.'

Yet he himself left Hebron soon afterwards: he missed

three months of school because of the curfew in the Old City, but he was determined to keep up with his work. 'I still have the power to be the first in my school.' He was at the best boys' school in Hebron, and he got the best results in his year. He won a place to study the International Baccalaureate at an international school called the United World College: he had a choice of going to Canada or America, but he chose Hong Kong. In 2003, he went home again, to study law in Jenin, in the north of the West Bank: it was the middle of the Second Intifada, and sometimes it took seven hours to travel to Hebron. He had another term to do to finish his degree when he came to the UK to study international politics.

Unlike many Palestinians he believed that the settlers have a right to live in Hebron. 'I believe that you have the right to live in any country, if you want to. At the same time, don't be aggressive. If you live in London and you're a terrorist, why do we need you here? Why do we give you rights? Same if you go to Hebron and you're holding a gun.' Besides, the settlers were not prepared to share the city on equal terms with their neighbours, and they were not content with reclaiming properties they used to own. 'They want also to take more, and every day you hear about a new house they buy or take. They want to have all Hebron.' Since he grew up opposite the Gutnick Center, he used to hear the triumphal song that the settlers broadcast every day through loudspeakers on top of the building, and he was baffled by the chorus 'Hebron, Hebron gilano – Hebron, Hebron is ours': 'Why yours? Why mine? Hebron is Hebron. Leave it in peace.'

He has lived in many countries around the world, but he still misses the house in front of the Tomb of the Patriarchs where he grew up: 'I love the history, I love the atmosphere;

even now, when there is no one there, because it's my child-hood, my history.' He loves the mosque, because of what it ought to stand for: 'Can you find any building in the world, where you can pray as a Christian, a Jew and a Muslim? Three faiths pray in the house of Abraham. The problem is who owns Abraham now? Everyone claims they have shares in Abraham. So we have to live together. We have to under-stand that we can live in the same city, we can go to the same mosque, we can do everything the same.'

For the time being, he has no plans to go back: 'I want to have my own life – I want to have a good life, you know, and I will come back when I am stronger. Now I want to do business. I might go to Dubai, or go back to Palestine and work there. I know it will be a lot harder – I can still work and do something, but now, after studying a long time away from home and everything, I don't want to come back to Israelis who are controlling my city and making my life harder, and Palestinians who are sometimes very harsh. The whole society, I see it as very backward.'

The repercussions of the massacre in the mosque were felt beyond the city. 'The murderer from Hebron opened fire on innocent people, but intended to kill the making of peace,' said the Israeli Prime Minister, Yitzhak Rabin. Less than six months earlier, Rabin and Yasser Arafat had signed a docu-ment that established a framework for limited Palestinian self-government and sketched out a path to statehood: the two sides had agreed in principle to partition the country, but before the next phase of the Oslo Accords were signed in May 1994 Hamas carried out its first suicide bombing inside Israel. One observer said that Goldstein's crime had persuaded Hamas to abandon the Islamic prohibition against causing indiscriminate harm against Israeli citizens, and another claimed that it 'directly and indirectly created the chain of suicide bombings and the appalling upward spiral composed of Israeli responses and Palestinian counter-responses.' The truth is more complex: the fact that the number of settlers nearly doubled between 1992 and 1995 suggests that Israel had never intended to relinquish the West Bank, and yet even so there were those who regarded Rabin's willingness to discuss the possibility of Palestinian statehood as treachery. 'It began after Goldstein,' Yigal Amir said after he shot Rabin at a rally in Tel Aviv on 4 November 1995. 'It's then that it dawned on me that one must put down [Rabin].'

Shimon Peres, Rabin's Foreign Minister, briefly succeeded him as Prime Minister, but Benyamin Netanyahu won the general election held in May 1996. Netanyahu had always been opposed to the idea of partitioning 'Eretz Israel' and there were fears that he would fail to meet Israel's obligation under the Oslo Accords initiated by Yitzhak Rabin: the IDF had left the West Bank cities of Jenin, Nablus, Tulkarem, Qalqiliya, Ramallah and Bethlehem in November 1995, and it was due to withdraw from 80 per cent of Hebron in January 1997.

The city found itself the focus of media attention again, and one day an Israeli woman called Yona Rochlin saw a newspaper story saying that the settlers had a map of the properties that used to belong to the Jews of Hebron. Since she was descended from two of Hebron's most significant Jewish families, she rang the journalist and asked if she could have a copy: 'It was a private call, really a private call,' she said when I met her at a cafe in a shopping mall near her home in Ranaana, a suburb of Tel Aviv. Yet the journalist was more interested in what she could tell him, for Hebron had suddenly become the most important city in the world: 'It was full of journalists, but nothing was happening, and all of a sudden, I open my mouth . . .' Yona Rochlin's laugh was a hoarse, throaty sound. The journalist rang her back, and asked her if she was prepared to be interviewed, and the next day her statement appeared in the paper beneath a bold headline: 'I don't want my son to die on my grandfather's grave'.

Fourteen years later, she described it as a peace statement: 'My son was about fifteen then, but whenever a child is born here you think about the army.' Yona was fifty-eight years old, and she had frizzy blonde hair and black glasses. Her English was far from fluent but very expressive, and she talked with engaging humour and directness. She was to get through at least half a dozen cigarettes in the course of the next two hours. We were sitting at an outside table within the glow of neon cast by the shop displays of the Kenon Arim mall. There were people drifting around the edges of the mall, like fish prospecting at the face of a reef, but there was no one sitting on the stone seats that ringed the empty plaza.

Yona had not meant to become involved in the debate over Hebron's future, but once she was she addressed the subject with what seemed like characteristic zeal. She does not like Hebron, and has no desire to live there, but she is proud of her connection with the Hasson and Mani families, for they occupy an important role in both the history of Jewish Hebron and the wider community of the Yishuv. Elijah Mani had come to Hebron from Iraq in 1856, and his son – Yona's great- or great-great-grandfather – was the Chief Rabbi of the Sephardic community. The second floor of Beit Hadassah was named after Suleiman Mani: 'Very Arabic names!' she said with another hoarse laugh. They did not have aristocrats in Israel – still don't – but if they did, the Mani family would have been amongst them. Even the Arabs regarded him as a '*haham*', or wise man. When he died in 1899, hundreds of Jews and Arabs attended his funeral, and the family had to post guards at his grave to stop the Arabs taking his body and re-burying him 'as one of their own'. Her grandmother's family, the Hassons, were no less integrated into Hebron's Arab life, and her grandparents lived in an Arab district of the city, rather than the Jewish quarter.

She used to joke that her father, who was born in 1912, was half Arab, for he spoke fluent Arabic and Ladino, and when she was growing up he always used to tell them that he wanted to go back to Hebron. Yona did not entirely believe he meant it – 'it was sort of a joke' – but she could see that it 'was a dream for him': Hebron seemed to exert the same hold on his imagination as it did on Haim Hanegbi's. Her father took her to the city for the first time in 1968, and she remembered the Arabs welcoming him 'like a brother': there were people stopping him in the street, and hugging him, and people crying. Yet on the same visit, her father went to see Rabbi Levinger in the Park Hotel, and told him he could have his family's properties in the Jewish quarter. 'He helped them,' she said. 'He belonged to the hard core of people who started the whole problem. He gave them the permission to stay – not that he had the official right, but who has?'

She believed that he would not have been so willing to help the settlers if he had known how vengeful and destructive they would prove to be, and as the debate over the city's future resumed, she did what she could to address the balance. In October 1996, she took a group of twenty-five descendants to meet the Mayor of Hebron. A couple of weeks later they published another statement in the press, saying that the settlers did not 'speak in the name of the old Jewish community' of the city, for their way of life was alien to that of 'the Hebron Jews, who created over the generations a culture of peace and understanding between peoples and faiths in the city'. Thirty-two descendants of some thirteen or fourteen families signed the statement, including Haim Hanegbi. Yona told a journalist at the time that it must have been a 'nightmare' for the settlers: 'they had been holding the history book of Hebron' for thirty years, and 'all of a sudden, we came out of the pages'. They had taken 'two days and ignored 500 years'.

Noam Arnon struggled to articulate a coherent response: he accused the petition's signatories of being agents of 'fanatical movements who want to destroy the Jewish existence in Hebron' and at the same time he dismissed them as a 'small group of leftist activists' who 'do not represent anything'. He accused the petitioners of 'bizarre activity to justify those who killed the Jewish community in 1929', and yet the only descendant of the old Jewish families of Hebron who supported the settlers' cause was a seventy-year-old man who had been less than a year old in 1929. Shlomo Slonim's father, Eliezer Dan Slonim, had been the director of the Anglo-Palestine Bank and a representative of the Jewish community in the Hebron municipality. The Arab mob had killed him and his wife and twenty-two people in their house with knives and machetes.

Yona's father's family had been more fortunate – 'by mistake, or by luck' they had left Hebron in 1929, because business was bad. Not all their relatives escaped. One of her father's uncles – a Hasson, and a rabbi – was killed. Her father's family moved to Jerusalem. Her grandfather had traded in fabric, which he went to Lebanon to buy; he

opened a shop in the Mahane Yehuda district of West
Jerusalem, where many of the Jewish refugees from Hebron
made their homes. Yona believed that they had attended the
same synagogue as Haim Hanegbi's grandfather, though she
was rather dismissive of Haim Bajaio's status: 'Really,' she
said, drawing on the proud heritage of the Hasson and Mani
families, 'they weren't that important then.'

Her mother's heritage was very different. She was not a
product of the Sephardic elite that dominated the old
Yishuv, but an Ashkenazic Jew from Riga, in the Baltic state
of Latvia, who had emigrated to Israel with her brother in
1934. Yona did not know when her parents got married –
there were many things about her mother's life that she did
not know. At first, she said they belonged to a generation
that did not talk much, and she and her brother 'were too
young and stupid to ask questions', but on reflection, she
said they did not ask for a reason: 'The past in my parents'
house was taboo because of the Holocaust. My mother left
her parents and her two sisters, and her aunts, and her other
relatives, and she survived alone with one brother – of
course we couldn't ask anything. And because we couldn't
ask her, we didn't ask my father.' It was a common trait
amongst the generation that had survived the Holocaust –
some of them became more prepared to talk as they got
older, but her mother always blamed herself for leaving her
family: 'So there was nothing to say.'

One thing she did know was that her father's family did
not want him to marry an Ashkenazic girl, which made
Yona laugh again: 'If you know the situation now in Israel,
when the Ashkenazim are the elite, then it's a joke. But it
didn't suit their class.' Her parents had other things in
common: neither was religious – Yona remembered being
ashamed that she was the only child at school whose father

never went to the synagogue – and both were right-wing.
Her mother was a member of Betar, the right-wing youth
movement established in her hometown by the prominent
Israeli politician Ze'ev Jabotinsky, who believed that the
Jews of Palestine could only negotiate with their Arab
neighbours from behind an impregnable 'iron wall', and her
father was one of the commanders of the Irgun, the militant
faction led by Menachem Begin that fought against British
rule in the last days of the Mandate. 'He was fighting your
father,' she said. It was said without reproach and yet with
such directness that I wondered if she knew something
about my family that I had forgotten.

Yet the Irgun did not confine themselves to fighting the
British, and Yona's father had a part in the *Altalena* affair,
which she called 'the most painful story in Israel's history'.
The *Altalena* was a ship purchased in Europe by Irgun fighters, and loaded with weapons donated by the French
government, which arrived on Israel's shores on 20 June
1948, at the beginning of the Arab–Israeli War. The Irgun
had been absorbed into the IDF, but the fate of the *Altalena*,
and the destination of its cargo, provoked a confrontation
between Begin and David Ben-Gurion, Israel's new Prime
Minister. Ben-Gurion wrote in his diary on 16 June 1948
that it contained '5,000 rifles, 250 Bren guns, 5 million bullets, 50 bazookas, 10 Bren carriers', and he ordered Begin,
who had boarded the ship at a beach north of Tel Aviv, to
hand over the weapons and 'cease his separate activities'.
When Begin refused to acknowledge the ultimatum, the IDF
shelled the ship and captured it by force. Sixteen Irgun fighters and three IDF soldiers were killed. Most of the several
hundred Irgun fighters who were arrested were released
after several weeks, but Yona's father, Moshe Hasson, was
one of five men who were kept locked up until the end of

August. He never forgave Ben-Gurion: 'He hated him,' Yona said. 'It was very personal.'

Unlike many of his colleagues in the Irgun, her father did not join the IDF, partly because he was in jail during the first part of the war, but his experience as a guerrilla helped him establish himself in the diamond business, which was dominated in the early years of the state by other Irgun fighters and immigrants from Antwerp. Yona was born in 1951, and she and her brother and sister grew up in Netayana, a coastal city north of Tel Aviv. Politically, the family's loyalties were divided – her mother's brother was a member of the Knesset for the right-wing party, Likud, but her mother's uncle, Abba Ben-Ya'akov, helped establish a kibbutz on the southern shores of the Sea of Galilee which was associated with Ben-Gurion's left-wing alliance, Mapai. Yet despite their contrasting allegiances, her mother's uncle and his family were the only relatives that she and her brother had left, and they were very close: her mother was the only person who was allowed to enter the kibbutz wearing the uniform of the right-wing youth group Betar 'because they loved her so much'.

Nonetheless, the political arguments were incessant: 'We were a very warm and loving family, but the political shouting, you know, was the sound of my childhood.' She was not interested in politics: she often visited the kibbutz, and she regarded her mother's uncle as the grandfather she never had, but she unthinkingly endorsed the right-wing views of her mother and father.

Yona was sixteen years old at the time of the Six Day War, and she remembered being very happy for her father when she heard they had captured Hebron. She went to the city shortly after the settlers had established themselves in the Park Hotel. She thought she remembered seeing refugees departing for Jordan, but she was too scrupulous to claim the memory as her own: 'I didn't even understand what I was seeing – just lines of people. And maybe it's a fantasy.' The visit to Hebron was a 'very great moment in her life', and yet it did not inspire her to act out her father's dream of returning to the city. Far from it: instead of following the right-wing settlers to Hebron, she moved to her uncle's socialist kibbutz instead. Her motivation was not political – she wanted to live on the kibbutz because it was 'a paradise for children' and she did not begin to question the political allegiances she had inherited from her parents until after they were dead.

She could not vote for anyone other than Likud while her father and uncle were alive, and the only time she broke her habit was in the middle of the seventies when she voted for an even more right-wing party, established by the Likud dissident Geula Cohen: 'It's so funny, I tell it as a joke, because it makes me laugh today. It was so stupid: let me tell you, I was not twelve, but I was so ignorant.'

The Lebanon War was a turning point for her, as it was for many Israelis, but it was not until the signing of the Oslo Accords that she began to vote for left-wing parties. Even then, she felt constrained by filial duty: supporting the party established by the man who sent her father to prison would have been like putting a knife in his back, and instead of taking one step to the left to vote Labour she took ten steps and voted for Meretz, a small socialist-Zionist party with links to Ha'tsomer Hatzair. 'Really, I tell you I felt like a religious Jew who eats pig.'

The sky didn't fall, as she put it, but her life was chang- ing in other ways: she had been living in Ranaana, a village near Tel Aviv, with her husband and their son and daughter, but in the space of two years she got divorced, went back to university to study political science and international relations and became a political activist. The thought of her son's political service provoked her into action. She became involved with a movement called Four Mothers, which campaigned against the Israeli occupation of southern Lebanon. She was not one of the original four founders: she thought she was the tenth person to join. 'They started in the north, and I was one of the founders when it came to the centre.'

The campaign attempted to enlist the parents of serving Israeli soldiers to bring about the withdrawal from Lebanon, and I did not doubt that Yona was right to say that the Israeli politicians were scared of Four Mothers: I could see that she would make a formidable opponent. Once, she was invited on a TV show, where she was accused of being a supporter of Hezbollah, and as she was leaving the studio she heard the next guest, Ehud Barak, say that if he became Prime Minister he would withdraw the IDF from Lebanon. He would not be in a position to act on the pledge for several more years, but Yona believed that he was sincere, and with the movement's aim secured her attention was drawn to Hebron.

She was one of the many people who believed that Netanyahu would refuse to withdraw from the city, though she knew that she would not have the same power to influence events as she had with Four Mothers. 'Hebron is much more complicated.' Haim Hanegbi hoped to kick the settlers out, but she knew it would not be possible. He had warned her that he would be a nuisance, and she soon realized why: she could present herself as a daughter of the Irgun chiefs, but Hanegbi's reputation as one of the most 'extremist leftists' in Israel attracted a great deal of criticism. Nonetheless, he came with them when they went back to Hebron in 1997, and met Jabril Rajoub, head of the Palestinian Security

Services in the West Bank, and a senior figure in the PA, who
had been criticizing the settlers and expressing doubts about
Israel's commitment to peace. Arafat himself wanted to meet
them, but Yona was suspicious of his motives: he wanted
them to say that they ought to be entitled to live in Hebron,
so that he could say Palestinians should be allowed to live in
Tel Aviv. She had a property deed to Beit Hadassah, but she
wanted to see the building converted into a museum docu-
menting the history of Arab–Jewish coexistence in Hebron.
'I always say, I give away my property for peace, because
peace is more important than a house.'

She felt they had achieved all they could, but Hanegbi
was 'mad at her' because he wanted the campaign to go on:
'He saw us as the most colourful or original peace movement, and he wanted us to continue. I didn't want to because
I had established something ad hoc and not a movement.'
Besides, nothing had changed – more people knew that the
settlers were living in houses that did not belong to them,
but it made no difference, for they were still there. Besides,
her orientation as an activist was as a mother and not just as
a citizen, and she said it was not 'in her blood' once she no
longer had a son.

After all she had said about him I was shocked to hear
that her son was dead. She had disclosed it in a very matter-
of-fact way, but her manner had changed: she suddenly
looked very brittle and frail, and she started tugging on her
cigarette, with short, distracted gasps. I didn't feel I could
ask her how he died, but when she started talking about his
military service I assumed I had my answer. He was posted
to Ramallah in 2000, which in itself was 'a punishment' for
her: unlike Haim Hanegbi, who wants to see a single unified
state for Israeli Jews and Palestinian Arabs, she believes
in the two-state solution, and she drew a clear distinction

between defending Israel and serving in the Territories. 'I went crazy – really. I live in Israel, I was born in Israel, we have wars here, unfortunately, but my son never went behind the Green Line before he went to service in Ramallah. It's immoral that we waste his life, not for his country, but for the foolishness of settlers and politicians, because the settlements are foolishness and mistakes – really, from the bottom of my heart, I say it's immoral to take my son to service across my borders. I told my cousin that the worst thing had happened to me – my son is serving across the Green Line. And he told me: it's not the worst thing. And after his funeral, I said to him, "So you were so right: it wasn't the worst thing."'

The only consolation was that he was not chosen to be a combat soldier: minor physical defects, such as a problem with his shoulder, meant that he was confined to his base. 'I was so happy about that, and he was very, very happy, so I shut my mouth.' Friends of hers joked that she would force Israel to leave the West Bank, but she did not get involved, and her son's years in the army were the happiest of his life. 'He liked the company, and he got all the compliments, because he was an excellent guy, and the moment he got there they saw it.' He served in the West Bank for two years between 2000 and 2002, at the height of the Second Intifada, but he had left the army, and he was studying at the Open University when he died in a car accident. 'Look, I was lucky that he wasn't killed in Ramallah. He was alone in his car, it was his mistake. I have nobody to blame. You see? If it happened to him in the army, I would have joined the Hezbollah. So emotionally, there is a difference. I have nobody to blame. I have only the pain, not the hatred.'

CHAPTER SEVEN

EMANUEL EISENBERG'S
RESCUE EXCAVATION

> As in many contested regions, the past is always
> present in the Middle East conflict. Here, however,
> the past has far greater weight than any other
> region, and archaeologists are those that give the
> distant past a palpable, physical expression. In this
> sense, archaeology and politics have always been
> intertwined.
>
> Raanan Rein, Preface to
> *The Present Past of the Israeli–Palestinian Conflict:*
> *Israeli Archaeology in the West Bank and East Jerusalem*
> *Since 1967* by Raphael Greenberg and Adi Keinan.

The events of Thursday 20 August 1998 will 'remain indel-
ibly embedded in my mind for as long as I remain in this
world', wrote David Wilder, in one of his periodic news-
letters from Hebron. Its title gave some indication of what
was to follow: it was called 'A Guiding Light: Rabbi Shlomo
Ra'anan, ZT"L HY"D', and most of its readers would have
known that the honorific meant 'of blessed memory', and
'may Hashem avenge his blood' – an incantation used of a
martyred Jew.

Wilder was in the Tomb of the Patriarchs when he heard
there had been a terrorist attack in Tel Rumeida. A former
Chief Rabbi of Israel, Ovadiah Yosef, the head of the Shas

Party, which represent the interests of Sephardic and Mizrahi Jews, was visiting Hebron for the first time in twenty years. His party had voted in favour of the Oslo Accords and the partitioning of Hebron, which hadn't created 'any great love for him among many people', Wilder said, but the rabbi was known as a great Torah scholar, and his 'return to the city of Abraham' was a significant event. Wilder had finished filming the 11 p.m. prayers led by the rabbi in the crowded Yitzhak Hall when a friend told him there had been a stabbing in Tel Rumeida: 'My heart missed a beat.' Wilder ran down the steps of 'the Ma'arat' and rang another friend. '"What happened?" He confirmed the rumor – someone had been stabbed – come fast. The victim – Rabbi Shlomo Ra'anan.'

The rabbi was a particularly significant figure for Hebron's Jews. He came from a family that has a claim to have founded 'modern Jewish religious Zionism': his grandfather Avraham Yitzhak HaCohen Kook was the first Ashkenazic Chief Rabbi of Israel, and the founder of the Yeshivat Merkaz HaRav, in Jerusalem, the seminary that propounded the religious justification for the settlement project. Rabbi Kook believed that 'the Land of Israel in its entirety', and the People of Israel, were holy, and that we were living in 'an Age of Redemption'. He believed that the borders of the state created in 1948 were 'strangling' the Jewish people. His son Rabbi Tsvi Yehuda HaCohen Kook called them 'Auschwitz borders'.

Tsvi Yehuda HaCohen Kook had led the 'return to the heart of Eretz Yisrael, to Judea, Samaria and Gaza', and his nephew Shlomo Ra'anan had followed in the family tradition – he and his wife, Chaya, moved to Tel Rumeida from Yamit, the village in the Sinai which was evacuated by the Israeli army when the peninsula was returned to Egypt in

1982. Although he was a less prominent character than his uncle or grandfather, he was nonetheless admired: Wilder said he was 'a quiet and seemingly unimposing man', who was also 'a great Torah scholar, whose modesty and humility characterized his life'. He represented 'the dedication and determination to Torah and Eretz Yisrael, willing to give literally everything, even his own life, to achieve these lofty goals.' The three men represented 'perhaps more than any other people the desire to return to Eretz Yisrael'.

Having heard the news of the stabbing, Wilder drove to the Avraham Avinu neighbourhood, where an army roadblock had been set up; he parked, and got out of the car. The soldiers tried to stop him going any further, but Wilder knew the system too well: '"Why – is this a closed military zone?!"' The punctuation conveyed his indignation. Other people 'showed up', and 'ignoring the soldiers' demands', they walked on together. Wilder called a different friend, who said he had been present at the time. He said he couldn't do anything: 'He was stabbed in the heart – there was a big hole in his chest – when I got there he still had a weak pulse, but the room was on fire and we had to pull him out . . . he just died.'

The soldiers at the bottom of the hill leading to Tel Rumeida tried to stop them going any further, but the settlers ignored them: 'We ran around them and continued up the road,' Wilder wrote. 'A few minutes later we arrived, and perhaps wished we hadn't.' It seems that he was still talking to his friend on the phone who told him that 'an Arab terrorist' had climbed into the caravan 'through the Ra'anan's bedroom window', where 'Rabbi Shlomo was getting ready to go to sleep'. The assailant had stabbed the rabbi three times and run into the living room where his wife, Haya, was sitting. 'When the terrorist tried to attack her, Rabbi

Shlomo stumbled out of his room and attempted to pull the terrorist away. The terrorist again stabbed the rabbi, this time in the heart. He collapsed in his wife's arms. The terrorist then fled back into the bedroom and hurled a firebomb into the living room before leaving the house as he had entered, via the bedroom window.'

Neighbours in the other caravans heard the screams, and ran to help. They saw Haya Ra'anan, who is a nurse, attempting to resuscitate her husband. One person pulled the rabbi outside; another tried to extinguish the flames. 'A neighborhood paramedic continued to treat Rabbi Shlomo Ra'anan, but it was too late. There was nothing left to be done. At 63 years of age, the six year resident of Tel Rumeida, father of two boys and one girl, grandfather, husband, brother, uncle, grandson and nephew of the spiritual leaders of the modern Zionist movement, was dead, another victim of Arab terror in Hebron, slaughtered in his own home.'

Four days later, Wilder was still shocked and agitated, but he had begun to formulate his response to the attack: 'What can one do after such an awful act of terror?' he said. 'The Hebron community has long demanded of the present administration fulfilment of promises of expansion and development in Hebron's Jewish neighbourhoods. The government decision confirming the Hebron Accords in January 1997 guaranteed reinforcement of Hebron's Jewish community. The Tel Rumeida neighborhood contains enough Jewish-owned land to construct 70 new housing units. What would be more appropriate than immediate building permits, allowing us to turn the tables on the terrorists whose sole objective is to eradicate the city's Jewish community. They are trying to destroy us – we will react by bringing in more and more people, building more and more houses. Rabbi Shlomo Ra'anan cannot be brought back, but we can see to it that his life and death were not in vain.'

Wilder said that 'building, building and more Jewish building, making sure that the Arabs understand that killing men, women, and/or children will only strengthen our resolve' was the only possible response. Fear and defiance propelled his leap into the sanctuary of the upper case as he concluded his newsletter with a hymn to Jewish existence in Hebron:

WE WILL NOT RUN AWAY, WE WILL NOT BE SCARED AWAY. WE WILL CONTINUE IN THE PATH OF RABBI SHLOMO RA'ANAN, WHO WHEN HE CAME TO LIVE IN HEBRON DEMANDED TO LIVE IN 'THE MOST DIFFICULT NEIGHBORHOOD,' WHO, WHEN ASKED WHERE HE LIVED, ANSWERED, 'IN A PALACE' WHO WAS LOVED AND RESPECTED BY ONE AND ALL, JEW AND ARAB ALIKE.

WE WILL FOLLOW THE PATH OF RABBI SHLOMO RA'ANAN'S GRANDFATHER, RAV AVRAHAM YITZHAK HACOHEN KOOK, AND HIS UNCLE, RAV ZVI YEHUDA HACOHEN KOOK, WHO WERE THE GUIDING LIGHTS OF RELIGIOUS ZIONISM AND OUR RETURN TO ERETZ YISRAEL.

RABBI SHLOMO RA'ANAN'S BODY MAY HAVE BEEN CUT APART BUT HIS SPIRIT LIVES ON. HIS SPIRIT, HIS BEING, WILL REMAIN A GUIDING LIGHT TO US FOREVER, HERE IN HEBRON.

It seems that Wilder's caps-lock outpouring was an attempt to inspire and fortify himself, as much as others. He had lived in Kiryat Arba for seventeen years, but in the weeks before the rabbi's murder he and his wife had been considering moving into the centre of Hebron. Another family had left 'due to a job opportunity', and there was a vacancy in Beit Hadassah. 'We had discussed it for a while and hadn't yet made up our minds,' he wrote, in his next newsletter. But then 'the unthinkable' happened, and Wilder told his wife that they had to move in – '"and the sooner the better."'

Some of their friends thought they were 'crazy', though 'a Gentile correspondent' offered an interpretation that Wilder appeared to prefer – he said they were either a 'little crazy, or very, very spiritual'. It did not seem to occur to him that they might be both. Living only minutes from the second holiest site in Judaism would be 'a truly spiritual experience', he said; but it had political implications as well.

Like many of the settlers in Hebron, Wilder was not born in Israel: he grew up in North Bergen County, New Jersey. He did not come from a religious background, but while he was at university he went to Jerusalem to study at the Hebrew University, and the experience 'turned his life upside down'. He did not intend to stay: 'I came to get away, and see something interesting, you know – just to do something a little different. And by the time I went back to the States, I knew that I wanted to come back. I hadn't decided exactly what I wanted to do, or if I would stay, but I knew I wanted to come back.'

Until then, he had intended to go to law school when he finished his history degree, but in his last year of university he got a 'teacher certification', and when he graduated he moved back to Israel and started working as a teacher. It seems that his conversion to the Zionist cause was complete: he got married in 1979 and two years later he and his wife, Ora, moved to Kiryat Arba. 'We wanted to, as you say, "practise what you preach" – not just talk about doing something, but do it. We went looking for some place where we thought we might be able to contribute – if by doing nothing else, just by being there.'

It was one of the best decisions they ever made: 'Arriving 2 weeks before the birth of our second child, we never regretted bringing up our family in this wonderful town, only five minutes from Ma'arat HaMachpela and the center of Hebron,' he wrote. 'In spite of the negative image portrayed by the media, Kiryat Arba is a fabulous place to raise children. The atmosphere is generally relaxed, the educational facilities excellent, and the people second to none.'

Wilder had soon realized that 'formal classroom education' was not for him, though he counts his work as tour guide and spokesman for the Jewish community of Hebron as education of a kind. He likes to start his tours on Tel Rumeida, because that's where the story starts: 'It's very exciting to be able to put your feet in the footsteps of the people that were the founders of your people, going back four thousand years. You know, American history, you're dealing with two hundred and fifty years – George Washington, Abraham Lincoln. Go back to Great Britain: I saw on the Internet that they were auctioning one of the copies of the Magna Carta, and that's a thousand years ago, a little less. Here we're talking almost four thousand years. The beginning of all people. The beginning of the modern Western religions. It's an amazing thought – that's the beginning, not only of Judaism, but of monotheism. If a person has any grasp whatsoever, it just blows them away.'

We were sitting in his small, cramped office in the basement of one of the renovated buildings that backs onto Al-Harem Street. I had walked through the souk, past the Tomb of the Patriarchs, and along the echoing avenues of green-shuttered shops, before turning into a dusty, rubble-strewn street overlooked by an army watchtower on the roof of an abandoned building. There was no one in sight, and no indication that the honeycombed fabric of fraying buildings concealed an area of neatly renovated buildings, faced with clean pale stone.

Wilder told me to call him when I arrived: I went through a courtyard where kids were playing football, and I met him in another courtyard at the top of a short set of stairs that led down to the basement. He held the door open for me as we went inside. He is a short man – so short that he once billed a publicity photograph of himself with a visitor to Hebron as 'the giant and the dwarf' – and he was dressed in a black shirt, a black cardigan and black trousers. He had a pair of glasses on a cord around his neck. His office was littered with files and newspapers. He sat down at an L-shaped desk bearing more papers, a computer and a printer. *Don't the Arab States Have Enough Land of their Own?* said the poster on the wall behind him. It featured a map of the Middle East, with the Arab countries shaded one colour, and Israel another. *Land Area Arab States – 2,291,833 sq miles. Land Area Israel (Including West Bank) – 10,084 sq miles.* It was a strange comparison. It failed to acknowledge that there are fewer Israelis than Arabs in the world, and it included Iran and Turkey amongst the Arab states.

He had started working for the Hebron municipality in 1994. To begin with, he was involved in administrative work, but he started to get more involved in giving tours and writing. 'And then as Oslo proceeded, and we started to go into the phases of the Hebron Accords, journalists sort of . . .' He paused. It was fascinating watching a press officer attempting to conceal his contempt for journalists – or rather, considering an attempt to conceal it, and then deciding not to bother: 'I don't know how you would want to describe

it,' he said. 'They started coming out of the trees. Parasites –
whatever you like.' He could barely summon up the energy
to despise them, and he did not think it worthwhile concealing how he felt from me. 'Vultures – they just swarmed
down here, and there was an overwhelming necessity to be
able to deal with them.'

Yet Wilder despises mainstream Israeli society as much
as he despises journalists. I had a feeling that he was mar-
shalling his opinions carefully, but when I asked why he felt
that most Israelis did not support the settlers of Hebron,
he was less diplomatic: 'Israel has to wake up. The Jewish
people have to wake up and pinch ourselves. For one reason
or another, people are unaware of the gem that's called
Hebron. Maybe they believe it doesn't belong to us, or
maybe we don't have a legacy here, or maybe there are
other factors that are more important from that legacy –
therefore they just sort of push it away, and try and close
their eyes to it. And that creates tremendous problems,
not only here, but all over the country. It's all the same
illness.' Wilder often branded those who do not agree
with him as 'sick', 'ill', 'deranged', 'poisoned', or 'impure'.
It seemed remarkable to me that the spokesman for a group
of people understandably preoccupied by the horrors of
the Holocaust should repeat one of the favoured tropes
of the anti-Semitic agitators, though it made sense in the
context of Wilder's racist views. The 'simple analogy' proposed in one of his newsletters reveals the nature of his
thinking: 'Take a big monkey, dress him in an expensive
suit, adorn a tie around his neck, and he looks just like
you, right,' he wrote. 'Except that it's still a monkey. Like it
or not. So too it is with our neighbors.'

It seems strange that a man drawn to live in Israel should
be so prejudiced about the vast majority of its indigenous

inhabitants, especially as he believes that the particular form of 'psychological insanity' that affects many Jews stems from the experience of exile: 'How can we regain our clarity, our peace of mind, our true national identity and with it our true way of life?' he asked. The answer was simple: making 'Aliyah' or returning to 'Eretz Yisrael' – 'breathing the air of Eretz Yisrael, walking the land of Eretz Yisrael', and presumably despising half the inhabitants of Eretz Yisrael – was the cure for this 'cancer'.

Living in Hebron was particularly important, for it was in the front line against the forces threatening Israel's future: 'their goal is to push us out of Hebron, and not only Hebron', he wrote in the New Year newsletter in which he recounted his decision to move into the centre of Hebron. 'Also, out of Haifa, Tel Aviv, and of course, Jerusalem.' A month after Rabbi Ra'anan's murder, Wilder restated the terms of the engagement even more explicitly:

> True, the Arabs have declared war on Hebron, but this is just the beginning. Should they be successful in this battle, the bloodshed will continue. First, throughout Judea, Samaria and Gaza. And then, into what is called 'Israel proper' . . . The declaration of war that began in 1948, with the creation of the State, is continuing. The present front is Hebron. The time has come for Israel's leadership to wake up and fight back, not only defensively, but also offensively and stop Arab expansion now, before the rocks, bottles and bullets and bombs that are flying here, reach the rest of the country.

In the days after the murder of Rabbi Ra'anan, many of the settlers rioted in the centre of Hebron, and a ten-day curfew was imposed on the Palestinian residents of H2. Wilder believed that populating the city with Jews was a more effective strategy, and as usual he returned to the massacre of 1929 as proof of the true intentions of the enemies of Am Yisrael: 'The massacre which left 67 dead led to the swift removal of the surviving Jewish residents by the British. They want us out again.' He did not specify who 'they' might be, but he knew how the settlers should respond to 'their' attempts to evict them. 'So we have to do the opposite, which is, to move in. Of course one family is not enough. We must bring in hundreds and thousands more people to live in the City of the Patriarchs and Matriarchs. And eventually we will.'

The settlers had lost patience with Prime Minister Binyamin Netanyahu when he signed the Hebron protocol that led to the partition of the city, but he responded to the murder of Rabbi Ra'anan in exactly the way they would have wanted: Wilder said that he visited during the shiva, or week of mourning, paid his condolences to the rabbi's widow and family, and 'upon witnessing the housing conditions in the neighborhood . . . immediately promised government approval to rectify the deplorable situation.' In September 1998, the Israeli government budgeted $3 million to construct permanent houses to replace the 45-square-metre mobile homes in which seven families had lived for the last fourteen years: 'This is our way of memorializing the memory of Rabbi Ra'anan', Wilder wrote. 'This is the true Zionist solution to Arab terrorism.'

One more task had to be undertaken before construction could begin. Responsibility for organizing the 'rescue excavation' at Tel Rumeida lay with a man called Dr Yitzhak Magen, the Staff Officer for Archaeology, who, despite his military title, is a civilian appointment within the military

government of the West Bank known as the Civil Administration. The post is a powerful one – according to Rafi Greenberg, Senior Lecturer at Avi Ofer's alma mater, Tel Aviv University, and director of an organization called the West Bank and East Jerusalem Archaeological Research Project, the SOA is not accountable to anyone in either the Civil Administration or the Israeli government, and Dr Magen, who has had the job since 1981, has come to see the West Bank as his 'personal fiefdom'.

Nazmi Al Jubeh told me that I ought to talk to Rafi Greenberg for a dissenting Israeli perspective on the dig. They had served together on a body called the Israeli–Palestinian Archaeology Working Group. It had been set up to formulate a plan for dealing with the region's archaeological heritage in the event of the creation of a Palestinian state, and Dr Greenberg had carried out the fieldwork that informed its research. Dr Al Jubeh said that Dr Greenberg was far more critical of Israeli archaeologists than he would ever be, and yet when I went to meet him at his office in Tel Aviv I did not find the pugnacious Israeli I was expecting, but a diffident, reserved man, short and pale-skinned, with receding hair, a round, freckled face and a prosthetic hand.

He said he did not want to be perceived as 'an anti-Magen figure', and yet he memorably compared him to Kurtz, the blood-bespattered anti-hero of *Heart of Darkness*, Joseph Conrad's novel about the Belgian Congo. Kurtz disappears into the Congo in search of ivory and never returns, and Rafi Greenberg remembered Dr Magen telling an archaeological congress that he had 'sacrificed himself' to the post of SOA.

Greenberg said: 'He sat there and said, "I am the last person excavating on the West Bank: after me, nothing will be left, it will be completely destroyed, looted, built over, etc., etc. So you can throw stones at me, you can say anything you want about me, but I'm saving this for posterity. You guys don't want to get your hands dirty, you want to stay in your ivory towers, and be ethical, but someone has to be out there to save the antiquities and that's me. I know how to get it done, and I'll do it. It's exactly analogous to this guy in the jungle saying, I'll get the ivory."'

Dr Greenberg's disapproval was plain, and yet he was prepared to concede that the legal and ethical status of digging in the West Bank was complicated – there wasn't a book of rules that told you how to behave. Paradoxically, he seemed to approve of the fact that the SOA was appointed by the military government of the West Bank, and wrote his own legislation 'in a very undemocratic way', for it preserved the distinction between sovereign Israel and occupied territory.

In practice, the divide was less clear. Since the Geneva Conventions stipulate that the occupying power has an obligation to protect antiquities for the local population, Dr Magen has repeatedly claimed that he would be prepared 'to turn everything over to the Palestinians' in the event of a political settlement, and yet he has not restricted his excavations to the kind of 'salvage' work required to meet the everyday needs of the local population: if he was intent on preserving the antiquities for the benefit of the Palestinians he would only dig at sites that were endangered by construction or road-building, but in fact he has maintained a 'very active programme'. When Avi Ofer's mentor Moshe Kochavi conducted his preliminary survey of the West Bank, in 1968, very few of the 800 sites he visited had been excavated, but forty years later there were more than 5,400 archaeologically recorded sites of which some 900 have been excavated, either as salvage work in advance of construction and development, or as part of research-orientated projects.

Rafi Greenberg knows that Magen has conducted hundreds of excavations himself and licensed Israeli universities and foreign institutions to do many more: 'Someone will say they want to write a seminar paper on Persian fortresses and they'd like to go and excavate a few of them, and Magen will say go ahead. Then that guy will go and punch a few holes in Persian fortresses.' Dr Greenberg believes that Magen got away with his cavalier approach because other Israeli archaeologists are very 'results-orientated' and wanted to hear 'a lot of information about stuff', but he has paid a price in terms of his reputation. Greenberg said that Magen is isolated internationally and ignored by the archaeological community at large, which does not regard his work as legitimate. I could not judge whether that is true or not. But Dr Greenberg has little sympathy for him. 'He chose his own path many years ago,' he said. 'He wasn't ever on track to be an international scholar and he decided to make the best of this post that he has.'

Yet even he did not want to excavate at Tel Rumeida, and he passed the job to the Israeli Antiquities Authority. Having gone to such lengths to define his territory in the 'dark continent' of his imagination, it might seem strange that he should choose to relinquish the most high-profile dig that came his way, but Rafi Greenberg believed he knew it was beyond his capabilities. It wasn't his period, and his small staff contained no one suitably qualified. Besides, it would be unlike any other dig he had ever undertaken: most of his excavations were conducted without much scrutiny, but Tel Rumeida would be different. 'He knew it would be under the magnifying glass and he didn't want to take the heat for it.'

Rafi Greenberg said the excavation was 'totally illegitimate on several fronts', and Nazmi Al Jubeh said that the decision to release the site for construction proved that the 'sons of Yadin' still hold sway in certain areas of Israel's archaeological establishment. He called the Israeli Antiquities Authority a right-wing organization, run by right-wing people in the interests of the settlers, and almost ten years after the dig had been completed he was still angry about it: 'How dare the Antiquities Authority allow anyone to construct over the site?' he said. 'How come they cannot prevent it, in spite of the fact that they are preserving sites much, much less important than this one? And the answer is just political – archaeology is just a tool: it could be good enough elsewhere, but not in Tel Rumeida. In Tel Rumeida the settlement is more important than history and archaeology, more important than Avraham himself.'

Even the archaeologist that the Antiquities Authority chose to carry out the dig was concerned by its ethical implications. Emanuel Eisenberg was an old friend of Yitzhak Magen's: they had trained together and started their careers at the Antiquities Authority, where Eisenberg had remained for the next thirty years. Yet when Magen and the Antiquities Authority asked him to excavate at Tel Rumeida, he refused. 'Of course I'll oppose building on a site like the tel of Hebron,' he told me. 'Can you imagine building a hotel on top of Tel Megiddo? Absurd, right? You don't have to be an archaeologist to understand.'

It did not take me long to find Emanuel Eisenberg, but it took a long time to get permission to talk to him. The Israeli government's emphasis on *hasbara* – the Hebrew word literally means 'explaining', though it's more commonly translated as 'public diplomacy' or 'propaganda' – generally ensures a prompt response to press enquiries, but the Antiquities Authority is not a front-line ministry engaged in the task of justifying Israel's actions to the world. When I emailed the press officer, and asked her to set up an interview with Emanuel Eisenberg, she asked me for more information about 'the purpose of my research', and then failed to acknowledge my reply.

Whether the IAA was being inefficient or deliberately avoiding the subject was not clear, but I decided to bypass it. Avi Ofer gave me Emanuel Eisenberg's number and I rang him during one of my first visits to Hebron. We agreed to meet in Jerusalem later in the week, though I should have known it would not be as easy as that – having done nothing for a month, the press officer called me as soon as she heard that I had called Eisenberg, and repeated her request for more information. I told her that it didn't matter because I had already found him and her reply was more characteristically Israeli than the blandishments of the courteous officers who staff the IDF press desk: 'Actually, it does matter,' she said. 'He can't talk to you unless I say he can.'

I sent her a more detailed account of my interest in the site but since I heard nothing more I decided to keep my appointment with Eisenberg at the Antiquities Authority's headquarters on an industrial estate in the north-west of Jerusalem. Har Hotzvim has the city's largest concentration of high-tech industries, and yet the presence of the Antiquities Authority amongst the offices of pharmaceutical firms and software manufacturers, and the sight of Orthodox Jews walking down the pavements, was a reminder that the attractions of modernity have not yet dispelled the lure of the country's ancient past or the traditions of the *shtetl*.

The building was scrupulously anonymous – it was a light-industrial warehouse like millions of others around the world, a pop-up construction as insubstantial as a flat-pack bookcase, seemingly stitched together by the strip lighting and ventilation ducts that ran along its whitewashed corridors. The walls were hung with a random collection of framed photographs – an Amsterdam canal scene; giraffes in a zoo; Buddhist monks at prayer. The photograph that hung outside one office door, of a blond man crouching in the bottom of an excavated pit with his arm around a dog, confirmed that at least one of the building's inhabitants was an archaeologist, though the significance of the decorations on Emanuel Eisenberg's door was harder to discern: the pink-framed mirror which said 'Go away!' seemed to belong in the bedroom of a teenage girl, while the clipping from the *New York Times* about the proofreader who had a coronary at his desk, and sat for five days before anyone realized he was dead – 'The moral of the story: Don't work too hard. No one notices anyway' – was from the same school of forced levity as the signs that say 'You don't have to be mad to work here, but it helps.'

I had plenty of time to study the decorations, for Eisenberg had a puncture and arrived an hour late. He was a stocky man with a round face, bright expressive eyes and thick curly hair, dressed casually in cords, brown shoes and a checked shirt. I wasn't sure what I was going to find when he unlocked the door – I would not have been surprised to find myself in a warehouse storeroom, but his office was like an academic's study, with a wide, paper-strewn desk and shelves stacked with books and files. The many photographs of archaeological sites that hung on the walls included an aerial shot of Tel Rumeida taken while the dig was under way and there were family portraits on the desk.

'We have a problem,' he said, as he dumped his briefcase, and sat down behind his desk: the press officer would not give him permission to talk to me. He was plainly frustrated, for he wanted to tell his side of the story. We talked for an hour, but only off the record, and it was testament to the unease that Tel Rumeida continues to provoke that it took another five months of intermittent negotiations before the Antiquities Authority finally gave him permission to speak to me. It was the middle of the summer when I went back to his office, and he was wearing a Bermuda shirt, sandals and the kind of khaki shorts that David Ben-Gurion used to wear, in self-conscious homage to the 'new breed' of Jew that he hoped would emerge in Palestine. Another archaeologist had told me that Eisenberg was 'an old Labour hawk', and he had internalized the spirit of Israel's founding father to the extent that he even dressed like him.

He also came from the same background as the Zionist pioneers: his parents were from Ukraine and Poland, and judging from the name he guessed his father's ancestors came from Western Europe. 'Jews moved to wherever they could make a living: they couldn't have land – it was forbidden – so they developed other skills.' He was born in Germany at the end of the Second World War: his parents could have gone to the United States or Canada, but his father, who was a doctor and 'would have done well anywhere', wanted to go to Israel for 'Zionist reasons'. He had learnt Hebrew in Poland, and he never spoke another language to his son.

Eisenberg blamed the British, 'who were in thrall to the Arabs and their oil', for the fact that they had to travel via the camps in Cyprus: it was cruel for people who had suffered so much to find themselves in camps again, and yet it did not stop them making a success of their new country.

'We came here as refugees – what was left of us after we were exterminated – and established all this.' He knocked on his desk to demonstrate the solidity of the Israeli state: 'To build what we built here in sixty years . . .' I agreed that it was a remarkable achievement, and he said that people should not be surprised: it was easy for the Jews because they had the tools and the skills. 'Everything was ready – we just didn't have the land and the peace of mind. The people around us never give us a chance, but once we got a chance it was done instantly.'

He talked slowly and clearly, barely acknowledging my questions or interruptions. He seemed very self-assured, and it was easy to see why Yitzhak Magen and his boss at the Antiquities Authority had felt that he would be able to handle both the dig itself, and the moral, legal, and ethical complications that would ensue. When Eisenberg turned it down, they told him to go away and think about it, which was a 'smart move'.

The fact that neither Avi Ofer nor Philip Hammond had published full reports of their excavations was one consideration, for the 'story of ancient Hebron' consisted of 'only a few lines, with many question marks', and he saw it as a chance to contribute something to our knowledge: 'Because archaeology has no borders. The boundaries of today don't belong to the past, especially not here – what you find in Hebron is like what you find in Jerusalem or in Beersheva. So what's the difference? It's not another country. It's the same history, the same place.' What's more, 'the people in charge of archaeology in the West Bank' – by which I assumed he meant Magen himself – had told him that they did not have to excavate at all: they could, if they wanted, ignore all the laws governing the protection of archaeo-logical sites – laws which had been established in the

Ottoman era and maintained through the British Mandate and the fifty-year history of the Israeli state – and simply allow the settlers to build on top of a site of national and international significance. Eventually, Eisenberg decided to treat it as he would any other excavation: 'I am just a soldier, as you know,' he said. 'They send me here and they send me there, and if I don't want to go, well, here's the door – go and look for another job.'

His use of a military metaphor was unfortunate in the context of Hebron, but regardless of how he chose to present the argument Rafi Greenberg believed that it was flawed. Greenberg and Eisenberg are friends: they used to work together at the Antiquities Authority, and they have co-authored several papers, but on the subject of Tel Rumeida they have agreed to differ. 'Emanuel's line is the standard one,' Greenberg said. 'If I don't do it, someone else will. He says, well it had to be done, the decision was taken elsewhere, we were just saving the archaeology for posterity. I don't accept that.' Greenberg believes archaeology should be a force for good – 'a bridge between cultures and periods, that allows people to explore the past as a shared asset, regardless of nationality or religion' – and he does not believe that it should be used for partisan leverage: 'The kind of archaeology that you do when you march into someone else's town under armed protection and start excavating – that's not how we should be doing archaeology.'

Eisenberg was not only facing criticism from those who felt he should not take the job: he was also facing a sustained campaign from one who wanted it for himself. Avi Ofer had never accepted Eisenberg's right to lead the dig: he objected to the dig, but if anyone was going to do it, it should be him, for he was the 'excavator', and Tel Rumeida was his 'intellectual property'. Ofer believed that he had been passed over for two main reasons: firstly, because it was known that he would insist on 'a strict veto on building on the site', and secondly, because of the 'internal political issues' that had interrupted his academic career. I still did not know what they were, and no one I spoke to was inclined to explain: Eisenberg went so far as to say 'there were some problems with his personality', but Greenberg, who was evidently pained to find himself discussing a former colleague, would only repeat Ofer's admission that there had been 'some issues'.

More relevant was Eisenberg's belief that Ofer was mistaken to claim Tel Rumeida as 'his': he conceded that he had some rights as the excavator, but he could hardly claim to possess it just because he had dug there fifteen years before, and it did not help that he had not published a proper account of his excavation. Ofer remembered Eisenberg saying he would have been glad to let him do it, or to do it together, but it wasn't up to him: if he did not excavate they would fire him, and he would lose his living. Ofer accepted that Eisenberg was in a difficult position. Yet he was so determined to get the dig himself that he took the Antiquities Authority to court.

The settlers were aware that Ofer was challenging Eisenberg's right to lead the dig. David Wilder had met him in the offices of the 'Jewish community' in Hebron, where he had made a statement that was 'still reverberating in [his] ears' weeks later: Ofer described 'Tel Hebron' as the second most important archaeological site in Israel, second only to the Temple Mount, but added that 'unfortunate as it may be' it belonged to 'Arafat and the Palestinians'. Not surprisingly, the settlers were pleased when Eisenberg's appointment was confirmed.

When the dig began, in May 1999, Ofer's suit was still

going through the courts, and he decided to pursue another line of protest: he drove to Hebron, parked his car near the settlement, and went on hunger strike. He said that he was protesting against the plan to build on the site, and against the fact that the excavation was being conducted by the authorities, and not by an academic – 'a scholar' – like himself. He slept in his car and refused to eat for a week. He didn't know how long he was going to continue. The first two days were hard, but after that it was easier than he had expected. He said it was not hard if you drink a lot, though after about three weeks it could become dangerous: 'You never know. It depends. Some people can do it for a longer time. Sometimes it causes a problem with the heart.' Shlomit said she would go with him, but they did not want to disrupt the children's schooling, and instead she visited him twice in the first few days.

Emanuel Eisenberg was bemused. 'He did a lot of strange things, a lot of wrong things,' he said: 'he's a strange fellow altogether.' Eisenberg had begun by surveying the entire site, and having established that the settlers' caravans had caused no damage, he started excavating the 'sliver' of land on the north-west corner of the tel. He had a team of sixty people, which included two other archaeologists – directors of the other areas – and fifty Palestinian labourers from Jerusalem. He said it was strange to find himself working with Arabs from Jerusalem in an Arab town in the West Bank, on a patch of land claimed by a group of extremist Jewish settlers, and the presence of an Israeli colleague who was both insistent that the dig should not proceed and equally adamant that if it did he should do it himself must have made it even stranger: 'I had to be nice to everybody, and that included him. So I was very friendly with him, I explained to him all the time, listen, if it wouldn't be me, it would be someone else. You don't have to look at me as an enemy. I'm a soldier. If I say no, they'll send somebody else, but it won't be you.' He decided there was no point in doing anything: 'If he wants to strike, let him strike – do what you feel like, he'll disappear. And this is what happened – in the end, he just gave up and left.'

Ofer did not stop because he could not continue, but because he recognized that it changed nothing. He decided to go home while he waited for the High Court to rule on his petition. Ten years later, he still maintained there were judges who would have decided in his favour, but the one who heard his case was known for never intervening in government plans unless it was essential. 'So they decided to do nothing – they did not decide that the government was right, or I am right, they just said, OK, the government is doing what it is doing, and there is no important reason to change their decision. So I gave up.' I said he must have been very angry to go to such lengths, and he agreed, though in

hindsight he saw it as part of a broader change in his life. He believed that he had been fighting for an important principle by resisting the Antiquities Authority's habit of excavating without respecting the intellectual property and rights of other excavators, but he did not get enoughsupport from his colleagues, and their 'patchy' response persuaded him that it was time to leave the academy: 'It was the last story,' he said. 'After that, I decided OK, enough.'

On 4 May 1999, as 'Israel's arch-enemy Arafat' was preparing to 'declare a state', David Wilder wrote that the Jews of Hebron were watching 'the uncovering of our ancient history'. He maintained that the land that Avi Ofer had ceded to 'the Arabs' was 'being bared for all to see', though he must have known that the excavation would unearth the site's history in reverse order, and, hence, that the early stages would have no bearing on its ancient past. On 7 May he reported that 'a winery', provisionally dated to the Byzantine era of the third to the seventh century CE, and several skeletons, had been discovered: 'It is clear that at some point in time the land was also used as a cemetery,' he wrote, though he was forced to concede that they did not know 'which people the skeletons belonged to'.

Avi Ofer was not the only unexpected visitor who arrived on the first morning – the two Canadian representatives of Temporary International Presence in Hebron who came to see Emanuel Eisenberg told him that the initials on their hats and armbands stood for 'Two Idiots Patrolling Hebron'. Eisenberg thought the name was apposite, and he was amused to discover that they intended to write a daily report on the dig, as if it was 'changing the status quo'. He would not have been there if there had been security problems, he said, though the journey from Jerusalem wasn't always straightforward.

Eisenberg was not religious – he shopped in the Palestinian markets because he didn't eat kosher food – but he seemed broadly sympathetic to the settlers' cause. He had insisted that they were right to call it Tel Hebron, not Tel Rumeida, and he commended their decision to give up the space beneath the building that had been allotted for parking in order to preserve the finds.

Since he was only excavating one of the two plots of land – the caravans are still sitting on the other – the area was no more than half a dunum, or 500 square metres, but it still took Eisenberg's team of sixty people six months to complete the dig. It was a much bigger expedition than Avi Ofer's – Eisenberg said that he had dug a couple of trenches, but elsewhere he had only gone through the topsoil and been lucky to find the sheep tablet. He was not unsympathetic: a proper expedition was expensive. The fieldwork was just the start – there was the post-excavation analysis, then publication of a full report. Salvage digs are usually regarded as second-best to a long-term excavation, but Eisenberg said it had been a proper expedition: if a typical university dig lasts for a month in the summer it was the equivalent of six seasons' work and made a significant contribution to the knowledge of ancient Hebron.

'You have to excavate in several places in order to get an average to understand the occupation much better, but at least I completed the excavations in my area all the way down to bedrock. We get a nice sequence, all the way to the end, and I can say that we were lucky with our finds. I found all kinds of important elements in the city, and all of them are preserved and protected by the roof from erosion and from weather. And you know what? I wish in other sites, in tels, that the finds will be protected in such a manner – not living above, but protected by a roof. At least it wasn't harmed, and those who want to see what was found can go and visit the place. That's if they are not afraid to go to Hebron. But that's a different story.'

PART TWO

CHILDREN OF ABRAHAM

2000–2009

CHAPTER EIGHT

A FINCHLEY SCRIBE

I will also make you a light of nations, that My sal-
vation may reach the ends of the earth.

Isaiah 49:6

I had been in Hebron for several days before I realized that
you can see the settlement of Tel Rumeida from the centre
of town. On my way back to my hotel one afternoon, I
stopped at the top of New Al Shalallah Street, and when
I looked up the hill towards the checkpoint I saw the pale
cream building through a gap in the flapping black awnings
that shade the market stalls. The setting sun was reflecting
from the windows in its eastern facade, and it looked clean
and bright and peaceful, set high above the busy streets of
Bab al-Zawia. I got out my notebook, and I was writing
something down when I was disturbed by an offer of hospitality: 'Welcome to Hebron,' said one of the nearby
stallholders, as many others had in the course of the day.
'Come – sit.' He gestured at a chair on the pavement: 'Drink
tea – write.' No visitor to Hebron would be able to accept
every cup of tea and coffee they are offered, but I had spent
all day walking around the slopes of Tel Rumeida, and
through the alleyways of the Old City, so I was happy to sit
and watch while the market was packed away.

The owner of the next-door shop was sprinkling the
pavement with water from a bucket and a man with a silver

coffee urn on a cart went past, ringing a bell. Two young boys on a donkey rode through the traffic, followed by two more on bikes, and two more pushing a shopping trolley. A breeze had begun to stir the black awnings overhead and the smell of charred meat overpowered the faint stench of rotting fruit. The heat of the day had only just begun to fade but the women gathered on the pavement, waiting for the service taxis to take them home, were wearing knee-length coats. At least half the buildings that hemmed in the square were disused, unfinished or falling into disrepair.

By the time I got up, and thanked my host for the tea, it was getting dark: most of the stallholders were packing up and people were gathering in lighted doorways beside the road. Black rings on the tarmac still marked the spots where tyres had been incinerated in the demonstrations and there were piles of litter in the gutter, waiting to be swept away. Hebron shut down at night: there were no restaurants or bars, and within an hour the stalls would be gone. The windows of the abandoned buildings would look out across an empty square.

I went inside the settlement twice, both times to talk to the only resident that David Wilder was prepared to let me meet: 'People really don't like journalists,' he had explained the first time we met, not attempting to disguise the fact that he shared their disdain. On reflection, he said there was one person who might make an exception. He was English, and although he was a busy man he might be prepared to spare me twenty minutes.

To my surprise Wilder offered me a lift up the hill from Avraham Avinu. A press officer helping a writer conduct an interview would not seem noteworthy in any other context, but this was David Wilder and Hebron. I wondered if it was a professional precaution: Hebron's internationals had repeatedly warned me against wandering around Avraham Avinu on my own, and I wondered if Wilder's motive was to prevent me meeting with the kind of treatment that would turn me irrevocably against the settlers.

His battered white estate car was parked in one of the abandoned streets in the market. It was so crammed with files that it looked like an annexe of his office, and I was not sure it was going to make it up the steep part of the hill to the checkpoint. I had never driven down Shoada Street before and it was strange to see the closed shops and military checkpoints through a windscreen. Wilder did not request permission to drive to the settlement: he waved at the soldiers at the bottom of the road as we chugged past. He drew up beneath the sentry post in the trees. The soldier who inspected my passport saw me getting out of the car, but even so he did not want to let me through: Wilder had turned round and driven away while I was still trying to persuade him that I had a legitimate appointment inside the building.

Eventually, he relented, and I went up the stairs that climbed the side of the building that overlooks the city walls. A plaque on the wall on the balcony identified the Ohr Shlomo Study Centre, which had been established in memory of Rabbi Shlomo Ra'anan. Inside a class of six or seven boys was in progress. To begin with 'the lights of Shlomo' yeshiva had occupied the room where Shlomo Ra'anan was killed and it remains a family concern, for it is run by his son-in-law, Yisrael Shlissel, who lives in one of the caravans beneath the settlement with his family.

I leant on the railings and looked out across the city. It was the first time I had seen the view from above. A staircase halfway along the balcony climbed through a deep well in the back half of the building, and I followed a trail of gourds, beads and dried plants hanging from the walls to Gabriel Ben Yitzhak's flat on the second floor. A child opened the door. There were more children helping themselves to pots of food set up on a long table in the middle of the room: counting at least five or six I thought I had arrived at a kindergarten or after-school club, but I soon realized that all belonged to the man who appeared from a room in the back of the flat.

Gabriel Ben Yitzhak was a short, thin man with a greying beard that almost reached his waist. He was dressed plainly in a black sweater and black trousers. He seemed very frail and nervous, which was no doubt why I had been allowed to speak to him: he was nothing like the stereotypical image of the bullying settler. He did not want to stop working and he invited me to join him in his study, which was as bare and clean as the rest of the flat: there were a few photographs on the wall and two woven baskets on the shelf above his head. David Wilder had told me that he was a rabbi, but in fact he was a scribe and he was working on a sheet of paper spread out on the plain wooden desk in front of him. There were more sheets laid out on another desk beside him and a timetable pinned to the wall marked out the schedule that lay ahead: it was divided into days and hours – each stage of his slow, diligent journey through the seemingly endless genealogies of Genesis, the epic narrative of Exodus and the complex legal and ethical prescriptions of Deuteronomy, the book of the Law, as he assembled a perfect copy of the first five books of the Jewish Bible.

A Sefer Torah, or handwritten scroll, contains 304,805 characters on sixty-two sheets, and a single misplaced stroke could render the work invalid. Each one took him 'many

months: less than a year – but many months'. The archaic
formulation seemed to suit the nature of the task. He had
only completed twelve scrolls in the eighteen years since he
had become a scribe. 'I never actually took the exams to be
a rabbi, but it depends on how you look at it,' he said, when
I mentioned Wilder's description of him. 'Rabbi is a term for
people with beards who have learnt a lot and things like that
– sometimes people call me rabbi.' He spoke very slowly, his
head bent low over the page. He put down his pen and
picked up a miniature sander, with a rounded, brush-like
head, to remove a blemish.

His name was not Gabriel Ben Yitzhak, either: he was
born Gabriel Dawson in the north London suburb of Finchley in 1956 but he decided to change it 'to something
Hebrew' – Ben Yitzhak means the son of Isaac, which was
his father's name – because the Israelis found it difficult to
pronounce. He understood how they felt: he had come
to Israel when he was eighteen years old and he had become
so immersed in its language and culture that he had lost his
fluency in English, and he often paused and waved his pen
in the air as he tried to locate the buried memory. Sometimes, he would give up and go backwards to rephrase a
sentence, sometimes several times over, giving into compulsive, stuttering revisions, and sometimes he would lapse
into silence as he contemplated his work.

Like David Wilder, he had not been planning on staying
permanently: he had been an ardent Zionist in England, but
he found it difficult to adjust to a world that did not meet
his expectations. 'I felt very foreign to the Israelis, to Israeli
society, the way of life and the attitude . . . What's the word?
The sort of oriental . . .' He did not finish the sentence.
'Now things are different – it's become more open.' He
started studying in a Talmudic institute. For the first two or

three years he missed the greenery, and tranquillity of England, but by the time he got married, at the age of twenty-four, he felt more at home. Now he feels no more affection for England than any other place in the world: 'It's strange because I had a very happy childhood but I never felt at home there – I was happy but I didn't feel that this was the place I wanted to live. There was no connection to Israel specifically, but I felt something didn't click.' It seems the same was true of the rest of his family, for his parents and his sister have moved to Israel and his brother lives in California.

He and his wife moved to Kiryat Arba in 1981 and stayed for six years. When they moved to the city in 1987 it was at his wife's prompting: she wanted to move to the Avraham Avinu area, but he refused, for it was still densely inhabited, with a busy market. 'Ideologically, we were both connected to the idea of settling Hebron, but it wasn't easy. In those days, there was no shooting, but there was lots of stone throwing. Security-wise, we were very, very vulnerable – extremely vulnerable.' He insisted that Tel Rumeida was the only place he was prepared to live, though they always shopped in the Arab markets. 'The Jews were walking around freely, and Arabs were walking around freely, there was employment. There were extremists on both sides, as they like to say, but most of the people who came to settle in Hebron were not interested in making a fuss, they wanted to live their lives, and the Arabs around lived their lives.'

Even after the First Intifada broke out they continued shopping in the markets. Security was lax; the army base was not created until the Hebron Protocol was signed, and the area was an empty field, with a few olive trees, and two reserve-duty soldiers sitting on chairs.

Yet the murder of Rabbi Ra'anan changed their lives: 'It was a real shock. You're not realistic – you think, it's OK, it won't happen to us, and when it happens it's a bit of a blow. It was a very severe knock to our feeling of security here. It's an awful thing to see someone, such a dear person, lying dead. Often you talk about people after their death as being very high, you know, but he was in his life a very, very special person. Very kind. I used to walk down with him sometimes and all the Arabs used to greet him, they used to call him the holy man or something like that.'

The man who murdered the rabbi was called Salem Rajib Sarsur. On 30 September, a month after the rabbi's murder, he threw hand grenades at a group of soldiers in Hebron, injuring fourteen, and in October he threw hand grenades into a crowd at Beersheva bus station, wounding sixty-seven people. Wilder said that Sarsur's repeated attacks were like Arafat's demands for more territory – he would keep coming back for more, until Israel itself was under threat – and the news that he had been arrested did not make Ben Yitzhak and his family feel more secure: 'We didn't know how we were going to continue living here. But you know, you get over it, like you get over all shocks in life.'

They were pleased that Netanyahu had approved the construction of the settlement, though in the short term it entailed further upheaval, for they were one of two families who lived in caravans on the upper plot of land, where the new apartment would be built. They moved the caravan down the hill, and since they had just had their twelfth child, and needed 'a little more room', as Wilder put it, they decided to bring in another to sit on top of it. The caravans were put in place before the dig began. They thought they would be in their new home for a year or two at most but they realized it was going to be for longer when Tel

Rumeida became a political issue in the run-up to the election in May 1999. 'We have clear red lines,' the Labour Party leader, Ehud Barak, told *Haaretz* in an interview in which he drew an explicit contrast between Tel Rumeida and places such as Gush Etzion and Ariel, which 'would be part of the State of Israel in the permanent settlement'. David Wilder came to the conclusion that Barak did not believe that Tel Rumeida was part of Israel and his fears were justified. Barak was elected Prime Minister on 17 May 1999 and his government refused to give permission to build on the site.

It seemed that Eisenberg's attempts to prepare the site for construction were wasted, and the outbreak of the Second Intifada presented an even more serious delay. Barak and Yasser Arafat had failed to reach agreement on a final settlement at the summit at Camp David in July 2000, and on 28 September Ariel Sharon visited the Al-Aqsa Mosque on the Haram al-Sharif. He said he was attempting to assert 'the right of every Jew to ascend the Temple Mount' but he had political motives as well. Sharon had resurrected his political career after the disastrous invasion of Lebanon and the massacres at Sabra and Shatila but Benyamin Netanyahu was threatening to displace him as leader of the opposition, and he feared that he would never become Prime Minister.

According to Idith Zertal and Akiva Eldar, the 'Palestinians' Public Enemy Number One' hoped that his visit to the Temple Mount would transform his prospects by provoking a crisis that would induce the Israeli public to seek the sheltering embrace of a man of war. Frustration provoked by economic stagnation in the Palestinian Territories, the lack of progress towards a Palestinian state, and Israel's ongoing programme of settlement building underlay the Second Intifada, but Sharon's intervention was decisive: 'The ground was indeed soaked with flammable materials, but it was Sharon, and not for the first time, who played the role of pyromaniac.' The next day, seven Palestinians were killed in violent disturbances after midday prayers at the Al-Aqsa Mosque, and the unrest spread rapidly through Israel's Palestinian Arab population, and the Palestinians of the West Bank.

In Hebron the settlers found themselves under fire from the hills above and the city centre below. 'To begin with we thought they would have a certain will to keep the order, because they wanted to prove that they were worthy of being given more land and more power. But it didn't work out.' Gabriel Ben Yitzhak gestured out of the window of his first-floor apartment in Beit Menachem at the buildings in the valley below. 'They were getting into windows down there, and shooting at us.'

A 'security expert' told them that they would have to hold out for two or three days until the army took control but it took much longer, and Ben Yitzhak was so agitated by the memory he could hardly bring himself to discuss it: 'Any normal country, you get attacked, you're getting shot at, you go back and *dadada* . . .' His account tailed off in a bat-squeak of fear and indignation. 'Afterwards, if you want to make talks, OK we'll talk. That was the idea, but it took the army a year or more. We have had very traumatic times. We had sandbags on our windows in the caravans. And we had a very difficult time because the army weren't allowed to go in there: they were just allowed to shoot back. It was a moral blow, to look out of the window and see the flag of the PLO, who we realized were out to destroy all of us. We were very worried.'

There were moments when Ben Yitzhak's confidence wavered, and he told his wife he thought they should go back to Kiryat Arba. 'For me, it was difficult, because I'm a bit of a nervy type.' It seemed an unnecessary confession. He had become visibly agitated since we had started talking about politics, and he was not getting much work done, yet he wanted to emphasize the resolve that had seen him through the fighting: 'We felt we had a mission to stay, because if we had collapsed Hebron would have collapsed, and it would have been given over to the Arabs, and who knows what else would have collapsed. And that it would get to other places, which in fact it did – in the end you couldn't walk around nowhere hardly in the whole country, the whole country became under danger.' The contorted English was further testament to his discomfort. 'So we felt we were doing a mission.'

It was not merely a self-interested one. Part of the settlers' frustration with their critics stems from the fact that they do not recognize their motives. One academic who had conducted many interviews with them in the days before they closed themselves off to outsiders concluded that they saw their actions as 'a righteous deed' that a 'particular people' undertook 'as a universal favour'. They believed that they were fulfilling God's plan for the world and, hence, hastening humanity's progress to 'universal redemption'. Rabbi Shlomo's grandfather had taught that settlement of the West Bank was a holy duty and the land of Israel and the people of Israel must be united in order to fulfil the commandments and redeem God's covenant with the world, and Ben Yitzhak believed that he had been 'guided' to live in Hebron. It would be a 'drastic step' and a 'spiritual loss' to leave the city, for they had a special blessing in Hebron.

Besides, the violence of the conflict was, in itself, nothing to be feared: Avraham Kook said that the destruction of war would release 'the light of Mashiach', the Jewish Messiah, and 'the greater the magnitude and force . . . the greater the revelation'. Ben Yitzhak attested that they had witnessed great miracles: 'Even without being a believer, there was absolutely no way of explaining how we many managed to stay there and relatively very few bullets came into the caravan. There were thousands of bullets flying around.'

Other Israelis were less inclined to trust to divine providence, or their elected leader. Many believed that Prime Minister Ehud Barak – the IDF's most decorated soldier – had gone too far in his attempts to secure peace with the Palestinians. As the violence worsened he found himself unable to govern effectively, and in May 2001 he resigned and called an election, in which Ariel Sharon defeated him. The visit to the Temple Mount had achieved the desired effect: it had won Sharon the premiership but at the cost of initiating what Idith Zertal and Akiva Eldar call 'an insane tribal war'.

Sharon proved himself the settlers' friend once more: before the election he had said that the settlers of Hebron had 'taken upon themselves a role for which we must all thank them', and on 19 November he ordered that work should resume on the apartments at Tel Rumeida. It hardly mattered that his government did not authorize the building permits for another six months, for the work could not have gone ahead while the country was trapped in an escalating cycle of internecine violence. In March 2002, dozens of Israeli citizens were killed in suicide bombings, and Sharon authorized the construction of the 'separation barrier' and ordered the Israeli army to repossess Palestinian towns and cities. 'Operation Defensive Shield' was the largest military operation in the West Bank since the Six Day War: in the next two months the IDF reoccupied Qalqiliya, Nablus, Bethlehem and Tulkarem, confined Yasser Arafat to the rubble of his presidential compound in Ramallah and demolished large sections of Jenin refugee camp.

Gabriel Ben Yitzhak could not understand why the army did not act so decisively in Hebron, though the testimony of those who have served in the city suggests that they were not entirely inactive. One soldier told the veterans' organization Breaking the Silence that they often drove up to Abu Sneineh in an armoured car 'just to make our presence felt' by shooting out streetlights and windows or blowing up a shop with a grenade launcher. 'Nothing like hearing a street light blow to bits after you've taken aim at it.' Another soldier remembered getting an order that the city was to be a 'ghost town', meaning that everyone had to get inside their houses while the army attacked the locations that could be used as firing points: 'I remember that we emptied magazines all night long, tons of ammunition, and I remember that I personally fired on an empty school, or empty windows, or street lights, just as a deterrent, just to instil fear . . . And this horrified me, because it wasn't justified, the quantity . . . it was grossly exaggerated.'

Yet Ben Yitzhak did not believe the army was doing enough and he concluded there was a secret agreement between the IDF and the PA, for the shooting always stopped during Jewish rallies and festivals at the Tomb of the Patriarchs. Eventually, a gunman broke the unwritten rule and shot at the crowd: 'Someone was injured, quite seriously, and the army took over.' The army reoccupied H1 and made some arrests, yet to the settlers' dismay, they withdrew after five days.

They felt that the situation improved when a new military commander was appointed. Colonel Dror Weinberg was a religious Zionist who took a more aggressive approach to policing the city. He told Ben Yitzhak that he had not reoccupied H1 permanently because he preferred to enter and leave as he liked. Weinberg allowed the settlers to reclaim the vegetable market, and shut down dozens of shops in the area, but on 15 November 2002 he was one of twelve soldiers and security guards killed in an ambush on the road between Kiryat Arba and the Tomb of the Patriarchs. He was the most senior military casualty of the Intifada.

Work on the apartment block began a month later. The building was supposed to have been completed within a year, but in February 2003 the High Court issued a temporary injunction while it considered a suit claiming that Israel was destroying ancient archaeological artefacts. The plaintiffs included Avi Ofer, Moshe Kochavi, Nazmi Al Jubeh and the Hebron Rehabilitation Committee. Yet the settlers ignored the ban: people told me that the Asian labourers who had been brought in to build the settlement hid when the police were called and resumed work as soon they were gone. In any case the legal challenge failed: the results of the suit were not 'wonderful', Nazmi Al Jubeh said, though Professor Chadwick's Zionist affiliations led him to conclude that the court had made the right decision.

The first tenants of the completed building were Shlomo Levinger, a son of Rabbi Moshe and Rebbetzim Miriam Levinger, and his wife Isca: 'What could be more fitting than to have a representative of Hebron's "first family" . . . be the first to move into this new edifice?' Wilder wrote on 10 April 2005. Gabriel Ben Yitzhak and his family moved in shortly afterwards. Their fourteenth and youngest child had been born in 2003, and they had been given a specially designed apartment in the new building. He had to count the number of bedrooms to remind himself how many they had: most of the flats contain four but the Ministry of Housing had given them an extra room. Even though five of his children had married and left home, living conditions were cramped, but Ben Yitzhak was happy in his new home: even when he heard shooting he thought, 'Let them shoot, I'm OK.' He does not regret staying through the difficult years when they felt so exposed. 'It's always very easy to say you should have left, you should have run away, but that's usually said against people living in places that are out of the consensus.'

He concedes that he has an incentive to move, for the five of his children who are married live on settlements near Nablus, in the part of the West Bank that he calls 'Samaria', where life is easier in some ways. 'On the roads it's dangerous, but where my two girls live for instance, is a nice, open settlement, and I have a son living on a very big farm there. So it's very different to Hebron: in Hebron, you can't walk – we have one road, and a bit down there in the market. It's a very closed society. It's not suited to everyone. Generally, you don't come here for a standard of living, although it's a very nice society, it's very friendly. So there is this attraction nowadays – to be with your own people, for your children to grow up with the type of friends you want them to grow up with. And schooling in this area is what you're looking for. But the early ones, you know, you couldn't come here if you weren't strong ideologically . . . The thing is you get used to anything. Life has its ups and downs and you forget where you are living. You forget the speciality of a place, because this is really a very rich archaeological and historical site for us. Sometimes, I go for a walk, and I walk down to the place where the water is . . .' He had forgotten the word for 'well': 'You know, the water thing that goes down the steps. There's a very deep pool there, and it's a Jewish custom to dip oneself in such things, and many people go into it in the summer. When I walk around, I think, so this was the place where Abraham walked. It's our land and I believe eventually that our way will be victorious. I believe that this is our land and eventually God will allow us to have it freely. What ups and downs there will be on the road I don't know. You may say I'm a dreamer, as John Lennon said . . .'

It was a poor attempt at a joke, and yet the cultural reference reminded me that I was talking to a man from Finchley. It was strange to think that I could walk more freely round the city where he has lived for more than twenty years than he could, and that I knew large parts of it better than he did. He may have overcome his perception of Israeli society as 'oriental', but he has never overcome his deeper fears and prejudices about his Palestinian neighbours. He said it was 'suicide' for a Jew to enter H1, which was undoubtedly true, but he dismissed the suggestion that he might miss the days when people mingled freely in the centre of the city. 'No, no, it's much better this way,' he said. 'We have no connection any more, really. And we have no wish to have any connection.'

He talked about the Intifada in the way that a child might describe a playground squabble: 'We didn't start it. They started it. OK, if they think things are better for them now than they were then they need their brains checked. But they started the Intifada, and I don't see that there's any way back, really.' There was another pause, while he bent over his scroll: 'You know, it sounds racist but people who grow up in Arab countries say you can't trust them. They can be friends with you but if they get incited they can stick a knife in your back – obviously not all of them, but it's a common characteristic of Arabs.'

His recognition that the remark sounds racist did not make it seem any less so. Noam Arnon was prepared to concede that the people who had lived in Palestine before the Zionists' arrival had rights, but Gabriel Ben Yitzhak wanted to deny their existence altogether: 'People talk as if the Palestinians have lived here for thousands of years. It's a load of nonsense – the Palestinians lived here . . .' He was becoming agitated again and his voice was becoming higher-pitched: 'At the turn of the century, when the Jews started coming in masses, there were a few thousand Arabs here, that was the whole story. It's all invented, this whole story of Palestinians. There are people who suffered, I don't deny it, but this whole story of millions of Palestinians . . . No one wanted it. It was desolate. It was a wasteland. There was nothing here.'

The idea of 'a people without land for a land without people' is Zionism's consoling myth, and the expulsion of the Palestinian population its guiltiest secret. 'Israelis, leaders and people alike, have a genuine psychological problem when faced with the refugee issue,' the Israeli historian Ilan Pappe has written. 'This is indeed for them the "original sin". It puts a huge question mark over the Israeli self-image of moral superiority and human sensitivity. It ridicules Israel's oxymorons, such as the "purity of arms" or misnomers such as the "Israeli Defence Forces", and raises doubts over the religious notion of the "chosen people" and political pretensions of being the only democracy in the Middle East which should be wholeheartedly supported by the West.'

Yet Ben Yitzhak was unmoved: 'We believe we have a right and duty to live everywhere we can. It's perfectly natural that we should be allowed to be in the centre of what we believe is our holy promised land. What to do with the Arabs is another problem. Basically it's a humanitarian problem – from a humanitarian point of view, someone who

doesn't bother me, I have no need to bother them, but it's much bigger than that, because we're dealing with millions, or hundreds of thousands, who don't want me here, so it's dreaming to think that we're going to live in peace together. It's not going to work out at all. Therefore the only solution is to persuade them to leave, as many as possible. Persuade them with money, or I don't know – it's not my business.'

It was not his indifference to the moral implications of requiring people to leave their homes, whether by force or inducement, that surprised me most – it was the impractical nature of his vision. The idea that, one day, the streets of Hebron would be filled with Jews was patently absurd, and yet no doubt he would have said that his God had accomplished more unlikely tasks. He leant forward again and picked up a pen, resuming the unending task of engraving the texts of the faith that licensed his presence in Hebron.

I was curious about the soldiers who guarded the settlement and patrolled the streets of Hebron. The city's international activists warned me against any kind of engagement with them, even insisting that I should not hand over my passport when they asked to see it, but I never found any of them unfriendly and I never saw the necessity of engaging them in psychological games. Many of them would want to talk when they saw I was from England – several said they had relatives in London including one who had spent a summer working at his uncle's bagel shop in Hendon. Some were embarrassed by what they were doing: on one of the rare occasions when an officer made me wait at the checkpoint for ten minutes one of the conscripts pulled a face and shook his head apologetically. Later in the day, I saw the same soldier lying on his back in the shade, head resting on his backpack. They were often eating sunflower seeds or joking amongst themselves. Yet I never forgot that they were representatives of an occupying army that subjected the Palestinians to degrading punishment and grievously impeded their day-to-day existence.

I could not talk to the soldiers on duty, but I could talk to some of their predecessors. I had got in touch with the veterans' organization Breaking the Silence before I arrived in Israel for the first time, and several months later, after many missed arrangements and unanswered emails and phone calls, I met one of their representatives.

Dotan Greenwald was in his late twenties, a slight figure, with widely spaced green eyes and thick black hair. He was wearing sandals, a checked shirt and a blue sweatshirt with orange flashes, and he had sunglasses propped on his fore-head. His father's parents came from Hungary – hence the name, which means 'green forest' – and his mother's parents from Egypt, which made him 'the perfect Israeli mixture', half Sephardic and half Ashkenazic. He grew up near Haifa, in a non-religious family, and at the age of fifteen he joined a socialist youth movement called Hanoar Halved ve Halomed, or 'Working and Learning Youth'. 'At the age of fifteen everyone talks about girls and punk stuff: I wanted to do something different. I wasn't into soccer. I wanted to find people who cared about values. I wanted a code to live by and I wanted to be surrounded by people who believe in that code,' he told me, when we met at a cafe in central Jerusalem.

He delayed military service by a year to work as 'a coun-sellor' or 'educator' at a commune, and when he joined the army at the age of nineteen he was selected for training as a sniper. Since I have been spared compulsory military service and have no sense of how it works I was surprised that he had qualified for such a brutal-seeming discipline, but Greenwald has grown up in a militarized society and did not regard it as incompatible with his previous experience: 'I don't know why they chose me,' he said. 'I guess I learn fast.' Besides, he did not like being in the army – 'run a lot, eat shitty food and not go home' was his pithy summary – and his vocation outlived his training: Breaking the Silence regards itself as an educational organization, and Greenwald invited me to hear him speak to an 'encounter group' of Israeli and Palestinian teenagers who were to meet in a room in Jerusalem's YMCA, opposite the King David Hotel, two days later. The evening started with a series of exercises and a round of singing and dancing, before the group settled down on chairs drawn up in a circle in the middle of the room to listen to Dotan, who was sitting with one foot drawn up beneath him. His mention of the commune puzzled one fifteen-year-old Palestinian boy, who put up his hand and said, 'You were a communist?' in a broad American accent. Some of the girls laughed but Dotan answered the boy patiently: 'We were socialists,' he said.

He and two thousand fellow members of the youth movement had joined the same brigade in the army: the Nahal Brigade, or Noar Halutzi Lohem, which means Fighting Pioneer Youth, used to encourage its recruits to combine military service with the task of establishing new agricultural settlements, and more recently it has accommodated idealistic youths like Dotan Greenwald. He spent six months in basic training at 50 Brigade's base camp in Arad, and he arrived in Hebron in February 2003. 'The big events of the Second Intifada were over, but the atmosphere of violence was still in the air.' Greenwald soon discovered that serving in Hebron was not what he had expected. 'I had the image that I'm going to the army to fight and defend my country, I'm going to fight the terrorist,' he said. 'Now of course I knew I'm not only going to do that but I never imagined I was going to do something completely different and something that is actually illegal in the name of the state.'

Like most Israelis he had not spent any time in 'the Territories', and he did not know anything about the settlers, other than what he had got from television: 'I thought they were regular people like you and me: they have one nose, two ears, they live, they get married, they have children. But it didn't mention that they would be so fanatical.' In his first days in the city one of the settlers' kids, who was no more than five or six years old, thanked him for killing all the Arabs, and he saw another spit in the face of an old Palestinian woman. 'And not because the five-year-old is a punk, but because this is how it is.'

In common with many of the soldiers who testified to Breaking the Silence, Dotan came to believe that they were terrorizing the city: 'Going into someone's house in the middle of the night, going through her stuff, going through her drawers – isn't that a sin? We don't know who is the enemy and so everybody is a suspect. And you start treating them like shit. I come to your house, I go inside your house for a routine check, I search your stuff – even if we were nice, in person, it's inevitable that you're doing an atrocity.'

He estimated there were seven hundred soldiers guarding seven hundred settlers, which meant that each of them had 'a special guard'. The army headquarters in Kiryat Arba was mainly concerned with logistics and supply, and there were four barracks in the city – the main one in the old bus station on Shoada Street, which was also a settlement, and others in Beit Romano, Tel Rumeida, and on Abu Sneineh. There were more in the countryside around Hebron. There were static positions and jeep and commando patrols. Special units also operated inside the city. Wilder claimed that it 'is quite possible that five minutes after killing Rabbi Ra'anan, the villain sat, calm and relaxed, sipping a cup of coffee, knowing that his home, in the H1–Arafat-controlled section of Hebron, is off-limits to the Israeli army', but Dotan said the army drew no distinction between H1 and H2: 'We didn't consider it a border – we go where we want: we did operations inside, outside, outside Hebron sometimes.'

It was the way his own behaviour changed that shocked him most. On his first day in the city, he broke into a house and 'terrorized' its inhabitants, and a week later he slapped a man because he was smiling too much. After each incident his reaction was the same: he sat in bed thinking that he had crossed another red line, and gradually he realized that he had changed. He had brought a set of slides to the YMCA, and he projected them on the wall to illustrate the process: the first photograph was of him in uniform, with shaved head and glasses, in his base in Hebron, the second was of a group of soldiers 'goofing around' like kids on holiday, the third was of a handcuffed, blindfolded man in a stairwell, and the fourth showed the forehead of a Palestinian man in the crosshairs of a sniper's rifle. Greenwald had taken it through his gun sight at the end of an eight-hour shift. 'No one got hurt – the safety catch was on – but I never thought I'd do anything like that.'

Greenwald had been taught that he should only use his weapon when he had to: during basic training one of his fellow recruits had been jailed for playing with his gun, but once his platoon arrived in Hebron discipline was soon forgotten. He read out a testimony from a soldier who described setting up a 'strangulation checkpoint' at the entrance to a village and controlling the flow of cars going in and out: 'Suddenly, you have a mighty force at the tip of your fingers, as if playing a computer game . . . You come here, you go there, like this. You barely move, you make them obey the tip of your finger. It's a mighty feeling . . . You know it's because you have a weapon, you know it's because you are a soldier, you know all this, but it's addictive.' The soldier realized that he was becoming addicted to 'controlling people', and Dotan told the group that everyone he knew felt the same.

There was little point looking to their commanding officers for guidance: most were scrupulous about enforcing orders, regardless of how unfair or absurd they were, and some were ruthless in punishing those who dared defy them. One soldier told Breaking the Silence about an incident in which they entered a house at 6 a.m. to arrest a teenage boy who had been throwing stones: 'You know, the way it goes when your mind's already screwed up, and you have no more patience for Hebron and Arabs and Jews there. We went inside and began to trash the house.' The commander, 'who was a bit of a fanatic', dragged the boy out of the house, and 'really beat the shit out of him'. As he dragged him away he kept pointing out holes in the ground and asking him, 'Is here where you want to die? Or here?' They took him to a 'concrete house which was under construction', where they beat him to the point he couldn't stand, and when his family came to look for him the commander put his gun in the boy's mouth and told them that he would shoot him if they came any closer. The soldier who reported the incident had done nothing to stop him: 'We were indifferent,' he said. 'It got to the point where we couldn't tell right from wrong. That's how it was in our platoon . . . If you even just looked at us in some way that irked us you'd get beaten up.'

The relentless routine – eighteen days with eight hours on and eight hours off, followed by a three-day break – contributed to the loss of empathy so many soldiers attested to: 'Serving in the Territories isn't about numbness, it's a "high", a sort of negative high,' one soldier said: 'You're always tired, you're always hungry, you always have to go to the bathroom, you're always scared to die . . . It's the experience of a hunted animal, a hunting animal, of an animal, whatever . . . ' 'Do you have any idea what shape people were in?' another said. 'You're fed up and everyone's a pack of nerves. And when you come down from the guard post you go: Fuck, I'm so sick of this town. You come down all nerves, and then you run into some Arab on the way, and slap his face . . . Guys would take the Arab into their post and beat him to a pulp . . . Just like that. Because, really, our nerves were gone and we said what the fuck . . . Some said: "I'll fuck with those Arabs like I'm being fucked with here." You know how it is. Not too cool there.'

What the stories had in common, Dotan said, was a 'lowering of standards'. The requirements of policing a city of 150,000 people meant that 'everyone was brought down several levels', and every day he found himself doing things he could not justify. The army imposed five hundred days of curfew in Hebron during the Second Intifada, which Dotan described as 'locking innocent people in their houses'. Another soldier told Breaking the Silence that there was no official prohibition on what they were allowed to do in a house, beside rape or murder: 'You were the emperor of the place,' he said. 'Really. Like some king. Ruler. You walk down the street with your hands in your pockets, your rifle hanging on your back even, and only because of your uniform no one dares talk to you.' If he felt 'like munching some cashews all of a sudden', the soldier would go into a shop and pick up a kilo of nuts. The shopkeeper wouldn't dare complain: 'Want me to trash your shop, what are you, fucked up or something? Give him a slap in the face and walk out.'

The soldiers were not allowed to arrest the settlers, regardless of what they did, and they were in no doubt that they were not there to keep the peace, or protect the Palestinians: they were there to protect the settlers, who were so appreciative that they would leave cakes in their guard posts. The fact that Dotan objected to their political views didn't mean he wasn't grateful: 'It's nice – it's real comfort,' he had told me. 'Why not? The settlers are part of your society – you might have disagreements, but you're still OK with that.'

Dotan believed that the most important legacy of the Holocaust ought to be the 'simple humanitarian lesson' that terrible things happen when one group of people begins to look down on another: 'Yet this is what I saw in Hebron – very clearly, and without shame.' It was not just the settlers who were guilty: Dotan himself began to look down on the Palestinians, as well, and he realized that he was as bad as the settlers, if not worse, for he was the one with 'the heavy boot, like any other oppressor in any other place in the world, in history'. He did not exempt himself, or his commander, or the military authorities, or the government, from blame, but the 'biggest sinner' was Israeli society: 'Every day something happened and everybody's OK with it in Tel Aviv, in Jerusalem, in Netanyu, in Haifa – that's the big fault.'

Yehuda Shaul arrived a couple of months into Dotan's seven-month posting as an officer in another platoon, but it wasn't until they had left the city and were stationed in

Bethlehem that they began to discuss what was happening in Hebron and the rest of the West Bank. 'We wanted to show Hebron to other people, to our families and friends, and we came up with the idea of putting on an exhibition.' It was held in Tel Aviv in 2004 and it combined the testimonies of serving soldiers with the kind of photographs Dotan had shown at the beginning of his encounter group. Dotan was still in the army but Yehuda and three other founding members of Breaking the Silence provided commentaries and explanations. It was a great success. Officially, the army chose to characterize them as 'rotten apples', but the attempts to dismiss the exhibition only confirmed its message. Dotan told the encounter group what a high-ranking commanding officer in his brigade had said: 'You call it dehumanizing people – I call it growing up.' That was precisely the point: 'They always say the army makes you more mature. They say you'll come out a different person. But they don't say why. Yes, we were different. Yes, we grew up. But we didn't want to grow up like that.'

One of the people who went to see the Breaking the Silence exhibition in Tel Aviv was an American-born lieutenant called Mikhail Manekhin, who gave his testimony to the group and went on to become one of its leading members. He was the man that I had spent the most time trying to track down, though when we did meet up I realized why he had been so busy. The British Embassy funds Breaking the Silence because it promotes dialogue between the Palestinians and Israelis, and the day before Mikhail Manekhin had taken a group of British diplomats on a tour of Hebron, which had attracted the attention of a notorious settler. Noam Federman – whom Manekhin described as 'one of the more criminal elements they've got there' – had chased them through the city in his car: having blocked them in, he got out and started kicking their car and when they pulled away he had raced after them and blocked them in again. They decided to leave the city, but the settlers would not let them through the checkpoint at Kiryat Arba, and when the police arrived Federman accused them of driving over his foot. 'We were very, very close to being detained,' Manekhin said. 'If high ranks hadn't been involved we would have been a Breaking the Silence representative and three British diplomats in the police station. It was very, very close.'

Such incidents were becoming increasingly common. Breaking the Silence had been running tours to Hebron since 2005 but recently the settlers had begun to disrupt them by attacking the groups with stones and eggs. The settlers seemed to reserve particular hatred for Yehuda Shaul, the Hebron veteran who founded the group: in the sixty years of its existence the Israeli state has only imposed capital punishment on one person, Adolf Eichmann, and David Wilder says that Shaul should be the second – he wants to see him tried and hanged for treason, as if his actions merit comparison with those of the architect of the Holocaust. For the time being, the settlers content themselves with following his tours and taunting him about his mother's suicide. The disruption became so extreme that the police began cancelling their tours and Breaking the Silence was forced to petition the state to assert their right to return. Manekhin said they were 'under terrible amounts of stress': 'Even on a personal level, we're getting attacked quite often – physically, harassing phone calls, in the media.' The day we met was his first free afternoon for several weeks, and even then he could only spare me half an hour.

I was surprised that their organization attracted such

criticism, for it did not offer a political perspective on the conflict, let alone attempt to come up with a solution – since Breaking the Silence speaks on behalf of the hundreds of soldiers who have given testimonies, Manekhin was determined to remain scrupulously neutral. He said its aim was simple: Israeli society wanted to ignore what was happening in the West Bank, and Breaking the Silence did not intend to allow it. 'They don't want to know but we're saying that you have to know – you have to know, and know, and know, and know.'

Manekhin had served in Lebanon and the West Bank in the early years of the Second Intifada, and he drew a clear distinction between the two halves of his term: in Lebanon he had been a soldier, but in 'the Territories' he had been part policeman and part administrative officer. In theory, the Palestinian Authority was running Nablus, but the army did what it liked and made frequent incursions into the city's refugee camps. 'I hated it,' he said. 'I thought it was bad for me, bad for the Palestinians, bad for Israel. Pretty quickly actually. But I still managed to do the same thing for a very long time: that's how powerful the system is, I guess – or how weak I am.' I asked him if it was an uncomfortable experience and he dismissed the question: 'Look, it's not about me being uncomfortable. If it was uncomfortable for anyone, it was for the Palestinians. I was heavily armoured and the boss of the situation. It was a wrong experience – morally, it was wrong, and I perpetrated it. I'm not the victim. I had a choice every step of the way. I could have said no, I could have done something different, I could have been somewhere else. I didn't. I'm an adult, I have to accept responsibility.'

What's more, he had signed up as an officer and done an extra year's service at the end of his term: 'I guess that means

I must have not hated it,' he said, as if the idea was still strange to him. Dotan Greenwald had laughed at the idea that he might have volunteered to serve for a moment longer than required, and when I pointed out that Mikhail Manekhin had done exactly that, he said, 'Yeah, but he was an officer,' as if he was still conscious of the difference in rank: 'I wasn't an officer. Look at me,' he said in his self-deprecating way: 'too short.' I had not noticed Dotan's lack of height, but I could see why he regarded Manekhin as officer class – his father and mother were academics who taught Jewish philosophy and history, and it was easy to see how his intelligence and privileged American-Israeli background had secured promotion to the rank of lieutenant, and given him the courage to present the army's failings to the world.

Manekhin was twenty-nine years old, bearded, with glasses, dressed casually in flip-flops, trousers and a short-sleeved shirt. He said he belonged to the diminishing group of Israeli 'leftists' who are also religious. Normally he would have been wearing a kippah, but we had met in a hotel on the edge of Palestinian East Jerusalem and he had removed it because he did not want to make people 'nervous'. Far from endearing him to the settlers, his religious faith seemed to make them resent his 'treachery' even more, but he was not unsympathetic to their cause. 'Hebron is an important place – Hebron has much more significance to me than Tel Aviv, not because I believe or don't believe that the patriarchs are buried there, but because my people wanted to be there for thousands of years and that has significance for me as somebody who's tied in with the history of my people.' It was not the idea of a Jewish presence in Hebron that he objected to but the form it took: 'I have problems with the specific Jews and the specific presence – because they're violent, because they don't believe in equality for all people, because they're misusing the texts I hold dear.'

Yet even the settlers' failings made Hebron an interesting place: 'It's not only a conversation about politics, it's a conversation about who we are as Jews, and that's very much part of the city for me.' Manekhin had told me that they took tours to Hebron for the simple reason that it was the only city in the West Bank Israelis could visit – the settlers had inadvertently turned it into a showcase for the occupation. Yet they were performing another service, as well – none of the Israelis that I spoke to said they would have trusted the Palestinian Authority to preserve Jewish access to the city's holy shrines. They believed that it was only the settlers' presence that allowed them to visit Hebron, and I saw for myself how much that mattered to some people when I joined one of the tours that the settlers ran as one of their ways of raising funds.

I had rung the tour organizers, who were part of the 'Jewish community of Hebron', to tell them I was coming but my name did not make it onto the list, so I had to introduce myself to the man with the clipboard standing on the steps of the bus in the car park of the Sheraton Hotel, opposite Jerusalem's main synagogue, at 9.15 on Friday morning. Yossi Baumol – the director of the Hebron Fund and our guide for the first part of the day – was a balding man in his fifties with a thin grey beard. He seemed amused to hear that I was a writer from England, and since everyone else in the group was American or Canadian I assumed that his first remarks were for my benefit: 'I'm not going to be speaking the Queen's English,' he said over the PA as the bus moved away into the rush-hour traffic. Baumol had lived in Israel

for thirty years but he could not lose the Brooklyn accent – and he assured us that he could not do political correctness. 'Jews bother people wherever they live. England in the twelfth century, Russia in the nineteenth, Germany in the twentieth . . .'

The monologue, which would continue with few interruptions until he left the bus an hour later, had two purposes: it was intended to address the prejudices of the settlers' critics and inform us where we were going. We had no other way of gauging our progress, for we were travelling in an armoured bus with toughened-glass windows rendered opaque by a misty sheen of tiny scratches. Since I had travelled back and forth between Jerusalem and Hebron at least a dozen times I knew the road reasonably well, yet I soon lost track of where we were, and Baumol did not help, for he was less concerned with observable reality than a mythic topography prefigured in the Prophets. He claimed that the Bible had even predicted the course of the Separation Barrier. 'In the end, everything falls together,' he said. 'Tremendous miracles are taking place here every day with the Jews returning after so many years to their homeland.'

Little of his talk made sense to me, and the difficulty was compounded by the fact that I soon acquired a second guide to complement the first – a surgeon from Long Island called Ari came and sat beside me and began explaining the difference between affiliated and non-affiliated Jews, his East Coast vowels merging with Baumol's in an aural blizzard as dense as the visual one that enclosed us.

The settlers had been using armoured buses since the beginning of the Second Intifada, when Route 60 came under fire. When the violence was at its worst the Israeli army had shut down the first place that we were going to stop at. Kever Rachel, or Rachel's tomb, lies on the edge of Bethlehem, where Rachel was supposed to have died after giving birth to Benjamin, the youngest of Jacob's twelve sons. Rachel was the third of the matriarchs who was infertile, and the only one of the 'grandfathers and grandmothers' not buried in Hebron. Yet she remained Jacob's best-loved wife, and the settlers were so attached to her memory that they adopted their favoured tactic to force the army to reopen the tomb – a group of women and children from Hebron and neighbouring settlements gathered every morning at an intersection that only Baumol and the driver could see, and 'marched their baby carriages under fire' to Kever Rachel.

The protests were another stage in what Jerold S. Auerbach calls the 'maternalist strategy' that revived the Jewish community of Hebron. Auerbach regards the women's actions, which were inspired by Miriam Levinger's role in reoccupying Beit Hadassah, as a statement of feminist independence in the face of the 'assertively masculine' values of the Orthodox communities from which most of them emerged. Other observers were appalled by the way they endangered their children's lives. The chief of police who arrived in Hebron in 2005 was astonished to find 'mothers from the Jewish settlement' using their babies 'as a shield' against police. 'I watch television, and I have never seen any population on earth that uses babies,' Commander Eli Zamir told the Israeli journalist Meron Rapaport in 2005. 'I don't understand by what right these mothers use one-year-old babies.' Zamir ordered his staff to 'find the section in the law book that will enable me to prosecute them', but the authorities have always found it hard to resist the women's tactics, and the Israeli army recognized that it had no choice but to

make it safer to visit Rachel's Tomb: 'That's when they insti-
tuted the use of bulletproof buses,' Baumol said.

Yet the reopened Rachel's Tomb was not quite as he
remembered – when he came to Israel in 1983 Baumol used
to put his fifteen-year-old daughter in an 'Arab taxi' and
send her to Jerusalem or Bethlehem to shop, but since the
'peace process', Rachel's Tomb looked like Auschwitz. I
assumed that he was exaggerating, but when I emerged from
the bus I realized that the comparison was not entirely inappropriate: Rachel's Tomb lay at the end of a narrow corridor
formed by two sections of the concrete blocks that make up
the wall, and only the rooftops of the fabled 'little town of
Bethlehem' were visible beyond another line of fortifications. An Israeli army watchtower had been built above the
entrance to the tomb, and the facing of Jerusalem stone on
the bunker-like building was the only concession to orna-
ment in the militarized landscape.

Unlike Christians, who tend to remove their headgear
when they enter a church, Jews cover their heads to pray,
and when I entered the room that housed the cloth-clad
cenotaph where Rachel is supposed to be interred I had to
resist the instinct to take off my baseball cap. I stood at the
back while the rest of the group 'davened' or prayed. They
were not praying to Rachel herself, Baumol explained, but
they believed that prayers said in her presence went directly
to heaven, and he exploited the connection by reading a section of the Psalms that would get him arrested for incitement
if he read it on the evening news.

When we got back on the bus I asked Ari what he
thought of Rachel's Tomb but he shook his head and did not
answer: his wife had forbidden him from speaking: 'She
thinks I'm bothering you,' he said.

His wife, Barbara, was a short, dark-haired New Yorker,

sitting two rows behind us. She stood up: 'I know he's bothering you,' she said.

'I should have married a British lady,' Ari said, loud
enough for her to hear. 'She would have appreciated me.'

Had they been English, then the volume and intensity of
the ensuing argument would have signalled the irretrievable
breakdown of the marriage. Ari lost, and obeyed his wife's
command to go and sit beside her, but a moment later, he
came back. He could sit next to me but he was not allowed
to talk.

Twenty minutes after we left Rachel's Tomb, the bus
drew up at the side of the road and Baumol, who lived in the
settlement of Efrat, got off and disappeared into the blur.
The bus seemed very quiet. I appreciated Barbara's efforts to
protect me from her husband but I missed Ari's commentary, and as the bus made its way through the outskirts of
Hebron I asked him how a surgeon equated evidentially
based science with his religious beliefs: did he really believe
that the world was created 5,768 years ago? He did, though
he could not explain why.

I could not tell when we passed Kiryat Arba, but I
guessed we had begun to descend the narrow road that runs
down to the Tomb of the Patriarchs when the dark shapes
of buildings began to hem us in. Soon afterwards Simcha
Hochbaum got on the bus. He was our guide for the second
part of the day; his dual role as rabbi of the Jewish community of Hebron and its director of tourism affirmed
the connection between its spiritual and financial needs.
Hochbaum picked up the microphone Yossi Baumol had
relinquished and said that we were not only coming to see
the people who are buried in Hebron, but the people who
live there today: 'There are four different Jewish neighbourhoods in Hebron, eighty-six Jewish families, five hundred

children, two hundred yeshiva boys – a thousand Jews. Unfortunately, we also have to share our area with fifteen thousand Arabs.'

Such an inconvenience might seem an unavoidable consequence of life in the largest 'Arab city' in the West Bank, but Simcha Hochbaum had no sense that the Israeli presence in Hebron was inconvenient to other people – all he could talk about were the constraints on Jewish movement in Hebron: 'Eighty per cent a Jew can't go, a Jew can't drive, a Jew can't walk,' he said in a New York accent as broad as Baumol's. 'God forbid, a Jew goes into any part of the eighty per cent, it's a one way ticket in.' His rapid, compulsive style made it sound like he was on the verge of breaking into song or prayer, and his voice hardly changed as he chanted Lamentations 5:2 first in Hebrew and then in English: 'Our inheritance is turned over to foreigners, our houses to strangers.' Yet even a visit to the restricted districts that the settlers controlled was a unique event. 'We're going to get off the bus in a moment and from this point and on I want you to realize the great privilege you have – every step you are going to take today with me I promise you that Abraham and Sarah

walked here before you, Yitzhak and Rebekah, Yakob and Leah. We are walking today in the footsteps of our fore-fathers, in 3,800 years of Jewish history.'

Tel Rumeida was the first stop of the day. As we gathered between the caravans and the railings that enclosed the two sections of the ancient city wall, Rabbi Hochbaum said he had come straight to Hebron from Manhattan fifteen years before, with no stopovers or absorption centres, and his patter was larded with references designed to make his com-patriots feel at home. He told us that the Middle Bronze Age wall was 'the giant's wall, though not the New York Giants' offensive or defensive line', and he said that when Abraham arrived in Hebron there was a famine in the land, which meant 'no more bagels and iced coffee'.

He 'sojourned in Egypt', before he settled in Hebron: 'Yitzak was born right over here, and Jacob was here, after that famous showdown with his twin brother Esau. You remember that Mike Tyson kiss?' He gave us Genesis 23 at great speed – 'Avraham Avinu comes to Ephron and says I want to buy the cave, and Ephron says, buy it, are you nuts?, you have tens of thousands of disciples: please let's not talk money, take my business card, give it out, recom-mend me, but Avraham Avinu insists' – as a prelude to his central point: 'This is where it all began. From here, Jewish history unravels. I want to ask you, isn't it very natural for a Jew to want to live here? Isn't it the most natural thing in the world for a yid to want to live where Abraham, Isaac and Yakob walked and lived?'

The back wall of the building was whitewashed and it still looked clean and newly built. A clothes rail hanging from one balcony was the only sign that it was occupied. Hochbaum said that families had lived in the caravans for twenty years, and that one of them was a 'spiritual visionary and special seer' who was 'stabbed to death again and again by an Arab terrorist screaming, "Slaughter the Jew."' His account of the incident was gruesomely detailed – 'His body hits the ground, his wife hears something in the bedroom, runs inside, finds her husband lying in a pool of blood, lifeless, motionless' – and he displayed the same gory relish when we arrived at the museum in the basement of Beit Hadassah.

It was called the Rose and Reuben Matteus Hebron Heritage Institute and it was dedicated to the memory of Lieutenant Colonel Yonatan Netanyahu, the brother of the Israeli Prime Minister who had authorized the construction of the settlement at Tel Rumeida. The elder Netanyahu was a decorated soldier and the commander of an elite unit who died in 1976 on a mission to rescue hostages held on an Air France plane hijacked by Palestinian terrorists, and diverted to Entebbe in Uganda. Inside, there was an assembly room decorated with crude paintings of the Tomb of the Patriarchs, and various rooms devoted to different aspects of Hebron's history. Hochbaum warned us that the room devoted to the victims of 1929 was 'very powerful', but he seemed more moved than anybody else. He explained that people had taken shelter in Beit Hadassah: 'They thought they would be safe here, but the mob came in yelling and screaming, and they raped the women, butchered the children.' He was standing in front of a dimly lit shrine in the corner: headstones rescued from the Jewish cemetery were piled on top of one another, and the wall behind was covered with photographs of the victims and their wounds. One showed a bearded yeshiva student called Elchanan Zeligroch lying in bed, his bearded bandaged head resting on the pillow, while an unseen woman held his forearm in her two hands, displaying the sutured stump to the camera. 'You can see, I don't have to spell it out – pictures speak louder than words: men, women, children, organ by organ, limb by limb.'

Another of the victims was an all-American kid from Chicago called Yacof Exler, whose father was inspired to send him to Israel when he heard a visiting rabbi's 'fire and brimstone' speech. Most people donated money but Exler's father told the rabbi that he had a far more precious gift: he wanted him to take his son and fill him with the love of the Torah. When the boy was killed in the 1929 massacre the rabbi felt guilty: 'Maybe I shouldn't have sent him to Hebron, maybe I should have realized the reputation of the Arabs of Hebron for being so barbaric,' Rabbi Hochbaum said, in his stuttering style. 'And therefore this rabbi avoids Chicago like a plague. One day, he's in New York, someone comes up to him and gives out his hand, and the rabbi looks up and he sees the father of the boy.' By now Hochbaum was on the verge of tears: 'The rabbi's stammering and stuttering, he can't get the words out, but finally the father says I didn't call you over to embarrass you. I called you over to thank you for what you did for my son. The gift that you gave to my son was not only in this world – you gave him a gift in the next world. Because we all know they have a place in heaven that no one else has: my son was always going to die and you gave him the gift of dying in Hebron.'

The rabbi led singing in front of the shrine of photographs. He said that hatred is generally taught, and he blamed the Mufti of Jerusalem for inciting the riots, in Hebron and elsewhere. 'During the Second World War, Haj al-Husseini went to see Hitler and told him to finish the job he had begun, not limb by limb, organ by organ, as he had done, but with gas chambers.' The Mufti's shameful record of courting the Nazis was inspiration for a battle cry of his own: 'God forbid when the non-Jewish world sees that it can kill us without a response. We ask Hashem to avenge the blood that was spilt here from '29 to the present.'

The next room commemorated the return to the city, and to Beit Hadassah, which had been inspired by the memory of the massacre – Hochbaum said that Miriam Levinger had led a group of ten women and thirty children through the market in the middle of the night, and he broke off his staccato account of their journey through 'shattered glass, dirt, stray dogs' to throw open a window in the middle of the display of photos in the back wall. We found ourselves looking down on one of the main streets in the new market, which I had often walked through on my way to my hotel. The new market was an attempt to revive Hebron's commercial life, but it had suffered just as much as the souk from the settlers' presence – the wide street beneath us was covered with a metal grille littered with bricks and bottles thrown from the upper storeys of Beit Hadassah. All I could see through the window was a roll of barbed wire, a concrete barricade and the rear wall of an abandoned house. Rabbi Hochbaum had hoped to illustrate the chaos of the Arab city that the settlers had found when they returned, but all he had shown us was the wasteland it has since become.

It wasn't clear what most of the settlers did for a living. Some had public roles: Baruch Marzel was a political activist of such an extreme and provocative kind that even other settlers tended to avoid him; Wilder and Arnon worked for the municipality, and Simcha Hochbaum augmented his work in Hebron by teaching evening classes at a yeshiva attended by American boys – 'no time to sin, right?' he told the tour group. There were teachers, and a doctor who ran a mobile clinic, but there were few other forms of employment: Idith Zertal and Akiva Eldar say 'the only industry that flourished in Kiryat Arba was the yeshiva industry', and the situation was even worse in Hebron itself. There were not enough people to open viable businesses and even if there were they did not have the space. The gift shop in the Gutnick Center and a small cafeteria in the Avraham Avinu neighbourhood were the only amenities. People shopped in Kiryat Arba, and commuted to and from Jerusalem for work.

Most of the Palestinians believed they subsisted on donations from abroad, and spent most of their time observing religious festivals: one resident described them as 'drunk people', though it may be that he had mistaken messianic religiosity for alcoholism. Other people said that their presence in Hebron was sufficient employment in itself: 'Their whole life is filled with purpose,' an American girl who had visited the city wrote on the settlers' website. 'They are living on a higher plane. It seems as if they are above time and space.' Even the settlers' children lived in a kind of heroic ecstasy: one of those who returned to Beit Hadassah with Miriam Levinger is supposed to have told a soldier that they were personal guests of Avraham Avinu, borne on the wings of eagles to Hebron. As Zertal and Eldar say, 'life, like death, is magnified, deprived of its reality, but rendered sublime, sanctified'. Yet that does not preclude the need for funds, and Hochbaum constantly pressed the tour group for donations to help the community that allowed other Jews to pray at the city's shrines: 'Don't just give the exact amount – add a little bit, to help the community out,' he said, when he collected payment for the tour after prayers in the renovated synagogue in the Avraham Avinu settlement.

The tourists had another opportunity to pray in the

Tomb of the Patriarchs and as they prepared to leave the eight-year-old daughter of one of Ari's friends from New York carried her two-year-old brother round the rooms that overlook the cenotaphs; she held him up to the grilled windows so he could blow kisses at the people inside. Abraham and his family were more real and vivid to her than the vast majority of the inhabitants of Hebron: 'Mommy, I saw an Arab!' she yelled as we got on the bus, though other concerns rapidly came to mind: 'Mommy, where's my chewing gum?'

As the bus pulled away, she noticed that someone was missing: 'Where's the rabbi? Why isn't he on the bus?'

'He's gone home, honey. To get ready for Shabbat.'

'What, here?'

'Yes, honey.'

'He lives here? In this city? With the Arabs?'

'Yes, honey. He told us so. Weren't you listening?'

'No!' The way she said this implied that 'not listening' was a virtue. 'Couldn't he come home with us?'

It seemed unlikely that Rabbi Hochbaum could be persuaded to leave quite so easily. I talked to the girl's mother on the way back. She had been to Hebron many times, though she could not imagine living there – you have to be made of stern stuff, she said. Her sister lived near the coast, in a new development, which was less pioneering. Her husband was a dentist and she spent the summer in Israel every year. She was a teenager when she went to Hebron for the first time: she just got on the normal bus in Jerusalem and got off in the middle of town. In those days there was no need for an armoured bus.

CHAPTER NINE

THE ANCESTOR OF ME

As for the racial origins of the city's inhabitants, although many of the family stories are mythical, the origins of a large portion of the population are clear. These include pre-Islamic Arab origins . . . Kurdish origins . . . Arab origins . . . in addition to Moroccan and Turkish origins. Furthermore, Hebron has received families which emigrated from various Palestinian cities (Jerusalem, Ascalan) or from towns located within the Hebron hills such as Doura and Yatta. Following the Catastrophe Day (*Yawm Al Nakba*, coinciding with Israel's Independence Day) in 1948, an unspecified number of refugees sought shelter in the city and blended in with the locals.

> *Old Hebron: the Charm of an*
> *Historical City and Architecture*,
> published by the Hebron Rehabilitation
> Committee, ed. Nazmi Al Jubeh

One of the most damning pieces of evidence about the nature of the settlement in Hebron emerged from a programme launched by the Israeli human rights organization B'Tselem in 2006. 'Shooting Back' was intended to discourage the violent activities of a small minority of thuggish settlers by giving Palestinians the means to document them. The Abu Ayshe family, who live in the caged house

opposite the settlement on Tel Rumeida, were one of those who received a video camera, and in the summer of 2007 one of the daughters shot a short video that dominated national news in Israel for several days.

The scene takes place in the street outside the settlement, and appears to begin in the middle, with a settler called Yifkat Alkobi walking away from the camera. 'She wants to lock us in,' says Mrs Abu Ayshe, who remains unseen, to the Israeli soldier standing nearby. Alkobi – a tall, solid-looking woman, with a round face and glasses – turns round and walks back towards the house. She is wearing the modest, hardwearing clothes favoured by women settlers – a striped top, a long skirt and a dun-coloured headscarf. 'Get in the house,' she says as she attempts to block the camera's wavering eye. 'Sit in the cage,' she says dismissively, and as the argument between the women escalates she presses her face against the bars and intones a single word in Arabic, stretching out its middle vowel in a prolonged cooing sound that imbues it with languorous intimacy: 'Sharmuta! Sharmuta!'

It is another of those moments when Tel Rumeida's present appears to collapse into its biblical past – Genesis does not record exactly what Sarah called Hagar when she cast her out after she had become pregnant with Abraham's oldest child, but it seems highly probable that it was what Yifkat Alkobi called Mrs Abu Ayshe. The subtitles scrolling across the bottom of the screen on the evening news provided a barely necessary translation: 'Whore – you are! Whore – you are!'

Gabriel Ben Yitzhak had told me that all 'the great anti-Semites' – including 90 per cent of the Israeli media – function in the same way: they take an isolated incident, blow it out of proportion, and blame the entire community, not the individuals involved. Yet a former Justice Minister called Tommy Lapid reversed the comparison in an op-ed article in the *Jerusalem Post*: he said that the images of Yifkat Alkobi gripping the bars of the cage and cursing Mrs Abu Ayshe in her soft, deep voice reminded him of someone. 'Gradually, from the cobwebs of my childhood memories, I dredged up the image of a Hungarian neighbour in Novi Sad, who used to stand at the entrance to her home and curse us every time we went into the street – just like Yifkat Alkobi.'

European anti-Semitism reached its height in Auschwitz, Lapid said, but it had existed for years before that, when 'shuttered windows hid terrified Jewish women, exactly like the Arab woman of the Abu-Isha family in Hebron.' He was not referring to crematoria or pogroms, but to the petty persecution of stone-throwing, spitting and public contempt: 'It was all of these things that made our lives in the Diaspora so bitter and harrowing, even before they began the wholesale killing of Jews.' Lapid said that he was afraid to go to school because little anti-Semites lay in wait on the way and attacked them: 'In what way is a Palestinian child in Hebron any different?' As Justice Minister, he had overlooked countless similar offences, and even now, he only 'piped up occasionally by means of articles such as this one . . . We are familiar with the excuse of "We didn't know." So, for the record: "We do know."'

The Prime Minister, Ehud Olmert, said the film made him ashamed, and the Defence Minister, Amir Peretz, asked the most senior military officer in the West Bank to investigate the harassment of the Abu Ayshes. The family was unmoved by their concern: when I met Mr Abu Ayshe, the family patriarch, in his shop in Hebron, he said that he told the military advisor sent to see them that worse things happened to them every day. I would have gone to the house if

I could, but the Abu Ayshes were not in the habit of receiving guests: the only person who was allowed to walk past
their house was the man who lived at the end of the road,
and even he had had to fight to win the right. At the start of
the Second Intifada the army told Hani Abu Heikel he was
not allowed to leave his front gate. He petitioned the Israeli
court three times and won a court order, but the Civil
Administration overruled it, so he shamed it into complying
by telling the TV crews that came calling at Tel Rumeida in
the wake of the Sharmuta scandal that it had ignored the
ruling of the highest court in the land. Even so, his short
journey is often punctuated by fusillades of eggs and stones.
He does not mind: he knew that the settlers hoped to force
him to leave, but he was not going to give in, for three generations of his family had been born in the house.

When I had gone to see Hani, his son had met me near
the mosque that the family had built on the far side of the
tel, and led me round the edge of the family's olive grove.
The Abu Heikel family owns a plot of 17,000 square metres
on the summit of the tel, beneath the army watchtower. It
used to be thickly planted, but the settlers had burnt down
the trees and the saplings that had been planted to replace
them were still no more than a metre high.

We went through the back gate into a yard, where the
family burns its rubbish: the only other way to get rid of it
is to carry it down the hill to the checkpoint, and the metal
barrel was filled to the brim. Hani always kept his front
door locked, but when I arrived he came outside and we sat
on the terrace eating grapes from the garden. A rich array of
plants, vines and fruit trees fringed the side of the balcony
that looked towards the Tomb of the Patriarchs, but the
view in the other direction was less appealing. The vines
planted in the front garden got thinner as they approached

the gate, and the earth around them was littered with rubbish discarded from the windows of the al-Bakri house, next door, which the settlers had occupied.

He said the settlers stoned his house almost every Saturday, and most nights he gets up two or three times to make sure the family is safe. We walked to the front gate and looked out: it was no more than twenty metres to the front door of the Abu Ayshes' house, but I could not walk down the street to go and see them, and Hani offered to take me to their shop in town instead.

Hani had been arrested during the First Intifada for his role in coordinating resistance in Hebron – in what capacity, I was not sure – but when he was released after twenty months in prison he decided that non-violent activism was a more effective way of fighting the occupation. He subsequently studied business administration, but he says he cannot keep a steady job because he has to be available if his children are arrested or his house attacked, and he runs a coffee stall because it gives him the flexibility he requires. When I met him at the Tel Rumeida checkpoint he was carrying an engraved silver urn and a stack of paper cups, which he kept filling and handing out to passers-by as we made our way back along Al-Adel Street, towards the fountains.

When Hani was a child the area we were walking through was full of orchards and it was still known as the 'valley of the apple trees', though it had begun to fill with houses in the nineteenth century, when Hebron began to expand beyond the confines of the Old City. Halfway down the street we turned into the alleyway where we met Abu Samir's second son, Taysir. He was wearing a checked shirt, khaki trousers, and a battered gold watch. He had a lean face, a moustache, and closely cropped black hair. He said

the harassment began soon after the settlers arrived in 1984, but it got worse at the beginning of the Second Intifada. In the winter of 2000, a group of settlers, including Baruch Marzel and Yifkat Alkobi's husband, Shalom Alkobi, broke into the house and attacked Taysir, who lives in the apartment on the first floor. They tried to drag him out into the road but his father, Abu Samir, who lives in the flat upstairs, beat them back with his stick. Taysir said the settlers have poisoned their wells, thrown hot tea in their faces, and shot at the house with air rifles. They swear at them, beat them with clubs, and spray them with water. The windows were broken so many times that they were forced to clad the front of the house in steel grilles. Abu Samir has been hit twice in the eye by stones and Taysir's daughter, Faha, has been beaten, stoned, and sworn at on her way to school. His daughter, Imam, was struck in the head by a stone when she was eight, and a year later Shalom Alkobi tried to run her over.

We had been talking for twenty minutes when Taysir's father arrived. Samir Abu Ayshe, who is also known as Abu Samir or father of Samir, the name of his oldest son, was in his seventies, and he walked with a stick, but he was an upright man, immaculately dressed in a white keffiyeh, a grey suit, and a long skirt. He had a tiny, neatly clipped moustache and brown eyes. When he was born in 1935 the hill was unoccupied; his father had begun building their house in the 1940s and they had moved in at the end of the decade, shortly after the Abu Heikels. Life on Tel Rumeida was 'sweet' before the settlers arrived: 'Amazing – just amazing,' Hani said, though I was not sure if they were his version of Abu Samir's words, or a wistful interjection of his own.

The family used to have a factory near the entrance to the settlement, which produced metal grilles for drains, door handles, and gifts for tourists. It employed fifteen people. The Abu Ayshes said it was the only one of its kind in Palestine, but the settlers filed a complaint with the army, claiming that it produced harmful smoke pollution, and in 2002 they were forced to close it down. Abu Samir had begun working as a farmer when the foundry closed – he had brought a bunch of grapes from his field – and since he had opened the shop he had embarked on his third career. It was such a hot morning that Hani and I had to keep moving our plastic chairs into the shrinking pools of shade in the alleyway, but Abu Samir was unconcerned: his keffiyeh kept him cool, he said, indicating the white cloth pinned with two neat black loops around his forehead.

I asked him if he could remember a time when Jews and Arabs lived in peace in Hebron, and the answer was a qualified yes: he was born six years after the massacre that shattered the city's Jewish community, but his family had close personal and business ties to the small number of Jews who returned in 1931. His father was a shepherd who had worked closely with Yaakov Ezra, the last Jew to remain in Hebron: he had sold him milk before 1929, and throughout the 1930s he helped him run his cheese factory in Beit Hadassah. The family had lived in Beit Hadassah until Abu Samir was twelve or thirteen years old, though the area was still known as the Jewish neighbourhood.

Of all the Palestinians I had met who pronounced affection for the former Jewish residents of Hebron, Abu Samir had the most direct connection, and yet he was also guilty of anti-Semitic prejudice of a kind I had not encountered before. He believed that the massacre of 1929 had been perpetrated by British agents seeking to rid their country of their obligations to the Jews. Britain had promised to create a Jewish homeland to repay the Jewish financiers that had funded its campaign in the First World War and when it defaulted on the debt it hired militias to destroy the Jews in Palestine. When I questioned this evident nonsense, he went on to elaborate an even grosser form of anti-Semitism. Hani translated: 'At that time all the world wanted to kill all the Jews because they bother all the world, and also they kill the prophets, Mossa and Jesus. They are very rich people and also they are the biggest troublemakers, so all of the world want to remove them. They are refugees all over the world, because any place they stay in they make problems.'

He illustrated the point with a garbled story about a Jewish plot to poison a German man who had married a Jewish girl, and a bizarre reference to the Nazis' predilection for forced sterilization, as if the desire to suppress the Jewish population was proof of Jewish crimes. Karen Armstrong maintains that anti-Semitism was a vice unknown in the Arab world before it was imported from Europe, and the best you could say for Abu Samir was that he had been corrupted by the contents of the worst anti-Semitic screeds. Even when Hani relayed my objections he was undeterred: 'In Germany there are Jews, there are Muslims, there are Christians, so why do they want to make the Holocaust for the Jews?'

Racist madness, I said, and the engrained habit of centuries of persecution.

'So why did they not kill the Muslims at the same time? They know that the Jews want to destroy the German people. Now they have the same aim but with different way – here, they kill this guy, they say this one is a terrorist, they follow the refugees from Jaffa and Tel Aviv to the Gaza Strip and kill them there. They have the same policy – they want to attack the people and kill them. Return back to the Jesus time. Hundreds of prophets killed by the Jewish – why?

Racists. That's his example.' Hani was keen to emphasize that these were not his views.

Palestine was a big country, Abu Samir said: why could they not agree to share it? 'But they came for the problems, not for the peace. They come to transfer us, not just to live. They believe that the world is created for the Jews, and all the people are their slaves. Any Prime Minister, any leader, of England or the United States, the first thing he says is we should take care of Israel. So all the world is their slave.'

When America attacked Iraq, saying there were nuclear weapons or chemical weapons, it was following Israel's instructions. 'So they search the whole of Iraq and they are not found. One of the generals says maybe in Saddam's mouth. But even in his mouth, there is no nuclear weapons.' He was referring to the famous image of a doctor taking a DNA sample from the dictator. Now America was planning to attack Iran on Israel's instructions: 'It's the order of the world.'

He asked me why people were so intent on protecting the Jews. I did not want to indulge his paranoid fantasies, but I could not deny that the West has favoured Israel in its confrontations with the Palestinians, and I suggested that the bias has evolved for several reasons, including the existence of strong cultural and familial ties with Israel, the Christian world's traditional suspicion of Islam and collective guilt at the centuries of anti-Semitic persecution that culminated in the Holocaust. Hani interrupted: so far, he said, he had only been translating what Mr Abu Ayshe was saying, but now he had a question of his own. 'I am Hani,' he said, meaning that he was speaking for himself. 'We feel sorry for what happened. We feel sorry for it. But why should we pay for it – is that our crime that we should pay for it?'

Besides, he did not understand why the settlers wanted to make others suffer, as they had suffered: 'So if I am a victim, did I do the same to the other, to make them victim? No, I should protect them. If anyone suffers, he will never make the others suffer. He will try to protect them.'

Most Jews would agree, I said.

'As I told you, the settlers are not Jews. Believe me. They are not Jews. I tell you why. On Shabbat they should pray, they should celebrate, but instead they attack the Palestinian houses. So you cannot tell me that they are Jewish: when I see their rabbi attack the kids, I'm sure he is not Jewish. He use the Jewish as a mask. He put the Judaism on his face, like a mask. He is not rabbi. He know nothing about rabbi.' Hani's family used to live in Beit Hadassah: he said it was not always a Jewish building, though he questioned the relevance of the term, since Judaism is a religion, not a nationality, and the Jews of Hebron were Palestinians as well. 'That time, the Jews were just like us – we have the same rights, the same life, the same food: they share everything. But these people they are not Jewish.' Hani had another question: 'We are killed, and nobody asks about it – one Israelian killed and all the world cry about it: why do they cry about the Israelian and not about the Palestinian? It's a question for you and the world.'

It was a better question than any that Abu Samir had asked me. Yet despite his espousal of the most grotesque anti-Semitic fantasies, Abu Samir was keen to insist that he felt no ill will towards the Jews: his family had sheltered Jewish residents in 1929, and if the settlers ever came to his house looking for shelter he would do the same again, even though they had spent years attacking him. Yet even this offer came clothed in prejudice: 'We have forgiveness for all, but as for them, no, they never feel forgiveness.'

He cited the two blue parallel lines on the Israeli flag as proof that they had no interest in peaceful coexistence: he believed that they indicate the Nile and the Euphrates and prove that the Jews hope to create a Greater Israel in the land between the rivers. 'So they do not want to make peace: they want to transfer the Palestinians, and after that they will continue with the Iraqi and Egyptian people. Palestine is not enough for them. They want to kill the people and make them leave the area – and they say the Palestinians are terrorists.' He had made the mistake of attributing the settlers' extremist views to Jews in general, but he insisted that he was aware of the distinction. After all, Jews and Arabs used to live in peace in Hebron. Even other Israelis could not live in peace with the settlers, he said, but if the settlers were replaced with normal Jews he would share his house with them. Hani picked up Mr Abu Ayshe's stick and banged it on the pavement to make the point. 'We used to live in the same house, Muslims and Jewish, we were like brothers. But these people, they are not Jewish.'

When he left his flat that morning a settler who was supposed to be studying at the Or Shlomo Yeshiva took off his son's dirty nappy and threw it at him. 'Where this happen in the world?' Hani began translating Mr Abu Ayshe's words again. 'A man of thirty-four or thirty-five years old has a mind to do this. He said that anyone who come to study Torah, he would not do that. We believe the Torah is from God, and God would never say do that.'

When they first arrived, Mr Abu Ayshe had taken them fruit and vegetables and they had responded by throwing stones at his house. He went to the Governor of Hebron to complain and the Governor had told him that the settlers needed psychological help: 'They should learn from the animals how to live: if you feed a lion he will not attack you.

Animals do not do what the settlers do.' The Governor also told him that he should buy a donkey to get supplies to his house, which prompted a wry response from Abu Samir: 'The world reach the moon, and I have to buy a donkey. That's democracy . . .'

The one thing that Abu Samir had in common with the settlers was his faith in divine protection: 'If all the world wants to hurt them, and the God does not want that, they cannot do it,' Hani said. 'So he has belief in God, and he will never leave his house.' During the Second Intifada, when bullets shattered all his windows, he told an American journalist that he was not scared because he had more strength and power than the United States. They looked at him like he was a crazy old man but he believed that his fate was pre-ordained: Islam teaches that an angel visits every baby in the womb, when he or she is four months, and presents what Hani called its 'CV', detailing every aspect of its destiny. 'So everything is controlled by the God – so why should I be scared?'

And yet Abu Samir's vision of the future was profoundly bleak. He saw no prospect of immediate reconciliation: the 'peace process' was empty words, and whenever he heard that they were planning an initiative to help the Palestinians, he feared a setback. Hani concurred: 'I said I am with you, believe me, when we hear that they want to take off a checkpoint it means we will have a settlement . . . So it's hopeless.' He had reverted to Mr Abu Ayshe's words: 'There isn't any hope with them.'

One of the policemen had asked him if it was written in the Koran that Muslims should kill Jews, and Abu Samir told him that it was not. The policeman said that he had heard that the Palestinians in Gaza said otherwise, and he replied that in Gaza they were refugees: 'Anyone whose

house is stolen from him, whose wife is killed – whose brothers, sisters, sons are killed – he will want to kill Jews because he wants revenge. We are not terrorists, no, but Palestinian refugees in Jordan, in Syria, in Iraq want revenge. If they not find a good solution for the Palestinian problem it will burn all the world, not just here. Think of all these refugees – what will they do? Even in a thousand years they will come back – they will never forget their land.' The situation in Palestine was like a fire in the jungle, and if it wasn't put out the conflagration would spread across the world: 'No one will be far from it, not England or France or Germany. Everyone will be in this war.'

Hani Abu Heikel was not the only member of the Abu Heikel clan who lived on Tel Rumeida: his cousins were part of the extended family who lived in a compound on the summit of the hill, next to the shrine known variously as Kever Yshai, the Tomb of Jesse, or Deir Arbain, 'the mosque of the forty witnesses'. In all, the Abu Heikels owned four of the six stone houses that stand within the line of the ancient city walls.

When they built the first one, in 1940, Tel Rumeida seemed as remote to the inhabitants of Hebron as Hebron did to other Palestinians. Feryal Abu Heikel – the former Headmistress of Cordoba School, and the matriarch of the clan – grew up in a house near the Ibrahimi Mosque during the period of Jordanian rule in the city, and she remembered people saying that only the strongest man in the world could reach Tel Rumeida. It was not its height or gradient that made it so intimidating. One night, a group of men dared one another to climb the hill and plant a stake in the earth to mark their conquest. Most of them turned back, but one man made it to the top. He was wearing traditional long-bottomed trousers, and when he drove his stake into the ground he trapped the flap of cloth between his knees. He thought he had been caught by one of the djinns that haunted the hill and he was so terrified he could not move. When his friends returned in the morning they found him pinned to his stake shaking with fear.

Yet far from being deterred by Tel Rumeida's isolation, Feryal Abu Heikel's future father-in-law seemed to regard it as an advantage: he was known as an antisocial man, and people said that he wanted to live on Tel Rumeida as a way of escaping unwanted guests. His family used to spend the summer months on their plot of land near the Tomb of Ruth and Jesse, and in 1940 they built a house. Naturally, his search for solitude proved self-defeating: once there was one house on the hill, others followed, though the first inhabitants were all related to him.

I had heard about the Abu Heikels as soon as I arrived in Hebron but the first member of the family that I met was an English activist who had married into it. David, or Dawud, as the Palestinians called him, was a deacon in the Church of England. He had trained as a priest but the role of deacon, who provides 'a bridge between the Church and the world', seemed a better way to fulfil his activist's instincts. He described himself as a 'Christian Muslim peacemaker', and I used to see him walking through the souk on his way to prayers in the Ibrahimi Mosque. He was a tall, thin man in his late forties, with light brown hair and greying beard, usually adorned with the keffiyeh and white hat that advertised both his Palestinian affiliations and pacifist calling. He was rather frail and suffered from a neurological disorder that often made him feel 'fuzzy and dizzy', but there was no doubting his courage: he went to Iraq as a 'human shield' before the American invasion of 2003 and had come to Hebron with the International Solidarity Movement, one of the activist groups that maintain a permanent presence in the city.

He had met Arwa Abu Heikel in the autumn of 2006 when he was helping the family with their olive harvest: 'You try and keep as many people picking as you can while you send one person to argue with the people who are trying to stop you,' he said, the first time we met. Police and soldiers had arrived followed by a random selection of the activists, peacekeepers and observers that cluster round Tel Rumeida. Dawud, or Deacon Dave, as he also liked to be known, said it was a 'huge circus' and it went on all afternoon. The soldiers were about to give in and give them permission to carry on when Arwa's mother, Feryal, called them in to eat: 'They were amazed that after all that we were just going to walk away. It was very funny.' Dawud was impressed with Arwa: he thought it took a strong woman to face down so many people, and she was impressed with him because he let her do the talking, which a Palestinian man would never do. They got married a year later and they lived in a house on the edge of the Old City, in the narrow alleyway that led into the Baladiya.

Dawud said he would introduce me to his wife's family, and we arranged to meet at the Tel Rumeida checkpoint. I got there first and sat on one of the graffiti-ed concrete roadblocks at the entrance to the street. A plaque inlaid in the pavement said the United States Agency for International Development – or USAID – had paid for the street to be repaved when the Hebron Protocol was signed, in anticipation of the day it would reopen, but eleven years later it was still cut in half by the checkpoint: only one of its many shops had remained open, and the taxis that used to collect

on Shoada Street gathered on the concourse below the concrete blocks, waiting to pick up passengers emerging from
the part of the city where Palestinians could only go on foot.

A man with pale skin and bright red freckles came and
sat beside me. A purple birthmark covered one cheek and
half his forehead. He said he helped the tourists for a living,
which must have been a precarious existence, and asked me
why so few came to Hebron. Dawud did not want to talk to
him – he was too polite to ignore him completely, but he
kept his answers short and turned his back on him. 'I can't
afford to be seen with him,' he said. 'The Palestinians think
he's a collaborator.' He must have felt that he had been
unkind for he added that the Palestinians weren't nice to
people with learning difficulties. 'Mind you, he does ask an
awful lot of questions.' Perhaps that was enough to incrim-
inate him – or perhaps it was the way he described his
activities: he had turned his blotched face outwards in the
hope of soliciting money from tourists, and found himself
portrayed as a traitor.

He would not have had a great deal of choice about how
he made his living: unemployment is high and Arwa is one
of many Khalilis who work for the Palestinian Authority.
When she came up the hill from the direction of the municipality, she was moving slowly, for it was a hot day, and
she was dressed in one of the long black coats favoured
by most Khalili women. The fact that she had married a
Western man seemed to cause many residents of the Old
City great amusement and prompted jokes that were a back-
handed tribute to her spirit – I assumed that she was joking
when she said she had a black belt in karate, but I could see
why people said I should call on the Abu Heikel sisters if I
needed help with the settlers. We went through the checkpoint and when we got beyond the turning to the settlement

we turned up another road that climbed between the Jewish cemetery that had been desecrated in 1929 and its replacement. The mosque at the top of the hill had been built by three generations of the Abu Heikel family. We went past the gap in the metal fence that led onto the summit of Tel Rumeida and walked down an unsurfaced lane that led though groves of almond and olive trees to the paved yard at the centre of the compound.

The original house was on the north side of the yard. We went up a covered staircase leading to a long corridor with windows that faced central Hebron. They had all been broken several times and were sealed with metal grilles. Arwa showed me a bullet embedded like a rivet in the frame. She seemed to think it was very funny. Half a mile to the west lay the blue-domed roof of the Russian monastery of Abraham's Oak – now the favoured site of the tree beneath which Abraham received his honoured guests.

We had sat down in the guest sitting room, which lay at the other end of the corridor from the family's private rooms, when Feryal Abu Heikel joined us. She was wearing a black headscarf with white dots, a grey checked sweater and a black skirt; she sat down on one of the sofas that formed an unbroken line against the walls and folded her hands neatly on her knees. When she and her husband had moved into the house in 1971 it only had a single floor, but their family had grown so quickly – they had had twelve children, including a girl who died aged six months, in the next seventeen years – that Mr Abu Heikel had added the floor where we were sitting. They moved in before it was finished – there was no electricity, and no doors or windows, but Mrs Abu Heikel was concerned by the way the soldiers were behaving, and she told her husband they should move in for the night. They fixed up an electricity feed and carried

mattresses upstairs. They slept in one room and sealed the
door with boards. When they woke up in the morning there
were soldiers on their land – they wanted to turn the house
into a military post, and Feryal Abu Heikel believed that
they would have requisitioned it overnight if the family had
not been sleeping there.

It was a sunny afternoon. Three of the glazed walls faced
inwards towards the courtyard, corridor and stairs but the
fourth faced the orchards and olive groves that lay beside the
path to the mosque. The family had been renting the fields
since 1949 but recently the settlers had attempted to claim
them for themselves. Mrs Abu Heikel said that a group of
settlers had entered the orchards with carpets, chairs, and
tables in 2006, and since then they had been attempting to
turn it into an open-air synagogue. On some Sabbaths as
many as eighty people came to pray. Dawud said the gath-
erings were very intimidating and he pointed out the
trampled path that led across the field from another hole in
the fence close to the road beside the mosque.

It was not entirely clear who owned the fields: Dawud
said he heard a different version of it every time, but it
seemed that the ultimate owner was the Tamimi *waqf*. The
waqf owns 20,000 acres of land in Hebron 'in perpetuity',
which no one can buy or sell, though they may buy and sell
the 'use' of it, including the right to pass it on to the next
generation. In theory, the *waqf* has to be consulted before
any sale, and even the government is forbidden from using
waqf land without a 'certificate of usage'. Both the Turkish
and the British rulers of Palestine had respected its terms of
ownership, and even the Israeli courts have upheld its rights
to the land, but most of the settlements in Hebron, including Tel Rumeida, and the army base in the old bus station on
Shoada Street, are on *waqf* land. In theory, it could sue to

get it back, but Ziad Jalala Tamimi had told me that a legal victory would not make any difference, for they had taken the land by force and the '*waqf* could not go against force'.

The Abu Heikels did not deny that the *waqf* used to rent the fields beside their house to the old Jewish community of Hebron. Feryal once saw a piece of paper confirming that Haim Bajaio had paid twenty-four Palestinian dinars in rent to the Tamimi *waqf* for the sixteen years between 1918 and 1934, but she also knew that Haim Bajaio's grandson, Haim Hanegbi, had refused to endorse the settlers' claims. The Israeli Guardian of Enemy Property had put up steel fences around the field in 2002 and said it was no longer going to rent it to them, but since the Abu Heikels had been renting the fields since 1949, Feryal felt their entitlement was secure.

She was used to dealing with representatives of the occupation. When the Israelis captured Hebron in 1967, Feryal was teaching in a school near the Ibrahimi Mosque and whenever a soldier entered she would order him to leave, telling him that without his gun he was a 'zero man'. She said there were many problems between her and the soldiers, and it was easy to imagine her confronting the Israeli youths sent to police the Territories: they might have tanks and guns, she said, but she was stronger because she was inspired by a love of freedom. When Feryal became Headmistress of Cordoba School in 1995, she set out to teach them that 'there were Palestinians in Hebron', as Arwa put it. On her first day at school she broadcast the Palestinian national anthem on a loudspeaker and dressed her daughters in the colours of the Palestinian flag – Arwa remembered going out in green trousers, a red shirt and white shoes to complement her black hair.

The family knew that the settlers meant to harm Feryal. They often gathered at the bottom of the steps opposite Beit

Hadassah and threw stones at staff and students or set their dogs on them as they left school. Yet she also confronted the settlers in her private life, as well as in her professional capacity: the Abu Heikels were so insistent that they would not leave their house that Arwa's father had thrown out 'an Arab spy' who had presented him with a blank cheque and told him to write any number he liked in exchange for the deeds. Arwa told a relative who suggested they should buy land elsewhere that if they were as weak as he was then God would not let them stay in Tel Rumeida.

Their attachment to the land seemed as profoundly felt as the settlers' messianic conviction that it was given to them by God: 'But we are here in Tel Rumeida,' Feryal Abu Heikel said. 'My feet, if it's not in Tel Rumeida, they'll burn. My lungs will seize up if I can't breathe its air. I feel that our roots are deeply in the ground and that there is a paradise here. The roses, and the flowers, and the almond trees . . . There is no choice. And my sons and daughters know this. They have the same feeling.' Arwa loves Dave, she said, but even if she moved to England, to live in the ashram in Sheffield that was his home when he was not in Hebron, she would still be in Tel Rumeida in her heart.

Arwa said she was relieved when her mother retired, for she felt that the job exposed her to constant danger. Yet Feryal was worried that the woman appointed to succeed her was not equal to the task. 'She was worried that the school would be lost,' Reem al Sharif told me, when I met her at her home near Hebron University, in the north of the city. Even Reem's boss needed persuading: she had told her that she could have the pick of any school in the city, but when Reem said she wanted Cordoba she was concerned. However,

Reem had made up her mind: 'It needs a strong woman and I believe in myself as a strong woman. It's not just like any ordinary school. It needs more than a principal.' When she started work in September 2006, Hamas had just won the elections and the international community had cut off its funding to the PA: many teachers had gone on strike because they were not getting paid. 'So during these two months I really worked very hard to know the situation, to visit the families and to get to know the people there. So far I believe I have succeeded, but I need to read more and study more. I can never stop.'

We were sitting in a formal sitting room, which she said was the coolest part of the flat: it had sofas ranged against three walls, in the usual style. On a low table there was fruit in a bowl, which she kept offering to me. Her youngest child was playing at our feet, or climbing in and out of a fenced-in balcony behind us. He was called Malik, and Reem said he was very spoilt, for she had named him after a boy who had died falling off the balcony. 'I got him after I lost the first Malik,' she said. They had been born ten years after her daughter, who was sixteen: 'Ten years of trying to have another child, and then I got the twins, and then I lost one of them, and I worked for three, four years for a chance to have a second boy. Then I named him after the first one I lost.' She indicated the iron bars on the windows: 'It's protected now, we have iron gates, windows everywhere – don't worry, it's safe. Inshallah, by God's help, it's never going to happen again, not to me, not to anybody.'

I was impressed by her calmness and conviction. She was a tall, good-looking woman, with black hair, casually dressed in knee-length jeans and an embroidered black shirt with a V-shaped neck. She had other visitors while I was there: her neighbour appeared in a pink dressing gown, with a tray of individual cheesecakes, a friend came round looking for some help with a proposal, and children kept appearing at the front door. She seemed calm and competent, and yet she was also capable of displays of emotion: when she said that 'the Jews' were welcome if they behaved, she put her hands to her heart and mimed warmth and enthusiasm with great vigour, and later, when she referred to something that happened during the British Mandate, she laughed, and apologized, quite unnecessarily, in case I was offended.

Her family are from Hebron and Dura, but she married a Sharif from Hebron, which made her a proper Khalili. She understood the significance of the school. Fifteen years ago it had three hundred pupils and had been one of the most important schools in Hebron but the presence of the settlers and the effects of the curfews had driven people away. At the height of the Second Intifada in 2004 Cordoba was only open for two months of the year, and the number of pupils fell to fifty. It started accepting boys shortly afterwards. When Reem started work in 2006 it had seventy-eight pupils, but the number had risen to a hundred and eighteen, and she was expecting more than a hundred and fifty to register for the autumn term of 2008. 'I am trying to do my best to keep the school open and the children safe, because if we lose these two elements then it means there is no education. So in our school I have this motto: "safety first, education second".'

She tried to ensure that the kids were safe while they were at school, but she could not control everything that happened outside its gates. At Cordoba the 'school run' is not the innocent activity that it is in other places – international activists accompany the kids to and from school in the mornings and afternoons, and Reem had arranged for a police car to be in the street outside Beit Hadassah for two hours every day. Even so, one of her eight-year-old boys was recently attacked on his way home by one of the settlers' dogs. He fell and broke his right hand in two places.

Cancelling school on Saturdays, when the settlers' kids were out on the streets and looking for trouble, had put a stop to one regular confrontation, but many of the problems happened at night. Sometimes a child came into school saying their house had been attacked and they hadn't got any sleep, or that a member of their family had been arrested. Life on Tel Rumeida was rarely peaceful. If the settlers were not fighting they were celebrating: 'They have *many* feasts, *many* celebrations, and every few days they have a party or something, with loudspeakers, so the children can't sleep during the night. So if the settlers are happy they don't sleep, and if the settlers are angry they don't sleep.' There were problems caused by poverty and problems caused by life under occupation. Once a week, the Palestinian Red Crescent sends two specialists to help prepare the eleven- and twelve-year-olds to grow up as normal

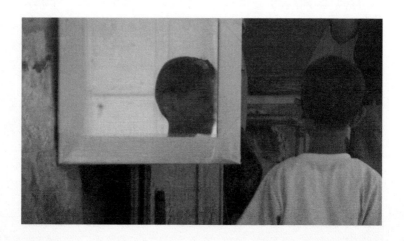

teenagers. 'We only have a hundred and eighteen children, but they need a hundred and eighteen people to help them. Every child has his problem.'

She seemed more pragmatic than Feryal Abu Heikel, and I wondered whether it helped that Reem did not live on Tel Rumeida in close proximity to the settlers. Even though it was the holidays, she said she was going to go in later in the week. She offered to show me the school and some of the historical sites on the hill, including the tomb of the man from whom the Sharif family are descended. I was on time but she rang to say that the soldier would not let her through the checkpoint. She sounded more affronted than annoyed: she had told me that such delays had become much less common since she had taken over Cordoba School. Some of the settlers' kids were playing in the street infront of Beit Hadassah and Noam Arnon was talking to an old man armed with an extravagant beard and an equally extravagant gun. There were two soldiers in the sentry post at the beginning of the empty avenue of shops. *Hevron Shalano* – 'Hebron is Ours' – said the graffiti on the wall.

This group of soldiers were relatively new: several Palestinians and internationals had told me that they had not had a chance to 'train' them yet, and there had been various incidents in the city. Two days before, the IDF had made an incursion into H1 and killed a Hamas militant. I had heard different versions of the story: Reem had told me that soldiers had surrounded his house, and he had refused to come out, even when his mother addressed him through a loudspeaker. They began destroying the house with a bulldozer and when they reached the room where he was hiding he started shooting, and was killed.

When she arrived ten minutes late, she was rather less

composed than normal. She was wearing a red headscarf, a black top and black trousers. She looked very hot. The soldier had wanted her to go through the metal detector; she had refused because she finds it humiliating. Some people believed that the soldiers press a button to trigger an alarm if they want to detain someone, and the fact that you pass your bag around the metal detector and pick it up on the other side seems to add weight to the suspicion that it is merely a means of restricting and controlling people's movement. Yet Reem took a different view: she believed that it was a real machine and the soldiers were able to control its sensitivity. Sometimes they would set it so it would beep for a nail in a shoe or a pin in a scarf.

She had told the soldier that her name was on the list of people who should be allowed to pass without being searched. She threatened to ring the DCO, or District Co-ordinating Office, the IDF's headquarters in Hebron. She had the numbers of all the people in charge and she kept in touch to ensure the safety of the children. She believed that if she always told them the truth then they would learn to take her at her word; she needed their help because the Palestinian Authority had no jurisdiction around the school. Whenever she called to say there was a 'situation', they would say, you're the boss, do your job, so she stopped calling them. Instead, she wrote to the DCO, the Red Cross and the Ministry of Education. The Governor of Hebron was very supportive: the fact that her husband works in his office presumably helps. She realized that the Israeli authorities were in Hebron on the settlers' behalf but she believed they could be prevailed upon to protect the locals, too. 'I believe that good relations and good arrangements can help to keep the school open and the children safe.'

We walked down a short concrete path that ran parallel

to Shoada Street. At the school gates Reem said she wanted to show me how the street got its name. Ibrahim Pasha, son of Mohammed Ali Pasha, the ruler of Egypt, invaded Palestine in 1831, and besieged Hebron in 1834. Six hundred people were killed in the fighting in the city and some of them were buried beneath the trees on the slope below the school. Reem stood on the side of the path pointing out the graves. She did not want to go too close to them: 'I do not have the courage to walk there, because they are the tombs of the Shoada – the martyrs who were killed for religious or for national reasons, but they were very, very old.' She laughed. 'Before the settlers came here.' She said that if you wanted to understand the history of the area you had to study the graves: there were ancient Islamic and Arab tombs on Tel Rumeida but not old Jewish ones.

We scrambled up the path to the front gates of the school. Inside, there was a paved courtyard enclosed with pale green walls that had been raised by the addition of a band of unpainted concrete and a fence. The raised flower beds were planted with trees and flowers – a miniature palm, a young olive, some cacti and a rose bush. In a sense, the garden was a gift from the settlers. In August 2007 they had tried to break into the school and when they could not get inside they had lit a fire on the balcony and burnt everything they could find. The school had raised $10,000 from various sources to make good the damage and built the garden at the front. The Governor of Hebron joined them at the ceremony to mark its rehabilitation on 14 November 2007, and Feryal Abu Heikel made a speech in which she said that the school was in good hands. Reem was pleased: she could not find the English translation of the Arabic word but said that Feryal was not just 'the mother of the school', but the mother of everybody in the area. 'It's nice to hear these words from such a great woman. It's like a certificate to me that I'm on the right track.'

Yet the garden did not last for long. On 25 November settlers attacked the school again and since they could not get through the metal gates fitted to the doors they destroyed the garden instead: 'Not one plant was left in its pot, or in its place. They killed all the plants. Everything.' Reem went back to fundraising again: she wrote to all the international institutions, the UN and the Israeli authorities, and raised the money to make the garden wall higher. 'It's like a prison now, but we can protect our garden. So you see whenever they attack I can get help to get more protection. So people are aware of what's happening now.'

We walked down the alley by the school, past the 'Gas the Arabs' graffiti, and climbed the steep path that leads up the side of the cemetery. We paused in the shade of a group of buildings that had been renovated with money from the Basque government. Many of the maps of Tel Rumeida show the route of a prospective road, running from the settlement down the eastern slope of the hill and cutting through the middle of the cemetery: since most of the graves were arranged in the traditional manner – flat tombs raised above the surface, their heads orientated towards Mecca – its construction will entail enormous damage.

There were two settlers immersing themselves in the spring – their clothes were hanging on the gate, and I looked over the edge and saw them sitting on the steps halfway down, drying themselves. 'The Arabs say it is theirs, they used to drink from it, and water the plants and olives, and the Jews say it is sacred water and it is theirs, and they go sometimes to wash, like Hindus do in the Ganges,' Reem said. 'As a result, we stopped drinking the water. But it's there and it's open for everybody, except for the day of celebrations, when they have special occasions, and we can't go there because there are Israeli soldiers everywhere.'

We scrambled up the dusty hillside until we reached the terrace below the ancient city walls. The Tomb of Sakawati was a low mound with green walls and faded terracotta tiles on the roof. It was surrounded by a low stone wall, patched with concrete. It looked a rather modest tomb, though Reem said it was better tended than any other in Hebron, which proved the esteem in which its occupant was held. He was known as Sakawati after the district of Morocco called Sakia al Hamra, in the disputed territory of Western Sahara, though the family had originated in Mecca. They were descended from Mohammed via the youngest of his four daughters, Fatimah, who married the Prophet's cousin, Ali, the fourth caliph, and his true heir, according to Shia Muslims: 'He is the great-great-grandfather of me!' She laughed: 'Sometimes, I feel proud.'

A strong sense of familial attachment is one of many qualities the Khalilis share with their neighbours in the city – their family trees do not stretch back as far as the matriarchs and patriarchs of the Middle Bronze Age, but they are more securely rooted. Reem believed that the Sharif family were punished for their proximity to the Prophet by his successors, and when the Umayyad caliphate came to power they fled to Morocco. 'They were there for a long time and then six hundred years ago this man came to Hebron. Because people here like the idea of having a relative from the Prophet's family, they used to deal with him as sacred – as a god. And he was a very religious man. The Sharif family are not the same.' She laughed.

People used to ask Sakawati to pray for rain, and after his death they came to his tomb and prayed themselves. They said their prayers were usually answered, though Reem believed their faith in his powers was based on the name which comes from the verb *sakar*, to water.

There was a pleasant breeze moving across the slopes of the hill. A man came out of the garden of the al-Bakri house, next door to Hani Abu Heikel's house, and walked past us, on one of the dirt paths that led to Beit Hadassah. He was leading two young girls by the hand, and he had a rifle slung across his shoulder. Reem did not recognize him: she did not recognize any of the settlers as individuals, and she did not try to talk to them because they would not listen: 'I talk to the people in charge. I talk to the Israeli government. I don't talk to a person who won't help me. I talk to the boss.' She said it was an Arab area and yet she did not dismiss the settlers' claim to the al-Bakri house: 'There's always two stories: the Arabs say that settlers occupied the place but the settlers say that they bought it, they have contracts, and they're allowed to live there. I don't like to say they occupied the place because I believe that they don't stay in a place if they don't really have papers.' Sometimes, she said, they take the house without papers – she clapped her hands to illustrate the coup – but more often than not there was a legal basis to their claim. Sometimes, there will be ten or more owners of a building and the settlers will get one signature. She believed that at least one of the owners of the al-Bakri house had agreed to sell it: after all, the settlers did not try to live in any of the other houses on the hill.

In theory, selling property to settlers or to Jewish institutions was a capital offence, and even if this penalty was never enforced people had been sent to prison. She was not surprised that some people were unable to resist the lure of the settlers' money: 'They try to take the land at any price. They sometimes give, as we say, a white cheque – you can write any number in it. Some people are very weak and they just do it. They don't live in the city, and if the place is abandoned and they are able to get good money for it, why not? So for people who don't live here, and they are not interested in coming back, why not? They can make all the papers in Jordan.' She mimes dusting her hands. 'Much of the Arab property was sold in this way.' She acknowledged that there was Jewish property in Hebron, but Shoada Street was 'a hundred per cent Arab', and she said that the settlers would never achieve their aim of driving out all the local residents: 'It's just a dream. Maybe they will be able to move some families, but not all. I'm not willing, for example, to give up Cordoba, which is not my property, to anybody – I'm willing to die for it. And so are my teachers and my students. And they will find so many Arab families also willing.'

CHAPTER TEN

ISSA'S HOUSE

There is an inescapable process in a population that is divided into two people, one dominant, the other dominated. No! The state of Israel will not be such a monstrosity!

Jacob Talmon

Hani Abu Heikel had said that one good thing came out of the Sharmuta incident, when Yifkat Alkobi was captured on film abusing the Abu Ayshe family: he used to think that all Israelis were the same but the reaction to Yifkat Alkobi's tirade convinced him that most of them were 'nice people', who had no idea what the settlers were doing in their name. He was adamant that the conflict was political, not religious or ethnic, and he became part of the loose cooperative of Palestinians and Israelis that set out to reclaim the house with the prow-shaped garden standing next to his on the eastern edge of the hill. Groups like Breaking the Silence and Children of Abraham brought their tours to the house, and Hani said they wanted to try to make a bridge between the religions, between the Palestinians and the Israelis: 'We want a human relationship between the people – not a relationship between the Israeli government and the Palestinian Authority. That's the idea. To return back for our Father Abraham, to be cousins.'

I went to the house for the first time with the elderly

English activist John Lynes. He worked for the Christian Peacemaker Teams and lived in its house in the Old City, which was marked by a multicoloured peace flag flying amongst the blue flags of Israel. I had noticed the building on my first visit to Hebron and contacted them before I came back on my own. They had agreed to my request to find someone who could talk to me about Hebron, though when the instructions for meeting John Lynes came they were like an assignation for a secret rendezvous. In the event, I found his basement flat in Hastings, via the unpaved track, the post box and the overgrown garden ('bring your mobile in case your courage fails!') more easily than he seemed to expect. There were old filing cabinets stacked in the hall, and the corridor opened into a series of small, dark rooms. John Lynes was wearing a check jacket with three pens in the breast pocket, a grey T-shirt and black trousers. His beard was grey, but he had a head of reasonably dark hair, and he looked fit and trim. Behind a pair of large glasses, his eyes were bright and his gaze was steady. I liked him immediately. He laughed a lot and considered every question very carefully: sometimes, he closed his eyes while he thought, and sometimes he began by asking himself a question – 'Now what can I tell you?' or 'How I can be honest about this?'

The settlers resented the activists, routinely accusing them of anti-Semitism and telling them 'to get back to Auschwitz', and they had particular reason to reproach John Lynes, for they felt he should know better: he had been born into a Jewish family in north London and used to worship at a Reform synagogue in Marble Arch. As he put it, he 'used to go to synagogue the way these guys go to synagogue' and it saddened him that they would not have anything to do with him. He understood their political views as well as their religious background. His parents had never been Zionists but he was brought up to believe that Jerusalem was special, and he was converted to the cause when people who had been in concentration camps began arriving in England at the end of the war: they had been sustained by the hope of a new life in Palestine, but they were not allowed to go because the British were restricting immigration into Palestine. 'And listening to them and knowing that this meant so much to them and that they had had nothing in life, I just couldn't shrug my shoulders and say, "Oh well, that's your affair."'

Yet his sympathy for his fellow Jews did not extend to affection for their religious practice. He discovered Quakerism in his early twenties, and he was attracted to the idea of worshipping in silence: 'It's so different from the Jewish liturgy, which is *so* busy, never a dull moment, full of symbolism and ritual and so forth, and what I felt then, totally cocksure, in the way that people are cocksure in their twenties, was all that is a load of drivel.' He also felt that worshipping in Hebrew was not a natural thing for him to do, so he abandoned Judaism and became a Quaker, though he did not join the Society of Friends until his parents died thirty years later.

He had had an active life – as well as his professional career as a lecturer in architecture, with a particular interest in 'daylight' and window design, he and his wife fostered a dozen children, and he had also found time for a busy schedule of 'illegal peace activities' that led to a spell in prison, when he was arrested at a protest outside the Ministry of Defence and refused to pay the £10 fine. Yet nothing in what he called 'a lifetime of mischief-making' seemed as valuable as the work he was doing in Hebron.

When he came to the city in 2002 it was not the most dangerous place in the West Bank – the Israeli army had reoccupied Bethlehem and Ramallah, and there was street-to-street fighting in Jenin and Nablus – but it was 'a terrible time' for curfews and closures. Often the only people on the street were the red-capped members of the Christian Peacemaker Teams and Médecins Sans Frontières, and the settlers often attacked them. CPT say it aims to bring the same discipline and purpose to making peace as armies do to fighting war, but John Lynes saw its work in simpler terms: 'It's so important that there's somebody who's friendly to both sides and who's able to be reasonable. There's no doubt that the Palestinians are so, so grateful for our presence, and so glad to see us.'

He was very clear about the risks he was taking: if he had not lost his wife in 1999, he would not have gone, but he enjoyed it so much he had kept coming back. When we first met he was reluctantly enduring a long leave of absence as he waited for an operation on a hernia, but two days later he was diagnosed with deep-vein thrombosis. He assured me that he would be back as soon as possible, and he meant it: the doctors told him to rest until the end of June, and he was back in Hebron at the beginning of July.

I was in the city at the same time and he took me on a guided tour of Tel Rumeida, with a silent red-headed American who was considering volunteering for a 'tour of duty' with CPT. We met in the Baladiya and walked through the new market, beneath the metal grid littered with missiles thrown from the windows of Beit Hadassah. We went through the Tel Rumeida checkpoint and onto the bottom of the hill. As we passed the well and began to climb the path that led past Hisham's sister's old house, John Lynes stopped and picked up one of the potsherds buried in its dusty surface: he believed they were the remnants of jugs that had been used to carry water up the hills, and since the tel had been abandoned by the end of the Byzantine era they must have been at least fourteen hundred years old. He resumed the climb, keeping up a slow, steady pace, his red hat floating above the clouds of dust stirred up by his feet, like one of the terracotta pots of water that he had imagined the city's women bearing on their heads.

He had been planning to go left when we reached the top of the path but he saw people on the terrace of the house to the right and said we should go and have a look. I assumed it was standard CPT practice to investigate though when we got back to the office his colleagues joked that he had done his best to get me killed. I felt that I could hardly have let an eighty-year-old man go somewhere I would not, though John had already confessed that he was adept at exploiting the fact that both Jewish and Muslim societies accord the elderly great respect. His colleagues complained that whenever the soldiers were annoyed with him they would hit one of them instead.

A pale, bearded figure was kneeling beside the gap in the fence that separates the front garden from the hill, and there were other people behind him. I would not have gone any closer but John walked up to the man and asked him what he was doing. His boldness was rewarded: there were at least a dozen people on the terrace, and they were not settlers. They were both Palestinian and Israeli, and they were dressed in matching T-shirts, and eating foil-wrapped chicken and pitta. They told us they were reclaiming the house on behalf of a local activist called Issa Amro. I felt ashamed of having been so timid, though three days later a group of settlers attacked the house and threw stones at Issa's brother. When I arrived the next morning, the house was still locked up and Issa was at the al-Hadad house at the top of the path that runs down to the spring, showing video footage of the attack to a group of uniformed observers from Temporary International Presence in Hebron.

The balcony looks west across the summit of the tel. I could see the roof of the settlement through the gaps between the flowerpots on the parapet and the splintered olive trees on the crest of the terraces. The blue and yellow flags flying above the army base framed the minaret of the Abu Heikel Mosque. Rough paths looped around the exposed walls of the ancient city, and there were deep pools of shade around the base of the olive trees. The tel seemed very small: I could hear the rising whine of an engine as a car climbed one of the slopes of the densely inhabited valley to the south, and I watched a woman walking home, carrying bags of shopping. She was only fifty metres beyond the edge of the tel, and yet she seemed far removed from the dusty landscape where biblical enmities still persist.

Issa said that he wanted to show people that it was still possible to live on Tel Rumeida but he did not deny that there were risks entailed: 'It's very, very dangerous and I am very, very scared,' he said, after the team from TIPH had left. He was twenty-seven years old, solidly built, and unshaven, his black hair cut in a sculpted flat-top. He was wearing jeans and a striped T-shirt, though he made the casual combination seem rather formal. He had just got back from a two-week trip to Turkey, where he had participated in a human-rights convention, and not surprisingly he was preoccupied by the contrast with conditions in Hebron: 'It's another life there,' he said. 'A beautiful life – I felt secure. It was like a dream for me, being with my friends, staying overnight on the beach, swimming. I don't have enough time for my private life here. And I am part of the story – I am not representing the people, taking their stories only, I am representing myself, too. Whenever someone tells me something, I feel it, because I suffer the same. This is my strategy: to live with the people who are suffering.'

Before he showed me the house we walked to the cyclopean walls at the gate of the city. He pointed out the ruined building silhouetted on the sky beside the Israeli army watchtower on the summit of Abu Sneineh. It used to belong to his mother's uncle, who had been a commander in the Mandate era and a political figure in the Jordanian era. When the army had reoccupied the hill in 2003 it had destroyed the house and built the watchtower on the site. Other members of his family have lived in the Old City for the last two hundred years and, until recently, Issa had lived with them. One of the reasons he had come to Tel Rumeida was because he had got married, and he wanted a place of his own, though his wife rarely came to the hill: she felt it was too dangerous, and Issa found it hard to watch her being harassed by the soldiers.

The damage was not as dramatic as I had expected, though the house was so well armoured it would have been hard to make much impression on it: it was built of solid concrete blocks, with an angled metal canopy on the roof shading the front door and terrace. The windows were barred and sealed in protruding metal boxes, yet the settlers had cut the rubber water pipes, splashed paint on the doors and killed a young olive tree in the garden. Some of the local kids had responded with graffiti of their own: 'Falestine' said the slogan on the front door. We walked round the house, photographing the damage. We did not go inside – Issa was not living there at the time, partly because he had been away and partly because he returned to his family at dangerous moments, and the next time I went there a new tenant had moved in.

It was November 2008, and the city was particularly tense, for the long-running saga of the settlers' latest acquisition was approaching a conclusion. In March 2007 they had occupied a 3,500-square-metre apartment block on Worshippers' Way, which was known by various names: the settlers called it the House of Peace, and Palestinians and Israeli activists called it the House of Contention. The settlers said they had bought it legally from a Palestinian man, who had subsequently denied selling it, and the usual arguments ensued. The Supreme Court had ordered the security services to evacuate the house while the case was reviewed, but the settlers were refusing to leave. The stand-off was perceived as a crucial moment in the Israeli establishment's attempts to control the extremist wing of the settlers' movement. Settlers from across the West Bank were converging on Hebron, followed by extra detachments of the Border Police and most of Jerusalem's international press corps.

The soldiers at the Tel Rumeida checkpoint were not admitting internationals to H2, but I had been told that I could get in the back way: the road that crossed the border between H1 and H2 on the far side of the hill was closed to traffic by concrete blocks, but there was nothing to stop a pedestrian or motor-cyclist passing between them. It was a five-minute drive in a taxi, but since it was a sunny morning I decided to walk. Beyond the tomb of Othniel Ben Knaz on Beersheva Street, I passed a butcher's shop where skinned and decapitated animals were on display, thick curly tails hanging from the fatty sides of flesh. The land fell away steeply beyond the half-built mall on the right-hand

side of the road and soapy water spilled into the gutter
from an open-fronted garage at the point where the road
turned back towards Tel Rumeida. It was much more open
than the other side of the hill: there were vineyards and
industrial-scale greenhouses and screes of loose stones
spilled across the pavement. The lights on the watchtower
on the border were on, though the cameras mounted on its
rim seemed to be monitoring the scrubby valley below the
road, and the only person who seemed aware of my presence
as I crossed into H2 was a young girl who emerged from
the doorway of a shop and handed me a chocolate bar called
U + Me.

Mi'chael Zupraner was working in the kitchen. I rang
him as I approached and he unlocked the door and came
outside. Until then, I had not realized that the house was
divided into two disconnected halves – the front door
opened into a short corridor which led past two bedrooms
to the kitchen at the back. You could only reach the room
above via the balcony at the back that overlooked the garden
of the al-Bakri house. He locked the front door behind him
and we went up the steps. The door to the other room was
locked, as well – inside, it had a tiled floor and whitewashed
walls, and thanks to the blinds on the windows it was dark
and cool. It served as the studio for HEB2.tv, the guerilla TV
station Mi'chael was hoping to establish. The ring of chairs
in the middle of the room had been arranged for a meeting,
and the whiteboard set up against the left-hand wall had a
list of projects they were planning.

Mi'chael had come to Hebron via a roundabout route.
He was born in Beersheva – another city with Abrahamic
associations – to an Argentinian immigrant and a *sabra* of
Lithuanian origins. He was taking a BA at Harvard in the
liberal arts programme and he was concentrating on film-

making. He had taken a leave of absence to make a film in Israel about house demolitions, but he had come to Hebron to film one of Breaking the Silence's increasingly contentious tours and decided to stay. He hoped that HEB2.tv would allow him to provide a more nuanced picture of life in Hebron than conventional media, which tended to see both Palestinians and Israelis as victims or aggressors. The weakness of most community TV stations is that they are forced to search for interesting material in places where little happens, but Tel Rumeida yielded endless riches: 'You have all these different aspects of the conflict and the history, and a lot of questions about Jews and Arabs living together and what coexistence can mean and how badly it can fail packed into this very small sector of Hebron,' he said.

He was hoping to make use of the mass of material that had been shot for B'Tselem's 'Shooting Back' project, a tiny proportion of which was used to support complaints against the army and police, and he was also encouraging people to shoot tapes that mixed family celebrations and family events with the aggravating and violent realities of life in Tel Rumeida. 'They'll be like home movies,' he said when we got back to the kitchen. 'Except the homes happen to be here.' He hoped that Hani's and Issa's involvement, and their privileged position at the heart of the community, would allow them to overcome what he called the 'Al Jazeera effect' – the tendency of so many in Tel Rumeida to internalize the representations of their lives that they see on television, and begin to play them back – though he must have been aware that starting a TV station was hardly the best way to counteract a surfeit of media coverage. As he himself put it, everything in Tel Rumeida was for the record – even our conversation, validated by the blinking red light on the tape recorder sitting on the table between us.

I was more interested in the way that he had placed himself in the experiment. He knew that some of his neighbours were suspicious of him and he recognized that, in some ways, he was no different from the settlers. Yet even the reactions of those who distrusted him were useful, for they gave him a better sense of what it means to be an Israeli in Hebron. Simcha Hochbaum's comment that a Jew could only enter H1 on a one-way ticket did not apply to Mi'chael – he could go if he went with Issa or Hani and pretended to be American – but he worried that he might be picked on by Palestinians who thought he was part of the settlement and by settlers who knew he wasn't: 'I'm kind of the exception.' He was a slight figure, in his mid-twenties, with a soft froth of stubble on his pale cheeks and a light tenor voice. 'I wonder how long that will last.'

He hardly went out any more, unless he was filming; he used to sit in the kitchen listening to the crackle of the army radio from the post in the al-Bakri garden drifting through the door in the wall. Mi'chael would not have been there if it had not been for the soldiers, though he had a strange relationship with them. Some of them used to swear at him. Eventually, he spoke to them and found out that the settlers' kids had spread a rumour that he was filming checkpoints and getting them arrested. 'One of them said I was living here to record the hours they change shifts. I told them, "Listen, I'm very busy, do you think I really care?" Also I explained many times, look around you, anyone with binoculars can do that anyway: you're totally exposed to the surrounding hilltops – you think they need me?'

He used the radio as a means of keeping in touch with what was happening in the city. It was the closest he had ever been to an army base, for he had been exempted from military service on health grounds, and he had worked at a shelter for children at risk. When I suggested that his self-imposed exile in Hebron was his substitute for serving in the army he laughed, but he did not reject the idea entirely. He felt that he was different from the Israeli activists of Breaking the Silence and other organizations who would come to Hebron with their awareness of their military service on their conscience, and become 'personally implicated' in what goes on. 'My involvement is broader – it's less about what I remember, more what I've done here personally. In a sense I'm kind of forcing myself on the city.' He would not join the army now, but at the age of eighteen he would not have objected – in fact, he was disappointed to be excluded when all his friends were joining up, and he still felt subtly disenfranchised in Israeli society because he had not served. 'It still plays a role, this idea that if you're not in the army then your right to speak politically is hindered.'

Hebron had also made him reconsider the other defining force in Israeli society. He came from a secular family, but he was becoming much more interested in Judaism, and he had begun reading the weekly Torah portion, or *parashah*. He believed that the change had been forced on him by the Palestinians, who never referred to 'the Israelis' unless they were making a political point: 'It's always "the Jews", which means that the discourse remains in the religious–ethnic arena. A lot of time I get the sense, not with everyone, not with people I actually know, but with others, that they think I'm different: they say "You're a good Jew, you're different, but the others . . ."'

He believed that the settler community had changed – 'It wasn't always people like Baruch Marzel setting the tone' – and he said there was no truth in the persistent rumour that the settlers were outcasts who had chosen to live in Hebron in lieu of going to prison. To the extent that it attracted racial supremacists, and the kind of people who enjoyed confrontations with Israeli activists, or 'Friday afternoon clashes' with a Palestinian farmer in an olive grove, it was 'a self-selecting community', and yet it raised interesting questions about the formation of extremists: 'Do people come with these positions, and Hebron lets them express them, or do they have all these positions because they've been living in Hebron and this is what they've experienced? Is that unavoidable? If you live among Arabs in Hebron and you're not fundamentalist, you're not racist, you're not violent – is there any way to live here without becoming something like that, or becoming part of the conflict? I'm trying to get a glimpse of the extent to which Hebron makes people hateful.'

Of course, not everyone had chosen to live in the city: two generations of Jewish children had grown up there. Mi'chael Zupraner did not think it was a coincidence that one of the inveterate rock-throwers and troublemakers in Tel Rumeida was the grandson of the murdered rabbi, Shlomo Ra'anan. He thought it must be like growing up in a bunker, surrounded by people with identical views, and the kids could hardly turn to their parents for help: in other parts of the country if a child spent their time throwing stones at the neighbours social services would step in, but in Hebron it was actively encouraged. He wondered how the settlers' children would ever find a place in wider Israeli society, and he feared that he would find it hard to adjust as well. 'Moving to Jerusalem would be kind of retreating from this. What would I do there?'

For a moment he seemed to entertain the idea that nowhere would seem as fascinating or invigorating as Hebron, until the memories of his former life came flooding back: 'But of course I'd like to do something else,' he said.

'It's exhausting being here, because everything is the extreme. It's a terrible place, Hebron. A terrible place.' His gesture took in the house and its surroundings: the Closed Military Zone outside the front gate, the tall white edifice of the settlement with its foundations enclosing the ancient city walls, and the stone houses of his Palestinian neighbours. 'This isn't life,' he said. 'This isn't normal. Hebron destroys your life. Everything else you had just rots away. It takes as much energy as you're prepared to give it – and it rewards you with diminishing returns.'

Mi'chael was meant to be going back to Harvard for the start of the autumn term in September 2009, but he was still in Hebron when I arrived at the end of the month, and I rang him up and arranged to meet him at Issa's house one afternoon. It was an unseasonably hot day: the Khalilis call it 'the short summer' – a brief autumnal blaze of heat that warms the cool mountain air to the temperature it reached in July and August. I went through the Tel Rumeida checkpoint at three o'clock in the afternoon, and I was sweating by the time I was halfway up the hill. A bus adorned with Hebrew slogans and a life-size image of a rabbi went past. There were kids playing in the abandoned army post on the far side of the road. A young settler with a machine gun slung over his shoulder came down the metal steps that led up to the summit of the hill. The long ringlets in his hair had solidi-fied into dreadlocks and he looked like a strange hybrid of militiaman and sadhu.

Noam Arnon had described Kever Yshai as 'an open place', which was testament to how oblivious he had become to the army's presence. I had never managed to get near it before, but the notorious soldiers of the Golani Brigade, who were back in town for another tour of duty, seemed unusually relaxed – the ones at the checkpoint and the bottom of the road that leads to the settlement had waved me through, and the one in the hut in the trees didn't even look up as I went past. It was like walking through a prison after a system failure has released all the locks and opened doors that had always been sealed. I looked down as I walked past the building and saw the pillars of the Israelite house through the barred windows in the front wall. A settler's child was playing in the front seat of a car parked outside Hani Abu Heikel's gate.

Even the soldiers in the street did not send me back – they rightly assumed that I was looking for Kever Yshai, and they ushered me towards a set of metal steps inserted into the concrete blocks forming the outer wall of the army camp. A plaster duck and a stack of pizza boxes were balanced on a gatepost, and army backpacks were piled on the ground in front of a Portakabin. I turned into a narrow alleyway, enclosed by white sheets of corrugated metal. I passed a yard filled with barbed wire, oil drums and rolls of camouflage netting, turned a corner, and emerged at the back of the base. Two soldiers were cleaning their guns in the yard behind the Portakabin. The Abu Heikels' olive grove was to the left, and to the right camouflage netting hung from the fence of an abandoned vineyard, where barbed wire had displaced the vines. Disintegrating stone walls enclosed the last stretch of path. I ducked through a metal-framed arch and emerged in the dusty yard on the summit of the hill that Jeffrey Chadwick had described as the 'elite zone' of the ancient city.

Its history was characteristically layered. The tower opposite the entrance was the remains of an old Crusader fortress, which had been built in the ruins of a Byzantine monastery that was supposed to have stood on the site of David's palace. The crumbling stone walls had been refortified by the city's latest conquerors. As so often in Hebron the military installation coexisted with a shrine: the arch in the left-hand side of the crumbling facade was decorated with script painted in the blue and white of the Israeli flag and inside there was a flat stone strewn with pebbles and burnt-out tea lights.

The cave was supposed to mark the grave of Jesse, David's father. When I squatted down and peered into it, I found myself staring at my reflection in a sooty pane of glass propped in a niche at the back. The Bible does not say that Jesse is buried in Hebron – Noam Arnon had told me that it would have made sense if he had been buried in Bethlehem, where he was born, yet he believed that David brought his father's bones to Hebron when he was crowned in the city.

The compound is also associated with Jesse's grandmother Ruth, a young woman from the kingdom of Moab, on the other side of the River Jordan. Ruth married a man who had come to Moab from Bethlehem with his family. Shortly afterwards Ruth's husband and her husband's brother and father all died, leaving her mother-in-law Naomi triply bereaved. Naomi decided to return to Judah and Ruth insisted on going with her. 'Entreat me not to leave thee, or to return from following after thee,' she says in the Book of Ruth 17:16. 'For whither thou goest, I will go; and where thou lodgest, I will lodge: thy people shall be my people, and thy God my God.' In Bethlehem she married one of her dead husband's kinsmen, Boaz, and had a son, Obed, who became 'the father of Jesse, the father of David'.

Her story has symbolic significance, as well: Ruth's acceptance of the ancient Israelites' faith is said to parallel the Jews' 'collective affirmation of the Torah', and it has become associated with the festival of Shavuot, or 'weeks', which commemorates 'the Sinaitic theophany', when Moses received the Ten Commandments on Mount Sinai. Arnon had told me that 'thousands of Jews' go up to Kever Yshai to read the book of Ruth on 'Shavuot afternoon', though not all at the same time. That was just as well – it was hard to imagine that the dusty compound would have accommo-dated more than a hundred people.

I thought I was alone, but as I sat down on one of the four plastic orange seats fixed to a metal frame opposite the shrine I became aware of singing drifting through a door in the building's facade. A moment later, the settler I had passed in the street came out and walked past me, staring straight ahead. Inside, there was a simple prayer room, with white walls and a domed roof. There were copies of the Torah on the table and a framed copy of the Book of Ruth on the wall.

By the time I went outside, the settler had left the com-pound and the young soldier sitting on a chair on the top of the watchtower with his rifle slung across his knees indi-cated that I could go up if I wanted. The fortress had been fortified with rusting metal sheets that turned its crumbling stone walls into a steel cockpit, and its walls were sur-mounted with aerials, CCTV cameras and floodlights. Noam Arnon had said the army had occupied the tower because it had a 'nice view', and its local name also acknowl-edged its value as a lookout – Deir Arbain is a reference to the forty '*shaheed*' or witnesses who testified to Abraham's purchase of the tomb, though Reem al Sharif translated it as the 'place from which you see things'. There were unim-peded views north and south across the city, and across the Abu Heikels' olive groves to the east.

It was my fifth visit to the city and I was not planning on
coming back again. My son was two years old and my wife
was pregnant again. I had not experienced a religious awak-
ening in Hebron, and I did not detect mystical significance in
the fact that our children had been conceived and born while
I was preoccupied by its history, but as our concerns about
fertility faded my interest in it had also begun to fade.
Besides, I had been everywhere I wanted, and met most of
the people with an interest in Tel Rumeida. I was confident
that there weren't going to be any more excavations in the
near future – ten years ago, Jeffrey Chadwick had hoped that
he would be the next man to dig on Tel Rumeida, but at the
age of fifty-five he had acknowledged that the chance had
gone: what we know now, he said, is what we will know for
some time to come. Even Nazmi Al Jubeh's incontestably
sensible plan of turning the tel into an archaeological park
and allowing it 'to reveal whatever story it can' was unlikely
to come to fruition, though everyone agrees that the hill and
the tomb that form the heart of ancient Hebron could
become one of the greatest tourist attractions in the Middle
East.

I walked over to the western edge of the watchtower.
Beyond it, a high stone wall cratered by deep holes that
looked like the sunken mouths of tombs formed the bound-
ary with the Abu Heikels' land. I had gone up to the Abu
Heikels' compound with a TIPH observer called Fazal earlier in the year, and one of Arwa's uncles had taken us round
the back of the house, and shown us the evidence of the settlers' latest attempts to annex the land: it was midday, and
seven or eight people were sitting at a table beneath a fruit
tree in one of the Abu Heikels' fields, guarded by a Border
Policeman with a gun that made the standard army rifle look
like a harmless toy. Arwa's uncle told us that the settlers had

produced a new military order banning the family from entering the field, and they were holding Bible classes twice a week.

It was characteristic of the settlers to assert their God-given right to the land through the supposedly ir-reproachable medium of religious study, and the Abu Heikels had responded in an equally characteristic way. Arwa's uncle pointed out the rows of spindly tomato plants, drooping with the weight of ripening fruit, that were grow-ing in front of a barbed-wire fence that ran between Deir Arbain and the set of steps that led down to the road in front of the settlement. He had been cultivating the land for a year. A couple of weeks earlier, the settlers had uprooted six rows of tomato plants and cut the wire frames that supported them. They had also stolen the pump that drives the well. He knew it would happen again, but even so he was plan-ning to expand. Fazal, who was translating for me, gestured at a patch of freshly turned earth beneath one of the olive trees beside the crumbling stone walls of the monastery: 'He said, "You see the corner there, I claimed it, and I started planting my plants. This is what they do with our country, so why can't I do it with my land? I'm going for it, a little bit there, a little bit there . . ."'

Such tactical manoeuvres will not lead to a decisive vic-tory: what was happening on Tel Rumeida, though neither side would acknowledge it, was the binding together, ever tighter, of Israeli Jew and Palestinian Arab – of the children of Isaac and the children of Ishmael. Earlier in the year I had sat in Noam Arnon's office, listening to him rehearse the familiar argument that there had never been an independent entity called Palestine, and when I pointed out that regard-less of its political status people had lived there for hundreds of years he had struck the desk and said: 'People lived, OK!

So they can live here still!' He and other leaders of the Jewish community had recently gone to a meeting at the home of Sheikh Abu Hader Ja'bari, nephew of the mayor who had reluctantly accepted Rabbi Levinger's presence in Hebron in 1967, at which they had discussed the prospects of peaceful coexistence in the city. Arnon said it was 'a very, very nice meeting', for it acknowledged their mutual interests: 'Happiness to one people can only bring happiness to another, and I hope that the Jewish community will develop, and will be big and happy, with all the other nations in this town.'

Such an assertion was heartening in the context of the dismal views held by many members of the community he represents, and yet Arnon did not envisage the restoration of the Palestinians' lands or liberty: he thought they would become disenfranchised citizens of an Israel that stretched from the river to the sea, unencumbered by such luxuries as the vote. Such an arrangement will never come into being. The fiction that the Palestinians' path to statehood is only impeded by their recalcitrance and immaturity licenses the occupation of the West Bank, but Israel's international allies could never condone the official creation of the kind of apartheid state Arnon hoped to see. Yet I agreed with one of his predictions: I do not believe that the country will ever be successfully divided into two. All of the attempts to partition Palestine since the Peel Plan of 1937 have failed, and the task has grown progressively harder, as the settlers' presence in Hebron makes plain. One day, it will be acknowledged that there will never be a separate state in the West Bank and Gaza, and then the Palestinian struggle will change from a national-liberation movement to a civil-rights campaign and the clamour for equal representation for all of Abraham's heirs – citizens of the indivisible country that is

beginning to emerge west of the Jordan – will be impossible to resist.

Getting to Issa's house was much easier than it had been the last time. As I walked past the settlement, I asked a soldier coming up the hill if I could walk round the hill beneath the Portakabins, and he said yes: he said he could not think of any reason why the soldier in the watchtower in the ruined house at the end of the path might send me back, which seemed to contradict the logic of the military zoning that governs most of the West Bank.

I had not been along the path since the morning when Noam Arnon had shown me around. It was getting dark, and there were lights showing in the windows of the Porta-kabins and the houses beneath the paths. A swing and a kid's bike had been discarded on the path, and further on a wall had collapsed, spilling stones across the path. Discarded palm leaves covered some of the rubble, and one of the set-tlers' kids was standing on the top of the slope at the corner, waving a branch. I passed a vineyard where barbed wire had displaced the vines and reached the gate at the end of the path that led to Issa's house. The call to prayer was echoing round the valley and the minarets on the Tomb of the Patri-archs were exuding their ghostly green glow.

Mi'chael was on the balcony at the back of the house, refilling the water tanks with a hose. It was good to see him again. 'I didn't think you'd still be here,' I said, and he said he didn't either. Issa and Hani were in the upper room working on laptops. A sheet of paper pinned to the wall listed the jobs they were trying to fill. Yet Mi'chael said they had almost given up on the project: in the last year they had only managed to post half a dozen movies on the website and produce two live broadcasts, including one covering the eviction of the 'House of Peace'.

He knew it was a poor neighbourhood, but he had been frustrated to discover that most people's response to HEB2.tv was to see what they could get from it. As if to make his point, a man came to the door and asked to use a laptop. Mi'chael went upstairs to set it up for him, and when he came down he said he had left him checking his Facebook account.

It was dark by the time I left. Mi'chael offered to escort me down, and I followed the glow of his cellphone as we walked past the Tomb of Sakawati. The rocky path emerged on the hill fifty metres above the checkpoint. We said goodbye, and Mi'chael went back to the house alone. I was not surprised that the project had not worked out as he had hoped. I admired his attempts to pioneer a new relationship between Israeli Jews and Palestinian Arabs in Hebron, but it had always seemed unrealistically ambitious. He hadn't come to the city in order to facilitate his neighbours' online habits, but for the time being such small acts of kindness were the most that anyone could hope to achieve.

Timeline

DATE *Biblical chronology* / archaeological / historical record

PRE-HISTORY

BCE

3760 *Creation. Birth of Adam and Eve*

c.3000 Chalcolithic era: first settlement on Tel Rumeida

c.2500 Middle Bronze Age I: first city on Tel Rumeida

City wall and steps beneath settlement built

c.2300 Early Bronze Age city destroyed

c.2300–2000 Intermediate Bronze Age: Tel Rumeida abandoned

1812 *Abraham born*

c.1800 Middle Bronze Age II: second city established on Tel Rumeida

Construction of city wall and gate-tower on south-east corner of tel

1735 *Abraham arrives in Hebron*

1675 *Abraham buys the Cave of Machpelah, after Sarah's death c.1500* *Jacob's sons follow their brother, Joseph, into exile in Egypt*

c.1300 *Exodus from Egypt*

c.1275 Late Bronze Age. Egyptian garrisons established in Canaan during the reign of Rameses I + II

c.1250 *Joshua conquers Canaan, and allots the land to the twelve tribes, the descendants of Jacob's sons*

c.1209 First reference to 'Israel' in Egyptian stele ('Israel is laid waste, and his seed is not')

1007 *David crowned in Hebron. Unites northern territory of Israel and southern kingdom of Judea to create the kingdom of Israel*

1000 *David moves capital to Jerusalem*

c.960 *Solomon inherits kingdom. Builds first Temple on Temple Mount*

c.920 *Solomon dies. Civil war over succession marks the end of the 'united monarchy'*

720 Assyrians destroy northern kingdom of Israel, and deport many of its inhabitants, giving rise to the legend of 'lost tribes of Israel'

701 Sennacherib, King of Assyria, attacks Judea, sacks many cities, including Hebron, and turns it into a vassal state

586 Babylonians invade Judea, destroy the Temple, sack Hebron and other Judean cities, and send the Jews into exile

Edomites occupy Hebron

Beginning of the so-called 'historical periods'

HISTORY

BCE

539 Persian Empire conquers Babylon. Allows the Jews to return home. The second Temple is built on the Temple Mount in Jerusalem, and the Bible begins to assume its final form. Patriarchal stories might have been located in Hebron as a means of reasserting Jewish control of the city. The prophet Ezra describes the attempts to rebuild the Temple, which is supposed to have been completed by 516 BCE.

330 Alexander the Great conquers Palestine

164 Hasmonean Revolt. Judah Macabee conquers Hebron, and establishes an independent Jewish kingdom

 63 Beginning of Roman rule in Palestine

c.39 Herod the Great appointed King of the Jews by the Roman senate

c.30 Herod builds the enclosure above the Cave of Machpelah

  4 Birth of Jesus Christ

THE COMMON ERA

CE

66–70 First Jewish Revolt, ending in the siege of Masada and the destruction of the second Temple. Many Jews sent into exile

132 Second Jewish Revolt. Suppressed by Hadrian, who renames Jerusalem Aelia Capitolina, and makes Judea part of the province of Palestine. More Jews sent into exile

330 Palestine becomes part of Byzantine Empire, the Roman Empire in the east, with its capital in Constantinople, the 'new Rome'

610 Prophet Mohammed receives first of divine revelations that constitute the Koran. Begins preaching in 612 CE

613 Persians conquer Palestine

622 The *hijrah*, or migration, Mohammed's journey from Mecca to Medina, where he establishes an Islamic community, marks the start of the Islamic era

629 Byzantine Empire regains Palestine

632 Muslim armies conquer Palestine. Roofed enclosure built over the Tomb of the Patriarchs

1099 Crusaders conquer the Holy Land and establish 'Kingdom of Jerusalem.' Romanesque church built over the Yitzhak Hall in the Tomb of the Patriarchs

1198   Saladin defeats Crusaders, and recaptures Hebron
        Church above the Tomb of the Patriarchs
        reconsecrated as a mosque

1250   The Egyptian slave dynasty known as the Mamluks
        capture Palestine

        Sultan Baibars bans Jews from entering the Tomb
        of the Patriarchs

        Jews begin returning to Hebron

1516   Jews expelled from Spain in 1492 buy property in
        Hebron

1517   The Ottomans conquer Palestine, and the Mamluk
        state becomes a vassal of the Ottoman Empire

1808   Haim Hamitzri buys more property in Hebron on
        behalf of its Jewish community

1881   Beginning of the 'first aliyah', or phase of mass
        Jewish immigration to Palestine

1897   First World Zionist Congress

1909   Tel Aviv – Hill of Springs – established on dunes
        north of Jaffa

1916   The Great Arab Revolt against Ottoman rule,
        assisted by T. E. Lawrence, aids British war effort
        in Middle East

1917   Balfour Declaration confirms British support for
        the creation of a Jewish homeland in Palestine

1922   Great Britain acquires League of Nations mandate
        to govern Palestine. Trans-Jordan created east of
        the River Jordan

1929 'Tarpat massacre': sixty-seven of Hebron's Jews murdered, others deported by British authorities

1931–1936 Haim Bajaio leads Jews back to Hebron. Community evacuated again in 1936, at the beginning of uprising known as the 'Arab Revolt'

1948 14 May: State of Israel declared. 15 May: Arab–Israeli War begins: forces of Egypt, Jordan, Iraq and Syria attack Israel. 750,000 Palestinian Arabs driven from their homes in the Israeli response.

1949 9 January: ceasefire declared. So-called 'Green Line', marking the position of the respective armies, forms Israel's internationally recognized border. Jerusalem divided; Hebron and the West Bank under Jordanian control

1964 Palestinian Liberation Organization created

1963–1966 The American Expedition to Hebron

1967 5–10 June: Six Day War. Israel captures East Jerusalem, West Bank and Hebron

1968 Rabbi Levinger re-establishes Hebron's Jewish community

1979 Settlers occupy Beit Hadassah

1980 Six Jewish students murdered on steps of Beit Hadassah

1982 Israeli invasion of Lebanon

1983–1986 Avi Ofer digs on Tel Rumeida

1984   Settlers set up homes in caravans on Tel Rumeida

1987–1990   First Intifada

1993   Signing of the Israel–PLO declaration of Principles on Palestinian self-government – better known as the Oslo Accords

1994   25 February: Baruch Goldstein murders twenty-nine Muslims in the Tomb of the Patriarchs

1995   Palestinian Authority created, acquires control of towns in the West Bank

1996   Hebron Rehabilitation Committee formed

1997   15 January: Hebron Protocol signed, dividing Hebron into H1 and H2

1998   Rabbi Shlomo Ra'anan murdered

1999   July–December: Emanuel Eisenberg's rescue excavation

2000   Ariel Sharon's visit to the Temple Mount incites Second Intifada

2005   Tel Rumeida completed. Building occupied

25 January: Hamas wins election victory in Palestinian Territories

International community refuses to accept the result, leading to division between Hamas, which seizes control of the Gaza Strip, and Fatah, which retains power in the West Bank.

13 July to 14 August: Second Lebanon War: Israel attacks Lebanon

2008   29 February to 3 March: Operation Warm Winter.
        Israel attacks Gaza Strip to stop militants firing
        rockets into Israeli towns

2008–2009   27 December to 18 January: Operation Cast Lead.
            Israel attacks Gaza Strip again

Glossary

Abraham — The patriarch from whom all Jews, Christians and Muslims claim descent. The settlers often refer to him as the first Jew; Muslims venerate him as a '*hanif*', a discoverer of monotheism, and a friend of God, hence the Arabic name for Hebron, Al Khalil, the friend. His oldest son, Ishmael, is believed to have been the father of the Arabs, while his second son, Isaac, became the father of the Jews. The first verse of the New Testament also asserts that Jesus Christ is 'the son of David, the son of Abraham'.

Abu, Umm — Abu means 'father of', and 'umm' means 'mother of'. Used in conjunction with the name of the first-born son, they form an honorific that is often substituted for a given name. Yasser Arafat was Abu Ammar, and Mahmoud Abbas is Abu Mazen. The patriarch of the Abu Ayshe family of Tel Rumeida is Abu Samir, after his eldest son, and his deceased wife was Umm Samir.

Aliyah — The Hebrew word for 'ascent' denotes immigration to Israel. The four phases of immigration that took place at the end of the nineteenth century, and the first half of the twentieth, in the years before the state of Israel was established, became known as the first, second, third and fourth *aliyah*.

Ashkenazim or Ashkenazic Jews — 'Jews of middle and northern Europe as distinguished from Sephardim or Jews of Spain and Portugal. (*OED*)' Left-wing Ashkenazic Jews were instrumental in the Zionist movement and the creation of the state of Israel.

Avinu — As in Avraham Avinu: Our Father Abraham.

Balfour Declaration — The communiqué which the Foreign Secretary, Arthur Balfour, sent Lord Rothschild, a leading member of
the British Jewish community, in 1917, the year before Britain was
granted the League of Nations Mandate to govern Palestine. The
full text is as follows: 'His Majesty's Government view with
favour the establishment in Palestine of a national home for the
Jewish people, and will use their best endeavours to facilitate the
achievement of this project, it being clearly understood that nothing shall be done which may prejudice the civil and religious rights
of existing non-Jewish communities in Palestine.'

Basilica — see Byzantium.

Byzantium — The eastern half of the Roman Empire, with its
capital in Constantinople, 'the new Rome', which inherited the
Roman possessions in the Levant, including Palestine. Christianity was the official religion of the Byzantine Empire, which
survived until 1453 when the Ottomans sacked Constantinople.
Their churches were called basilicas.

David — The divinely chosen shepherd-boy who became the
second king of the biblical kingdom of Israel. He was crowned in
Hebron in 1007 BCE, and the ruins of his palace are believed to
lie on the summit of Tel Rumeida.

Dunam — A land measurement used in the Ottoman Empire. In
Israel and Palestine it denotes an area of 1,000 square metres, or a
quarter of an acre.

Eretz Israel, or Yisrael — The land of Israel, usually taken to refer
to the territories on both sides of the River Jordan, which Joshua
allotted to the sons of Jacob, founders of the twelve tribes of
Israel. The use of the term Eretz Israel implies a certain perspective – one opposed to the idea of partition. The phrase 'Eretz
Yisrael belongs to Am Ysrael', meaning 'the land of Israel belongs

to the people of Israel' often appears in David Wilder's news-letters from Hebron.

Green Line — The ceasefire line marking the position of the forces of Israel and the neighbouring Arab states of Iraq, Jordan, Lebanon and Egypt on 11 January 1949, at the end of the first Arab–Israeli War (see *Nakba*). Until 1967, it formed the borders of the state of Israel. Since 1967, it marks the division between sovereign Israeli territory and the territory occupied in the Six Day War, including the West Bank, the Gaza Strip and the Golan Heights.

Haganah — The Jewish militia, 'half underground, half-official', as Avi Ofer put it, which protected Jewish settlements in the days of the British Mandate and later became the backbone of the IDF.

Haram al-Sharif — The Holy Sanctuary, the Arabic name for the enclosure on the flat summit of the hill in Jerusalem that Jews know as the Temple Mount, where the first and second Jewish temples were located. The site was abandoned when Omar captured the city in 632 CE and, subsequently, the Muslim rulers of the city built two mosques in the Haram: the Dome of the Rock, and Al-Aqsa, or the Furthest Place, where Mohammed supposedly tethered his steed, Al Buraq, before he ascended into heaven for an audience with God.

Hebron — The Hebron Rehabilitation Committee estimates that the population of the city is 185,000. It is divided into two parts.

H1 — The larger part of Hebron, in which the PA has control of administration and security. It is home to approximately 165,000 Palestinians.

H2 — The smaller part of Hebron, including Tel Rumeida and the Old City, where the IDF has control of security. It has a population of approximately 20,000 Palestinians and 600 settlers.

IDF — Israel Defense Forces, or the Israeli army.

Israel, ancient — The biblical kingdom of Israel that David bequethed to his son, Solomon. After Solomon's death, it split into two halves. The northern kingdom was known as Israel, or Samaria. It covered an area roughly equivalent to the northern half of the West Bank. In 720 BCE, the Assyrians conquered Israel and deported many of its inhabitants, prompting the legend of the 'lost tribes' of Israel. At the beginning of the Common Era, when Jesus was born, the term 'Israel' was sometimes used to describe the kingdom controlled by the Roman client-king Herod. See also: Judea; Palestine.

Israel, modern — Came into existence on 14 May 1948, the day after the British Mandate expired, and was attacked on 15 May 1948 by forces of Jordan, Egypt, Syria and Lebanon. When the fighting ended on 11 January 1949 the 'Green Line' marking the respective positions of the opposing armies became Israel's internationally accepted border. Accepted as a member of the United Nations on 11 May 1949.

Joshua — Moses's successor as the leader of the Israelites, a ferocious warrior who led the conquest of Canaan in approximately 1250 BCE, according to the traditional biblical chronology.

Judea, or Judah — The southern kingdom of the so-called 'united kingdom' of Israel, created by David. After the destruction of the northern kingdom by the Assyrians in 720 BCE it became 'the sole inheritor of the pan-Israelite identity'. In 586 BCE, the Babylonians conquered Judea, destroyed Solomon's Temple, and deported its inhabitants. In 539 BCE, the Persians defeated the Babylonians and allowed the Jews to return home. The Bible took its final form in post-exilic Judea. Judea was conquered by the Hellenic Empire of Alexander the Great in 332 BCE. It became an independent kingdom under the Hasmonean dynasty in c.163 BCE but in 63

BCE it was absorbed into the Roman Empire. See also: Israel, ancient; Palestine.

Khalili — A native of Al Khalil, 'the friend', the Palestinian Arab name for Hebron.

Kiryat Arba — The other name by which Hebron is known in the Bible, and the name given to the new town or suburb built to house the settlers who returned to Hebron in 1968. It is located on the north-east edge of Hebron, above the Tomb of the Patriarchs. It was completed in 1971. Its population in 2008 was 7,200, according to the Israeli government.

Memshal Tzvaii — Hebrew for military compound. The settlers lived in a military compound in Hebron known as the '*memshal*' between May 1968 and September 1971.

Midrash — 'An ancient Jewish homiletic commentary on some portion of the Hebrew scriptures, in which free use was made of allegorical interpretation and legendary illustration. (*OED*)'

'Nakba' — The 'catastrophe': the Palestinian term for the events of 1948–49, when 750,000 people were expelled from their homes in the fighting that followed the creation of the state of Israel. Their descendants now number 4,500,000 people. The Israelis call it the 'War of Independence'. Most neutral observers refer to the 1948 Arab–Israeli War.

Occupation — The term used to describe the Israeli military occupation of the West Bank, which facilitates the maintenance and expansion of the settlements.

PA — The Palestinian Authority. The interim government created under the terms of the Oslo Accords of 1992, and granted control of most Palestinian cities of the West Bank and the Gaza Strip. The envisaged transition to full statehood has not materialized. Some doubt that it ever will: the Palestinian poet Mahmoud Darwish summed up the terms of the agreement with the dismissive phrase 'Jericho first and last', while Edward Said wrote that by agreeing to Oslo, 'the PLO had transformed itself from a national liberation movement to a form of small-town government, with the same people still in charge'.

Palestine — In David's time, Philistia, or Palestine, in Greek, was the area of Philistine settlement on the coast from Gaza to Jaffa. At the beginning of the Common Era it was a Phoenician settlement, unconnected to Israel, Judea or Galilee. When the Emperor Hadrian suppressed the Bar Kochba revolt of 132–136 CE, he suppressed the practice of Judaism, sent many Jews into exile, and renamed the entire region Palestine, to emphasize that Jews had no place in it any more. Jerusalem became Aelia Capitolina. Modern Israel, pre-1967, is centred on ancient Palestine and Galilee, while the West Bank covers the area known in the Bible as Judea and Samaria, the heartlands of the biblical kingdoms of the Jews. See also: Israel; Judea.

PLO — Palestine Liberation Organization, the resistance movement dominated by Yasser Arafat's Fatah Party.

Sephardim or Sephardic Jew — 'A Spanish or Portuguese Jew, a Jew of Spanish or Portuguese descent.' (*OED*) The term originally denoted the followers of the 'Spanish rites' who had been expelled from the Iberian Peninsula, though in time it came to encompass all the Jews who lived in North Africa and the Middle East before the advent of the state of Israel.

Settlers — The term used to describe the Israeli citizens who have colonized the land which Israel captured from Jordan in the Six Day War of 1967. By 2010, there were approximately 250,000 settlers in East Jerusalem, and the same number in the West Bank. Many are drawn by the cheap rents and subsidized living provided by the Israeli government, but others – such as the settlers in

Hebron – are motivated by the idea of settling Eretz Israel (q.v.), or the land of Israel. It has been estimated that approximately 75 per cent of the settlers would be prepared to leave if offered comparable housing at comparable rates within the boundaries of Israel, but there is a significant minority who would not. The settlements are illegal under international law, which prohibits an occupying power from transferring a population into occupied territory. Even Israel does not acknowledge the legitimacy of some of the outposts, such as those established by the so-called 'hilltop youth'. The settlement programme and the military occupation that facilitates it have destroyed any realistic chance of partitioning the country, and hence prevented the implementation of the 'two state solution'.

Six Day War — The brief campaign, lasting from 5 to 10 June 1967, in which Israel defeated its largest Arab neighbours, capturing East Jerusalem and the West Bank from Jordan, the Golan Heights from Syria, and the Sinai peninsula from Egypt. The Sinai was returned as part of the Camp David peace agreement with Egypt, but Israel has retained control of the rest of the land. It began settling the West Bank soon afterwards. See also: Settlers.

SOA — Staff Officer for Archaeology. A civilian appointment within the military government of the West Bank, which is known as the Civil Administration.

Two State Solution — The plan to divide the land into two separate states, which forms the basis of negotiated attempts to end the conflict. It envisages a Palestinian state in the West Bank and Gaza, and an Israeli state within the Green Line. It was accepted by both parties after the Oslo Accords, but no progress has been made towards its implementation. See also: settlers.

UNRWA — The United Nations Relief and Works Agency for

Palestine refugees, the body created in 1950, and mandated with providing aid for the refugees of the 1948 Arab–Israeli War, which Israelis call the War of Independence and the Palestinians refer to as the 'Nakba' or catastrophe. Still in operation sixty years later, and now responsible for the health, education and housing of 4,500,000 descendants of the original refugees, who make up the Palestinian diaspora in Jordan, Lebanon and Syria, as well as the West Bank and the Gaza Strip.

Wall — The wall built to divide Israel from the West Bank, also known as 'the apartheid wall', or the 'separation barrier'. Construction started during the Second Intifada, supposedly to prevent suicide bombers and other terrorists entering Israel, though Palestinians regard it as a means of annexing more territory, for in many places, it deviates inside the Green Line. B'Tselem estimates that approximately 12 per cent of the West Bank lies to the west of the wall, on the Israeli side, or is 'completely or partially surrounded' by it.

War of Independence — The Israeli term for the 1948 Arab–Israeli War. See also 'Nakba'.

West Bank — The term for the area on the west bank of the River Jordan, between the Israeli town of Beth Shean and the Palestinian city of Jenin in the north, and Hebron and the Dead Sea in the south. It lies on the far side of the Green Line. Home to 2,500,000 Palestinian Arabs and approximately 250,000 settlers. Religious Jews call the area Judea and Samaria, in reference to the northern and southern kingdoms of ancient Israel, which occupied the same territory.

Western Wall — Judaism's holiest shrine, 'where the divine presence always rests'. Solomon built the first temple on the Temple Mount, the flat mound in the south-west corner of the Old City of Jerusalem, which is traditionally identified as Mount Moriah, where Abraham was prepared to sacrifice Isaac. The first temple was destroyed by the Babylonians in 586 BCE, when the Jews were taken into exile, and rebuilt by the returning exiles. The second temple was destroyed by the Romans, when they put down the first Jewish revolt, which began in 66 CE. The Western or Wailing Wall is its last redoubt. Tensions over rights of worship at the Western Wall provoked the riots of 1929. See also: Haram al-Sharif.

Yishuv – or the old Yishuv — the community of Jews who lived in Palestine before mass Jewish immigration began at the end of the nineteenth century (see Aliyah).

List of Illustrations

Selected Bibliography

BOOKS

Abu El-Haj, Nadia, *Facts on the Ground: Archaeological Practice and Territorial Self-Fashioning in Israeli Society*, University of Chicago Press, 2001

Adler, Elkan Nathan, *Jewish Travellers*, 1930, republished RoutledgeCurzon, 2005

Amnon ben-Tor (ed.), *The Archaeology of Ancient Israel*, trans. R. Greenberg, Yale University Press, 1992

Armstrong, Karen, *Muhammed: A Biography of the Prophet*, Victor Gollancz, 1991, republished Phoenix Press, 2001

———— *Islam: A Short History*, Weidenfeld and Nicholson, 2000

———— *A Short History of Myth*, Canongate, 2005

Auerbach, Jerold S., *Hebron Jews: Memory and Conflict in the Land of Israel*, Rowman and Littlefield, 2009

Barghouti, Mourid, *I Saw Ramallah*, trans. Ahdaf Soueif, Bloomsbury, 2004

Bellow, Saul, *To Jerusalem and Back*, Viking Press, 1976; Penguin Modern Classics, 2008

Benvenisti Meron, *Sacred Landscape: The Buried History of the Holy Land Since 1948*, trans. Maxine Kaufman-Lacusta, University of California Press, 2002

Conder, Claude Regnier, *Tent Work in Palestine: A Record of Discovery and Adventure*, Vol. 2, Palestine Exploration Fund, 1878

Conder, Claude Regnier and Kitchener, Horatio Herbert, *The Survey of Western Palestine, vols 1–3, Memoirs of the topography, orography, hydrography, and archaeology*, ed. with additions by Palmer, E. H. and Besant, Walter, Palestine Exploration Fund, 1881–83.

Davis, Thomas W., *Shifting Sands: the Rise and Fall of Biblical Archaeology*, Oxford University Press, 2004

Finkelstein, I., and Silberman, N., *The Bible Unearthed: Archaeology's New Vision of Ancient Israel and the Origins of its Sacred Texts*, Touchstone, 2002

Gil, Moshe, *A History of Palestine, 634–1099*, Tel Aviv University, 1983, Cambridge University Press, 1992, trans. Ethel Broido

Gilbert, Martin, *Israel: A History*, Doubleday, 1998; Black Swan, 1999

Goldberg, David and Rayner, J., *The Jewish People: Their History and Their Religion*, Viking, 1987, Penguin, 1989

Grossman, David, *The Yellow Wind*, trans. Haim Watzman, Jonathan Cape, 1988
——— *Sleeping on a Wire: Conversations with Palestinians in Israel*, trans. Haim Watzman, Vintage, 2010
——— *Writing in the Dark: Essays on Literature and Politics*, trans. Jessica Cohen, Bloomsbury, 2008

Hourani, Albert, *History of the Arab Peoples*, Faber and Faber, 1991; 2002

Josephus, *The Jewish War* trans. G. A. Williamson, 1959, Penguin Classics, 1981
——— *Jewish Antiquities*, trans. William Whiston, Wordsworth Editions, 2006

Krämer, Gudrun, *A History of Palestine: From the Ottoman Conquest to the Founding of the State of Israel*, trans. Graham Harman and Gudrun Krämer, Princeton University Press, 2008

Laughlin, John C. H., *Archaeology and the Bible*, Routledge, 2000

Leavitt, June, *Storm of Terror: A Hebron Mother's Diary*, Ivan R. Dee, 2002

Malouf, Amin, *The Crusades Through Arab Eyes*, Editions J.-C.
    Lattès, 1983; trans. Jon Rotschild, Saqi Books, 1984
Milton-Edwards, Beverley, and Farrell, Stephen, *Hamas: The
    Islamic Resistance Movement*, Polity Press, 2010
Morris, Benny, *1948 and After: Israel and the Palestinians*,
    Oxford University Press, 1990, 1994
———— *The Birth of the Palestinian Refugee Problem*,
    1947–1949, Cambridge University Press, 1987
Murphy-O'Connor, Jerome, *The Holy Land: An Archaeological
    Guide from Earliest Times to 1700*, Oxford University Press,
    1980, revised edition, 1986
Pappe, Ilan, *A History of Modern Palestine: One Land, Two
    Peoples*, Cambridge University Press, 2006
Philo, Greg and Berry, Mike, *Bad News from Israel*, Pluto Press,
    2004
Rogan, Eugene, *The Arabs: A History*, Allen Lane, 2009
Rosenberg, David, *Abraham: the First Historical Biography*, Basic
    Books, 2006
Roth, Philip, *The Counterlife*, Jonathan Cape, 1987; Vintage, 2005
Said, Edward W., *Orientalism*, Routledge Kegan Paul, 1978;
    Penguin, 2003
———— *Out of Place: A Memoir*, Granta, 1999
Saunders, Trelawney, *Introduction to the Survey of Western
    Palestine: Its Waterways, Plains and Highlands*, R. Bentley
    and Sons, 1881
Segev, Tom, *One Palestine, Complete: Jews and Arabs Under the
    British Mandate*, trans. Haim Watzman, Keters Publishers,
    1999, Abacus, 2001
Shami, Yitzhaq, *Hebron Stories*, ed. by Moshe Lazar and Joseph
    Zernik, Labyrinthos, 2000
Shehadeh, Raja, *Palestinian Walks: Notes on a Vanishing
    Landscape*, Profile Books, 2007
Shlaim, Avi, *The Iron Wall: Israel and the Arab World*, Allen
    Lane, 2000, Penguin Books, 2001

Silberman, Neil Asher, *A Prophet from Amongst You: The Life of Yigael Yadin: Soldier, Scholar, and Mythmaker of Modern Israel*, Addison-Wesley Publishing Company, 1993

Thompson, Thomas L., *The Historicity of the Patriarchal Narratives: the quest for the Historical Abraham*, Walter de Gruyter, 1974; Trinity Press International, 2002

Twain, Mark, *The Innocents Abroad*, the American Publishing Company, 1869; Penguin, 2002

Van Seters, John, *Abraham in History and Tradition*, Yale University Press, 1975

Weizman, Eyal, *Hollow Land: Israel's Architecture of Occupation*, Verso, 2007

Wiesel, Elie, *Messengers of God: Biblical Portraits and Legends*, trans. by Marion Wiesel, Random House, 1976, republished Simon and Schuster, 2005

————— *Wise Men and Their Tales: Portraits of Biblical, Talmudic and Hasidic Masters*, Schocken Books, 2003

Zertal, Idith, and Eldar, Akiva, *Lords of the Land: the War Over Israel's Settlements in the Occupied Territories, 1967–2007*, Dvir publishing house, 2005, trans. Vivian Eden, Nation Books, 2007

ARTICLES

Archaeology

Chadwick, Jeffrey R., 'Discovering Hebron: The city of the Patriarchs slowly yields its secrets', *Biblical Archaeology Review*, September 2005

————— 'The Archaeology of Biblical Hebron in the Bronze and Iron Ages: An Examination of the Discoveries of the American Expedition to Hebron'. Dissertation submitted to the Faculty of the University of Utah, June 1992

Greenberg, Raphael, & Keinan, Adi, 'The Present Past of the Israeli-Palestinian Conflict: Israeli Archaeology in the West

Bank and East Jerusalem since 1967'. Research paper
published by the S. Daniel Abraham Centre for International
and Regional Studies, Tel Aviv University

Hammond, Philip C., 'Hebron', *Revue Biblique 72*, 1965, 267–70

—— 'Hebron', *Revue Biblique 73*, 1966, 566–9

—— 'Hebron', *Revue Biblique 75*, 1968, 253–8

—— 'Ancient Hebron, the City of David', *Natural History*,
May 1966, pp. 42–9

—— 'The Search for Ancient Hebron', *Dominion*, December
1966, pp. 31–41

Na'aman, Nadav, & Anbar, Moshe, 'An Account Tablet of Sheep
from Ancient Hebron', *Tel Aviv*, 13–14, pp. 3–12, http://www.
tau.ac.il/humanities/archaeology/publications/pub_telaviv.html

Ofer, Avi, 'All the Hill Country of Judah: From a Settlement
Fringe to a Prosperous Monarchy'. In Finkelstein, Israel, &
Na'aman, Nadav (eds), *From Nomadism to Monarchy –
archaeological and historical aspects of early Israel*, Jerusalem,
1994. Based on his Ph.D. thesis, 'The Highland of Judah
During the Biblical Period'.

—— 'Hebron', *New Encyclopedia of Archaeological
Excavations in the Holy Land*, vol. 2, pp. 607–8.

—— 'Tell Rumeideh (Hebron) – 1985', *Excavations and
Surveys in Israel 1986*, Vol. 5, English edition of *Hadashot
Arkheologiyot*, Jerusalem, Israel Dept. of Antiquities, 1986,
pp. 92–3

—— 'Tell Rumeideh (Hebron) – 1986', *Excavations and
Surveys in Israel 1987/88*, Vol. 6, English edition of *Hadashot
Arkheologiyot*, Jerusalem, Israel Dept. of Antiquities, 1988,
pp. 92–3

Other subjects

Hanegbi, Haim, *My Hebron: A Story of a Different Love*,
Koteret Rashit, 20 July 1983

BOOKLETS AND ONLINE SOURCES

The quotes from the soldiers who served in Hebron come
from two booklets published by Breaking the Silence:
'Soldiers Speak Out About Their Service in Hebron' (2004),
and 'Soldiers' Testimonies from Hebron' (2005–2007).
They are available online at http://www.shovrimshtika.org/
publications_e.asp.

Noam Arnon's history of the Jewish presence in Hebron,
'Hebron: 4000 years + 40', is at http://www.hebron.com/
english/article.php?id=422 His account of 'Entering the Cave
of Machpelah' is at: http://www.hebron.com/english/
article.php?id=282.

David Wilder's blog is at: http://davidwilder.blogspot.com/.
His articles on Tel Rumeida, including 'Hebron: the Real
Tel Aviv' and 'The Roots of Tel Rumeida', are at: http://
www.hebron.com/english/article.php?id=241 The Hebron
Chronicles, which contains 500 newsletters dating to 1995,
can be downloaded at http://www.hebron.com/english/
data/downloads/hcbook.pdf.

The account of Rabbi Moshe Levinger's trial for manslaughter in
Chapter Six comes from a 1994 B'Tselem report called 'Law
Enforcement on Israeli Civilians in the Occupied Territories',
http://www.btselem.org/publications/summaries/199403_law
_enforcement.

Eyal Weizman's essays on 'The Politics of Verticality' are at:
http://www.opendemocracy.net/conflict-politicsverticality/
article_801.jsp.

The Hebron Rehabilitation Committee's book about the city,
*Old Hebron: the Charm of an Historical City and
Architecture*, is unpublished in the UK. It was edited by
Nazmi Al Jubeh, who also wrote the chapters on the history
of the city, and the history of the Tomb of the Patriarchs.

Index

as mosque, *82*; cenotaphs, *91–3*;
divided, *91–2*, *103*, *184*; Muslim
entrance, *91*; Yitzhak Hall (Isaac
Hall), *92–4*, *103*; explored, *93–6*;
Islamic worship objects, *97*; Jews
barred from entering by Sultan
Baibars, *103*; security checks,
104; synagogue, *104–5*; truces at,
244; *see also* Tel Rumeida
Peace Now (organization), *157*
Peel Plan (1937), *332*
Peres, Shimon, *184*, *187*
Peretz, Amir, *278*
Persia: conquers Babylon (539 BCE),
79
Phalangists, *157*
Philip (English member of
Palestinian Solidarity Project),
31
Philistines, *73*
Potiphar, Pharaoh, *106*

Qalqiliya: Israel reoccupies, *243*
Qawasmi family, *145*, *148*, *152*
Qawasmi, Ala, *144–5*, *152*
Qawasmi, Fahed, *148*, *150–1*
Qawasmi, Khaled, *143–4*, *147*,
151–2
Quakers (Society of Friends), *313*

Ra-eed (Palestinian), *180*
Ra'anan, Rabbi Shlomo: murdered,
199–200, *202–4*, *209–10*, *238*,
326; memorial study centre, *234*;
on settlers' holy duty, *244*;
descendants, *314*, *324*
Rabin, Yitzhak, *183–4*, *186–7*
Rachel (Jacob's wife): marriage, *105*;
barrenness, *106*; birth of children
and death, *106*; tomb (Kever
Rachel), *265–7*
Rajoub, Jabril, *195*
Ramallah, *196*, *198*, *244*
Ramat Aviv, *114*
Ramban, the, *128*
Ran'anan, Haya, *202–3*

Rapaport, Meron, *265*
Rebecca: cenotaph, *97*; marriage to
Isaac, *101*, *105*; bears twins, *105*
Rechab (Ish-bosheth's soldier), *75*,
77
Red Crescent, *303*
Rein, Raanan, *199*
Rochlin, Yona: life and views,
187–96; son's death, *196*, *198*
Rogan, Eugene, *122*
Rome: Jewish revolts against (66 CE
and 132 CE), *82*, *138*
Rose and Reuben Matteus Hebron
Heritage Institute, *270*
Rosenholz, Shmuel Halevi, *125*
Roth, Philip, *169*, *174*
Rothschild family, *136*
Rothschild, Lionel Walter, 2nd
Baron, *120*
Ruth (Jesse's grandmother), *328–9*

Sabra refugee camp: massacre, *157*,
242
Saddam Hussein, *285*
Sakawati, Tomb of, *307–8*, *335*
Saladin: recaptures Hebron
(1187 CE), *95*; shows respect for
Tomb of Patriarchs, *97*
Salah, Qa'id Hasan, *172–3*
Salih Muslim (collection), *85*
Samaria: biblical sites, *139*, *143*
Sarah (Abraham's wife): death and
burial, *5*, *42–3*, *46*; infertility, *9*;
hostility to Hagar and children,
10–11, *277*; Abraham finds at
spring in Hebron, *56–7*; travels
to Canaan with Abraham, *56*;
God promises child to, *68*, *99*;
tomb and cenotaph, *88*, *91–2*; in
Hebron, *268*
Sarsur, Salem Rajib, *238*
Saul, King of Israel, *64*, *72–3*
Sefer Torah, *237*
Segev, Tom: *One Palestine,
Complete*, *123–4*, *128*
Sennacherib, Assyrian king, *48*

Acknowledgements

I am grateful to everyone who agreed to be interviewed in the course of researching and writing this book. I owe a particular debt to the archaeologists – Jeffrey Chadwick, Emanuel Eisenberg, Rafi Greenberg, Nazmi Al Jubeh and Avi Ofer – who shared their knowledge of Tel Rumeida very freely.

I am also grateful to the many people who helped me during my visits to Israel and the West Bank. Alex Cooke organized the conference at which Eyal Weizman alerted me to the existence of Tel Rumeida. Charles Asprey, Sacha Craddock and Samar Martha of Art School Palestine organized my first trip, and provided a great deal of help on subsequent visits. Emad Hamdam, Khaled Qawasmi and Walid Abu-Hallawa of the Hebron Rehabilitation Committee were consistently hospitable. Hisham Sharabati was an informative guide. Ronit Sela translated Haim Hanegbi's article 'My Hebron'. Mi'chael Zupraner acted as my interpreter on other occasions. Jason Cowley commissioned me to write articles for *Granta* and the *New Statesman*. Pia Hannini of TIPH, Giovanni Fontana Antonelli of UNESCO and Hillel Cohen were very generous with their insights.

I would also like to thank the following people for various kinds of advice and support: Paul Baggaley and all at Picador; Caroline Dawnay; Alexa de Ferranti; Charles Fernyhough; Tim Franks; Angela Godfrey-Goldstein; Simon Grant; Caspar Hall; Leo Hollis; Josh Lacey; Matt McAllester; Nick Pelham; Catherine Platt; Aimee Shalan; Bella Shand; and my parents. I am grateful to the Authors Foundation, which gave me a grant during the writing of the book.

Thanks to Sarah Beddington for the inspiring photographs.

Above all, thanks to Sophie, Benjamin, Eliza and Ava, who were involved in the making of this book in many different ways.